"*Healing the Heart, Healing the Body* contains such profound insights that it forms a solid bridge between psychology and spiritual knowledge. I highly recommend it to anyone who desires more from life."

John Farrell, Ph.D., Dept. of Psychiatry,
University of California at Davis Medical School

"This book teaches us about the negative impact that fear has upon our bodies, and reveals how to tap the force of love within us to heal that fear and create health and well being. This is a book that needs to be on anyone's shelf who wants to live a healthy, creative life."

Donald Marrs, Corporate President,
Author of *Executive in Passage.*

"*Healing the Heart, Healing the Body* is one of those rare books that helps us tap into our deeper wisdom and bring it into conscious awareness. It helps us use that wisdom to make our individual and collective journeys through life more healthful, more loving, and more fulfilling."

Douglas Ternand, M.D.,
Critical Care Specialist

"*Healing the Heart, Healing the Body* is the most comprehensive treatise on health that I have ever read. It shows us how to achieve and maintain a truly healthy, happy, and spiritually fulfilling life."

Vicki Rowe, Educator, Founder: Creative
Awareness Center, Sacramento, California

"This book is a profoundly helpful 'user's guide' for the human mind, emotions, and body. It awakens us to the wonder of ourselves as it gently penetrates, with the reader in tow, the depths of our very existence. I highly recommend *Healing the Heart, Healing the Body* to anyone seeking a deeper understanding of health, of healing, and of life itself."

Ellen Seely, MFCC,
Psychotherapist

"What a wonderful
helpful in daily life.
the human spirit."

D1512067

at is so
ness of

'ilczek,
_____swoman

HEALING THE HEART, HEALING THE BODY

Also by Ron Scolastico, Ph.D.

THE EARTH ADVENTURE
Your Soul's Journey Through Physical Reality

HEALING THE HEART, HEALING THE BODY

A Spiritual Perspective On Emotional, Mental, And Physical Health

Ron Scolastico, Ph.D.

Hay House, Inc.
Carson, California

HEALING THE HEART, HEALING THE BODY
A Spiritual Perspective on
Emotional, Mental, and Physical Health
by Ron Scolastico

Library of Congress Cataloging-in-Publication Data

Guides (Spirit)
    Healing the heart, healing the body : a spiritual perspective on emotional, mental, and physical health / Ron Scolastico.
        p. cm.
    ISBN 1-56170-039-8
    1. Spirit writings.   2. Spiritual healing—Miscellanea.
3. Health—Miscellanea.   I. Scolastico, Ronald B. (Ronald Barry)
II. Title.
BF1301.G96   1991
133.9'3—dc20   91-58888
                                                              CIP

Library of Congress Catalog Card No. 91-58888
ISBN: 1-56170-039-8

92 93 94 95 96 97   10 9 8 7 6 5 4 3 2 1
First Printing, February 1992

Published and Distributed in the United States by:

Hay House, Inc.
P.O. Box 6204
Carson, CA 90749-6204

Printed in the United States of America
on Recycled Paper

You do not stand in the world as a finished, self contained spatial being, but you stand within continual happening, continual becoming, within processes continually going on and continually proceeding.

Rudolph Steiner

To Susan,
my beloved companion,
and to all those who
seek a larger vision of life.

Contents

Preface

For a number of years, I have noticed a growing dissatisfaction with our traditional scientific approach to health and healing. Many people, particularly those who are frustrated by the inability of medicine and science to heal humanity's various "incurable" diseases, have been experimenting with alternative approaches to healing.

However, in spite of a determined search that has ranged from an exploration of ancient healing techniques, through the development of new, and often unusual ways of manipulating the physical body, no single approach has been demonstrated to be consistently effective in healing *all* people at *all* times. I believe that the reason there is no such universally effective healing method is that, even though our *physical bodies* might be relatively similar, there are complex *psychological* and *spiritual* factors that make each individual's healing a unique circumstance.

xvi HEALING THE HEART, HEALING THE BODY

Most of us know something about staying healthy by working with the *physical* aspects of our lives, such as diet, exercise, and rest. Some of us may understand the psychological factors that affect our bodies. However, many of us lack a clear understanding of how the nonphysical, *spiritual energies* in life can affect our health.

The spiritual energies that continually interact with our human existence dramatically influence our bodies, our thoughts, and our emotions. Yet, such energies are difficult for us to understand because they are usually hidden from our ordinary awareness. The purpose of this book is to help bring the hidden spiritual energies into a clearer focus so that we may consciously draw upon them to create emotional, mental, and physical health in our lives.

The knowledge presented in the following chapters has been drawn from a source of wisdom that lies beyond ordinary consciousness. Therefore, it can address the usually hidden spiritual realities that influence us as human beings.

I first learned to draw upon this source of wisdom in 1978. At that time, I developed a way to put aside my ordinary awareness and enter into a greatly expanded state of consciousness. (I wrote about this in detail in my book, *The Earth Adventure: Your Soul's Journey Through Physical Reality*.) From this expanded state of consciousness, I was able to align with a vast source of knowledge, and I eventually learned how to speak that knowledge out loud. This enabled me to conduct spiritual guidance sessions, or "life readings" for other people.

Since 1978, I have done more than 13,000 such readings for individuals and groups throughout the world. The knowledge that has come forth during these readings has addressed many areas of human life, as well as the spiritual realms of existence. This information has been collected on numerous audio tapes and in books, making up what is now a vast body of spiritual, psychological, and metaphysical knowledge that provides insights into many aspects of our being.

While doing a reading, I believe that I am drawing upon a non-physical source of knowledge that is available to everyone. I believe that we are all inwardly connected to that source, but it is often difficult for a person to become *consciously* aware of the knowledge that is available there.

During the course of the readings that I have done, the source of the knowledge has identified itself as *spiritual guides* to human beings. Thus, I call the source of these readings, simply, "the Guides."

We have many different ideas and concepts about the inner knowledge that lies beyond our conscious awareness. The idea of "spiritual guides" is only one way to describe the source of that knowledge. Many psychologists prefer such terms as "collective unconscious," or "race memory." Some people think in terms of "guardian angels." Others prefer more vague terms, such as "intuitive wisdom," or simply, "inspiration." I use the concept of spiritual guides because that is what has been used in the readings that I do, and because I personally believe that each of us is inwardly guided by souls who help us fulfill ourselves as human beings. However, since we cannot objectively verify and precisely describe the nonphysical source of knowledge that is available to us, I encourage each person to use whatever concept or explanation seems true to him or her.

In the following chapters, the wisdom of the Guides is focused specifically upon spiritual and psychological factors that will help us more fully use our abilities to create health. From the Guides' teachings, we will learn how illness and disease are caused, how our personality patterns can interfere with our health, how to assess and heal problems that we might have with our health, and how to draw upon the spiritual forces of life to create health in our emotions, our thoughts, and our bodies.

All of the information in the following chapters comes from tape-recorded readings that I have done for this book. I have organized and edited the transcripts to make the material easier to read.

I do not claim that what is contained in this book is the ultimate "truth" about life, nor do I present the perspective of the Guides as the only way to look at health and healing. This knowledge is presented for your consideration, in the hope that the ideas and suggestions will inspire you to discover your own truths about your health and your life.

As you read this book, you will notice that there are many different methods suggested for working with various aspects of your life. Obviously, it would be difficult to work with all of the suggestions at the same time. I believe that the best way to use this material is to first read through the entire book, then, go back to the parts that are most important to you and begin to work with any specific methods that are given. When you are satisfied with your work in that area, then you can begin to work with some of the other methods that are suggested.

There are a number of step by step procedures suggested for working with your thoughts and emotions. Many people find it effective to read the instructions for such work into a tape recorder, allowing enough silent time after each step to carry out the suggested inner work. Then, when they actually do the work, they play back the tape, and their own voice guides them through the various steps of the work.

Of course, the knowledge presented in this book should not be used in the place of any professional therapeutic or medical assistance that you might need to resolve your health challenges. If you have problems with your health, mentally or physically, it is important to consult a qualified physician or health professional.

It is my hope that this book will help you understand health as a natural expression of powerful spiritual energies that live within you. I believe that by working sincerely and patiently with this knowledge, you will be able to experience those spiritual energies inside yourself as inspired feelings and thoughts. Once you learn to feel those energies, then you can begin to use them more effectively to create the healthy life that you desire.

RON SCOLASTICO, PH.D.

The Wisdom
Of The Guides

Chapter 1

Your Health
And Eternal Forces

—To manifest the fullness of health intended for you in this lifetime, you need to learn to feel that there are portions of you that are larger and wiser than your body. Rather than the usual human belief that you are only a vulnerable physical body that eventually will be destroyed by death, you need to understand that you are an eternal being with an existence rooted in that which is quite magnificent and extraordinary, independent of your present physical reality.

As we begin with you now a study of health and healing in human life, your first task will be to gain a deeper understanding of the vast spiritual realities that underlie your health. To accomplish this, you can begin by creating *a new vision* of yourself as a human being living in the physical world. This new vision is necessary because of certain distortions that have unintentionally been created by human beings in the past, as they have attempted to understand themselves and their lives.

At the present time on earth, these distortions manifest as narrow attitudes, confused thoughts, and habits of negative action that have come from the influence of preceding human generations. Even though what you have been taught about life has, at times, been infused with the idealism, the love, and the wisdom of your ancestors, much of it has been confused by the fear and the misunderstanding of those who have lived on earth before you.

As a consequence of these distorted influences, human beings in your modern age have been fed a kind of "deficient diet," in terms of the input to the mind and to the emotions. That input has not included enough knowledge about your *eternal* nature. This has resulted in widespread human teachings about life that are marked by *a preoccupation with physical matter.*

This preoccupation with the physical has brought about a pervasive belief throughout the earth, and particularly in the United States, that all things can be manipulated by physical, scientific means. In relation to the health of the human body, this results in a kind of over-dependence upon the use of certain healing chemicals and substances, as well as surgical and other physical manipulations of the body.

Yet, for the most part, as you can observe, all of your physical areas of healing are quite beneficial to the human race. The ways in which the ones of medical knowledge heal and correct deficiencies, malformations, and various diseases are generally quite effective. Clearly, without medical and scientific knowledge, there would be much less health within the physical bodies on earth.

However, there are many confused attitudes that human beings have adopted *because* of the effectiveness of your medical and scientific methods. Many of you have come to believe that those are the *only* reliable ways to heal yourselves.

As a result of this widespread human preoccupation with physical ways of healing, there has come about a certain temporary loss of your deep, intuitive capacities that could bring you knowledge of ways in which *eternal energies* can manifest health in a human body. This loss of intuitive capacities has occurred over a long period of time, through many human generations.

Also, through many generations, human beings have inadvertently created distorted *human* energies that have begun to manifest diseases that now defy healing through medical and scientific manipulations. You now manifest certain conditions, such as diseases of the immune system, and cancerous responses in the physical body, that, from your point of view, are *incurable* by the medical and scientific means.

Such diseases have come about because rigid human attitudes toward physical bodies, along with certain negative inner energies created by human beings, over time, have caused some unusual changes to take place in the inner structure of the human bodies themselves. In other words, *certain human thought energies and emotional energies have actually interfered with the evolution of the physical body.* As human beings have over-focused upon physical reality, generation after generation, and, as they have ignored the deeper realities of the inner life, by consistently creating patterns of negative thought and emotion, they have unknowingly created *energies of human negativity* that have interfered with the eternal forces that sustain physical matter. This has caused a disruption in the various cellular functionings of the human body, created abnormal responses in the blood structures, and generally affected the glandular functioning of human bodies in ways that bring about new diseases. (We will explore this more fully in later parts of these teachings.)

To put this human distortion into symbolic form, we would say that it is as though you are standing on a mountain top, and you find that the wind is blowing extremely hard. You have a "natural" impulse within you that prompts you to seek shelter from the wind. However, let us say that you have created a *belief* that the wind is wonderful, and you should never resist it. Thus, you stand still, the wind blows harder, and you are blown over and tumble down the mountain. Even though, ordinarily, the wind can be wonderful, your rigid belief went against what was beneficial for you in that moment, which was your inner impulse to seek shelter. The result of following your confused belief was the creation of unnecessary suffering and pain.

In the same way, the human belief that only physical manipulation can bring health, and the belief that you should give yourself to such healing no matter what—giving yourself to the wind, even though it is about to cause you pain—goes against a natural, inner knowing within you that could help you create health by guiding you toward creative, wise, and loving ways to live your life—an inner impulse urges you to seek shelter from the wind of over-reliance upon physical matter. It has been the development of rigid human beliefs about physical reality and health that have blocked the inner knowing to such an extent that human beings have created the negative human energies that have interfered with the evolution of the human body. We could call these negative energies, "disease energies." These disease energies have brought about a great deal of unnecessary pain and suffering to the human race.

You must understand that disease was not *intended* to be a part of human existence, nor has it come into human life accidently, or through bad fortune. Disease is the result of certain *human choices* made over long periods of time, involving many human generations. Later, we will explore with you fully the ways in which human choice created the negative energies that have invited disease into human existence.

Even though your preoccupation with physical matter does create some confusion, at this present time you would need to continue your scientific and medical explorations. And, when you are personally ill and challenged, it is beneficial for you to go forth to those of medical and scientific knowledge to use all that you can find there to help yourself. However, at the same time, you can remind yourself that, just as human beings as a race have *created* disease and illness, so can you *heal* those creations. In time, you will even heal the diseases that you presently consider to be incurable.

Those of you who desire full health at the present time can learn to accelerate the processes of healing in *inner* ways that can lead you out in advance of your present scientific accomplishments. You can learn to make adjustments within your own personality that can eventually lead to the full health of your physical body, your thoughts, and your emotions. It is not a simple path. It requires a determination, a patience, and a lovingness. But, for all ones who dedicate themselves to the task, it is possible to create the fullness of health that was intended for you by the eternal forces that have manifested human life.

To begin this pathway toward full health, you will need to build a foundation for your work by creating a new vision of yourself. You must learn to see yourself as a being that is much larger than your present physical body.

YOU ARE MORE THAN YOUR BODY

The creation of health in your life depends a great deal upon your ability to stimulate a feeling inside yourself that you are much more than your physical body. To manifest the fullness of health intended for you in this lifetime, you need to learn to feel that there are portions of you that are larger and wiser than your body. Rather than the usual human belief that you are *only* a vulnerable physical body that eventually will be destroyed by death, you need to understand that you are an eternal being with an existence rooted in that which is quite magnificent and extraordinary, independent of physical reality. For the fullest manifestation of your health as a human being, *you need to feel that you are an eternal soul.*

It is very important for you to know that *you have a continuing soul existence in a non-physical realm of being, and your soul existence cannot be diminished by any challenging experience that you may have in this lifetime, including illness, disease, and even the death of your physical body.* If you can adopt this as your attitude and feeling about yourself, even in a small way, this can become the base for strength and wisdom that can eventually lead to the creation of full health for you in this lifetime.

To clearly understand how your present human life is linked to your eternal soul existence, you must realize that you have within yourself an extraordinary kind of inner structure that ordinarily remains invisible to you. We can call this non-physical structure your *personality matrix.*

Your personality matrix is composed of inner realities that have to do with your *human* experience, as well as your existence as an eternal soul. For the simplicity of human communication, let us say that your inner personality matrix is formed of strong "energies" that stream forth from your own soul. The link between your soul and your physical body is maintained by these energies that constantly flow from your soul into your personality matrix. Your personality matrix also contains the energies of all that you are as a self-aware human being—your thoughts, emotions, ideas, beliefs, memories, perceptions, and so forth—all infused with the eternal energies from your soul.

Often, this vision of the link between the human personality energies and the eternal soul energies is lacking in human beings who create illness for themselves, particularly the diseases that come forth in ways that seem mysterious or unexplainable to your conscious minds. Many times, that which is seen, from your point of view, as an incurable illness, can be healed by those who are able to penetrate this deeper level that you might call the *spiritual* level of life, in which powerful eternal energies continually interact with your personality and your physical body.

Therefore, an important first step in maintaining full health in your own life—and in healing your physical body when it is malfunctioning or manifesting illness—is to strive to bring forth a feeling that within your personality matrix, there is not only your human experience and human energies, but there are also powerful eternal energies that constantly stream into you. Such feelings bring forth the sense that there is a portion of you that is stronger than any illness that might manifest in your body. You can stir a feeling of inspiration that there is something *within* your body that can heal it; that there is a larger reality that can work upon your body to dissolve and eliminate any symptoms that you might manifest, and that can restore the strength and health of your body.

This first step of believing that eternal energies live within your personality matrix is extremely important, but, it is often difficult for human beings to achieve. As an ordinary human being, you will not usually have conscious awareness of these deeper spiritual areas of which we speak. In later portions of these teachings, we will help you become more aware of the eternal energies that flow into your personality matrix and into your physical body. However, for now, we must look more closely at the way in which your personality matrix and your physical body are linked to a certain kind of *perfection* that streams forth from your soul.

THE PERFECTION OF YOUR SOUL

In the beginning of the physical earth, the intention of the eternal souls who created human life was to make a place for *portions* of themselves to come into a physical form in order to experience life on earth. The vehicle that the souls created for such expression was the human body.

It was intended by the souls that human bodies would function according to the perfection of the divine patterns inherent within the realm of the souls, those patterns being expressions of the force that you would understand as *God*. In essence, it was intended for the human bodies to function in full health, without the limit of illness and disease, as a reflection of the perfection of God itself.

Thus, in the beginning of human life on earth, the

souls placed what could be called "perfect energy patterns" into the personality matrix and physical body of each human being. *Such perfect energy patterns still continue to live within all present human beings.* They are the *ideal* patterns that human personalities were given to enable them to manifest the perfection of the forces of God in physical reality. At the present time, the result of fully *living* such ideal patterns in human life would be the manifestation of goodness and health in the emotions, the mind, and the body, just as intended by the souls.

In order to understand the present *limited* human manifestation of emotional, mental, and physical health, in terms of what was intended by the souls, you might ask, "What went wrong?" What are the *human* contributions to the earth realities that have resulted in less than a perfect manifestation of health in human life?

As we have mentioned, in the earth affairs of the past, there have been certain choices made by human beings that have actually altered the course of human evolution, particularly in terms of the physical bodies. The kinds of confused patterns that were generated by early human beings, many generations ago, literally interposed themselves between the perfect energies of the souls, and the human bodies that those energies feed. Without that human intervention, those soul energies would have stimulated a perfect functioning in all bodies. However, because human beings have been given a mastery over the physical reality—a freedom to *choose* in earth through their *will*—human choices in those early generations were allowed by the souls to *come between* the energies of the souls and the human bodies.

To put this in a clearer context, let us make a simple vision for you. Imagine that you are a young child who is thirsty. You have a small cup that you have been given by your mother. Your mother intended for you to use that cup only for drinking, but, you decided to use it to play in the mud. Now, you are thirsty, and you come to a fountain of clear, pure water. You reach out your cup, fill it with water, and you drink. Because your cup is muddy, the water is dirty and does not taste good.

You could see the cup as the physical body that your soul has given you. The pure water represents the perfect eternal energies that constantly pour into your body from your soul. The mud in the cup would be the distorted *human* energies of thought and feeling that you have unintentionally created by playing in the negativity of fear and misunderstanding of human life. The perfect eternal energies that pour into you (the pure water pouring into the cup), and that could bring health to your body, are mingled with the human negative energies (the mud), with the result that your body is fed an "impure" influence that can disrupt the health of the body. This is a very simple way of putting it, but it can help you establish a beginning understanding of some of the complex interactions between your personality, your body, and your soul.

As we go further in these teachings, we will explore this more fully. We will show you how to adjust for the distortion caused by human intervention in the perfect energies of the souls. We will also help you to adjust your own negative personality energies that you yourself have created in this lifetime, energies that can often come between your body and the perfection of the energies of your soul.

However, for now, we must create a preliminary understanding of the way in which the perfection of your soul interacts with your personality and your body. To begin this, we need to refine the understanding of your personality matrix. Let us say that your *human personality* is the collection of thoughts, feelings, ideas, beliefs, memories, perceptions, and all of the other inner experiences that you have had as a human being in your present lifetime. In your human personality, these experiences create *human energies*. Your *personality matrix* is a larger "energy structure" that *includes* all of the energies of your *human personality*, but it also receives the *eternal* energies from your own soul, as well as energies that stream into you from other souls.

The energies of eternal souls are the perfect energies of God itself. These are energies of such extraordinary magnificence that there are no human words that can adequately describe them. These perfect soul-God energies are constantly being poured forth into all human physical bodies, and they will continue for as long as there are human bodies on the physical earth. But, before these eternal energies flow into your physical body, they must pass "through" your *human personality*. Let us describe this in a simple way: the perfect eternal energies of your soul flow into your *personality matrix* on their way to your physical body, but, inside your personality matrix, standing "between" those perfect soul energies and your physical body is your *human personality*—your collection of human thoughts, feelings, desires, beliefs, perceptions, and so forth.

Therefore, *what you do within your human personality will determine whether the perfect soul-God energies get through fully to your physical body, or whether they will be blocked.*

To clarify this further, imagine the perfect soul energies as a ray of brilliant white light. This light is intended to shine upon a wall, which represents your physical body. Then, your human personality can be seen as a magnifying glass through which the light must pass in order to strike the wall. If the glass is clean and clear—if your human personality is relatively free from the distortions of negative personality patterns—then the light will appear clear and bright on the wall, and will actually be enhanced by the magnifying glass. Your body will receive the full perfection of the eternal soul energies that feed it, with those energies being *augmented* by the clarity of your human personality. If, on the other hand, the glass is dark and dirty—your human personality is constantly filled with unhealed negativity—then the light reaching the wall will be very weak. The perfect soul energies reaching your body will be diluted and diminished, in a *physical* sense.

Thus, it is possible for your human personality to stand as the *barrier* to the perfect soul energies that are projected toward your body, causing disruptions that can accelerate illness and disease. Or, your human personality can stand as the *enhancer*, or the *creator of augmentation* of the soul energies that stream into your body. This can fill your physical body with all of the magnificence, perfection, and health that were intended for it by your soul.

YOUR SOUL'S PLAN

As we have mentioned, it is often difficult for human beings to become aware of the fact that, even as you presently exist as a human being within your physical body, *you are also simultaneously existing in a non-physical realm as your eternal soul.* As difficult as it may be, it is very important for you to try to open yourself to perceiving your present existence as an eternal soul. In fact, the manifestation of *full* health in your life depends upon your willingness to patiently work toward the realization that you *are* your soul.

Further, to fully understand your present human personality, your physical body, and the way to bring those two aspects of yourself together to create a healthy life, you will need to understand how you, as an eternal soul—participating with all other souls in the beginning of the manifestation of earth—did *intend* the human personality to exist and function in its relationship with the physical body. By understanding the intentions of your soul, you can become aware of the energies of the souls that were implanted into all human personalities, and that are now present within your own personality matrix.

To speak of the intentions of eternal souls, whose

existence is very different than human experience, we will need to begin with some quite simple descriptions. As we do this, it is wise to remind yourself that the words of the human languages are not yet large enough in meaning to fully convey the unique realities of eternal existence.

To begin, we would say again that the energies of the souls have always been *perfect*, even as they were infused into human beings in each generation of human life. And, in the ancient beginning of humanity, human beings were able to clearly and fully manifest the perfection and goodness of the soul energies in their earth lives. There was no human distortion of the souls' intended perfection. Using our earlier vision, we could say that the ray of white light representing the soul energies would pass through a clear magnifying glass (the undistorted human personality) and shine brightly on the wall (the physical body).

However, as we mentioned earlier, in time, there came about changes in human life that were caused by human choices made in fear. Individuals began to fear one another for many reasons—particularly the fear that others would steal their highly valued physical possessions—which eventually led to strife between families, and then between larger groupings. This was the beginning of human negativity on earth. The magnifying glass of human personality became dirty, and only a part of the perfect soul energies were able to get through to the physical body.

Since, from the souls' point of view, there is no *badness* in human negativity, and since it was the intention of the souls to allow human *will* to determine the course of earth life, after human beings began to create negativity, the souls needed to alter their original intentions and adjust the way in which they sustained human life. This adjustment was solely in response to the negative choices being made by human beings. Thus, simply put, the souls' perfect creations needed to be different, in order to take into account the changes in human life caused by human negativity—the human pain and suffering, and the growing struggles between human beings.

Using our image of the magnifying glass, let us say that, in a way, because the white light shining on the wall was being blocked by a dirty glass, the souls began to shine a second ray of light, or energy, whose brilliance would illuminate the distortion of the human personality, thereby pointing up the need to heal that distortion—to clean the glass.

Let us explore this more fully by looking at the way that the souls have adjusted for the human negativity, and the way that they *now* intend the human personalities to function. To do this, we will need to ask you to take a rather unique viewpoint. Begin with us by imagining *your own soul*, as it is about to engage in the process of manifesting the energies that have now come to be your present human personality in this lifetime. This would mean that *you*, as your soul, would be standing *before* your present human birth.

Then, imagine yourself as a soul joined together with vast, extraordinary eternal energies that you will weave together in order to create the energies that will form your present human personality.

As you now imagine yourself as your soul, we will attempt to describe for you your soul's unique viewpoint. This viewpoint will include a clear vision of all of the various energies that will go into your present human personality, as well as the way your soul would *intend* for your present personality to function in this lifetime.

First of all, you as your soul will have a perfect and complete knowledge of *all that you have ever been, as a human being, through many past lifetimes of walking upon the physical earth.* Thus, as you create your present personality, you will draw upon a vast reservoir of past *human* experiences that you have had in your past earth lifetimes.

You as a soul will also draw upon past *eternal* experiences that you have had as a soul. These are such vast experiences that they simply cannot be described in present human words.

You will then bring the past human experiences and the past soul experiences together with certain "desires" that you have as a soul. These soul impulses that we are calling desires would be much different than what you know of as human desires. These "desires" would be your soul's *patterns of intention* for the kinds of accomplishments that you as a soul wish to create on earth through your forthcoming human personality.

You as a soul, by drawing together the complex energies of past human experiences on earth, past eternal soul experiences, and your "desires" as a soul, will then create what, crudely put, could be called a *soul plan*.

Since it is not possible to express the entire fullness of an eternal soul in only one human lifetime—you could not fit your entire soul into one human personality—you as the soul, necessarily, must narrow down the possibilities to the ones that you consider to be most important for the lifetime of the forthcoming human personality. This is an extensive narrowing process because many different things need to be put aside in order to refine the focus to a narrow enough point of energy to enter into the human personality. Thus, you as your soul, taking into account all that you have ever been as a human being through many past lifetimes, will align with all of your past human abilities and you will choose the ones that you consider to be most important to manifest in your forthcoming human personality. This might possibly include strong intellectual abilities, deep emotional capacities, various creative abilities, shrewdness, wisdom, sensitivity, diligence, on and on—so many different qualities to choose from.

Then, after you, as the soul, have manipulated all of the various energies of thought, feeling, tendencies to believe certain things, to assume certain things, certain levels of creativity, sensitivity, intuition, and all of the other inner qualities that will be implanted into your new human personality, you will design an *energy package*, so to speak. This energy package will establish what you might call the "positive" aspects of your *personality matrix*. It will include the positive *human* qualities that you as a soul consider most important to manifest as the new human personality. It will also include certain perfect *eternal* energies that you as a soul will infuse into the personality matrix. These eternal energies are intended to inspire the new human personality.

Next, you as a soul must address the fact that human beings have created *negativity* in human life. Therefore, you must adjust your creation of the new personality matrix to take into account the negativity that human beings have created in the past. To accomplish this, you look at all of the past lifetimes that your many human personalities have lived on earth, and you observe the various *challenge* patterns from your past human lifetimes that have been left in earth as "negative human energies." Using our vision of the magnifying glass again, you as a soul will see that some of your past human personalities have "dirtied" the glass of personality in certain ways, causing the past personalities to distort the soul energies passing through them.

Therefore, even though the *main* purpose of your new human personality is to manifest joy and love in earth, you as a soul will also try to use your new personality to *transform* certain threads of those negative human energies left from past lifetimes. To accomplish this, you will implant certain impulses into the personality matrix that hopefully will inspire your new human personality during its forthcoming life on earth to clean the magnifying glass whenever it becomes dirtied by negative personality energies. In doing this, you as a soul will focus upon the remaining negative energies from past lifetimes that you decide are the most disruptive to present human life on earth.

In order to address these negative human energies, you as a soul will weave into your new personality matrix the tendencies that will most likely influence the human personality toward certain kinds of *challenges* in life. Then, you will give your human personality some particularly potent energies of strength, courage, and creativity that will help the personality heal those challenging situations when they later arise in day to day life. It is these potent "extra" energies that we have symbolized as *a second ray of white light* from the soul that will illuminate the dirty magnifying glass. These powerful, positive qualities within your human personality can be drawn upon to illuminate and transform the negative human energies that have dirtied the glass.

You and other souls give all of this attention to the preparation for the healing of challenge because *human negative energies need to be transformed from inside of human personalities*. Thus, the human personality, which is what *created* negativity on earth in the first place, must now be used by the souls as the vehicle sent into physical reality to transform that negativity.

Then, you as a soul, considering the positive abilities that you have orchestrated, along with the chosen tendencies toward certain challenges, and the powerful abilities to heal those challenges, will create your particular personality makeup for this lifetime through an extraordinarily complex weaving of eternal energies with human mental, emotional, intuitive, and other inner energy patterns. In the process of creating the energies of your new *human personality*, you will infuse into your new *personality matrix* the perfect forces of God. Thus, your new *personality matrix* becomes a vast complex of energies that are initially *created* using the forces of God, and, the *human personality*, for as long as it remains in its new body, will be *constantly sustained by the perfection of God itself.*

Then, you as your soul will bring your new personality matrix of energies into alignment with the souls of your new father and your new mother. And, in unimaginably complex ways, *all of the souls involved in your forthcoming physical birth will align the human personality energies of yourself, your human father, and your human mother, in order to influence the physical bodies of the father and mother as they conceive the child that will be you.* The result of this will dictate what you would call the "hereditary" influences upon your new fetus form.

Then will come your physical birth as a new human being. Through your birth, all of the physical, mental, and emotional *intentions* that were implanted into you as energy patterns by your soul, as part of its plan, are transformed into an extraordinary synthesis of human personality energies merged with a new physical body.

Now, it is important to understand that, even though you as a human being will naturally desire full health throughout your life, the perfect way that your soul would *intend* for your human personality and body to unfold might not always have to do with perfect health. Some souls do not desire perfect health in the new physical body. Some souls desire *moderate* health, or even *illness*. Thus, in your soul's plan, there can be soul intentions for you that do not always move toward physical health. (We will explore this fully in a later section.)

What your soul *intends* as the perfect way for your human personality patterns to integrate with your physical body could be described in the following manner. First of all, your soul would intend what we could call, *steadiness*. In other words, your soul, while allowing for a broad range of intense inner experiences for you in your human life—knowing that you would desire that as a human being—would also plant within your personality certain tendencies toward steadiness, stability, and harmony, intending them to help you feel secure, stable, and unthreatened during your physical life. These forces of steadiness are intended to reassure you by helping you feel that you are not in danger of being destroyed during your temporary life as a human being on earth.

These soul impulses of steadiness have to do with the human emotional qualities of patience, feelings of safety and security, feelings of harmony, and so forth. Your soul would plant tendencies in you to stir up such feelings throughout your human lifetime.

Of course, there will be factors in your life, from other human beings, and from some of your own challenge patterns, that will tend to disrupt your feelings of steadiness. Therefore, your soul would also plant within you a certain level of *intelligence* that will enable you to analyze and understand your capacities for steadiness, for patience, for harmony, even in interaction with the disruptive forces that tend to shake your steadiness. Your soul would *intend* for you to draw upon this stream of intelligence when challenging experiences shake you.

The next area of patterns intended for you by your soul could be described as a kind of *clarity* that is gained from *human experience.* In other words, your soul did not intend for you as a human being to always have the feeling that each moment of your life is perfect. Your soul would know that in human life, your tendencies toward challenge, placed into you by your soul, would lead you into some difficult situations in which you would not feel that life is perfect. Thus, your soul would instill within you an impulse to desire clarity about your life, and this desire for clarity will stir up your honesty, your patience, and your willingness to manifest the courage necessary to fully live *all* of your human experiences, particularly the challenging ones, in order to learn and grow from them. Your soul would implant in you an inner knowing that qualities such as honesty and patience will eventually lead you to clarity, intellectually and emotionally.

Your soul would also implant within you a force of *communion,* or *cooperation* that would be intended to align your personality with other human beings in your life as a way of helping you interact with them in a manner that brings about the steadiness, security, and clarity that your soul intended for you. This tendency toward cooperation with others, if carried out by you in the way intended by your soul, would also lead you to create experiences of harmony in your relationships with other human beings, and that would result in the *happiness* and *joy* that would promote your health, and would stimulate the perfect functioning of your physical body.

Another tendency placed into you by your soul is the tendency to *love*. This goes beyond harmony with others. This is a force that is intended to stir you to have the courage to love yourself and other human beings, even when all is not steady and clear in your day to day experience—even if there is temporary chaos and confusion in your life.

This tendency to love is one of the most important patterns that you ones have been given by your souls. (We will look deeply into the area of love in a later chapter.) When you are able to nurture the tendency to love, and follow it in your relationships with one another in each day, then all of the other perfect patterns placed into you by your soul are more likely to be stirred into manifestation.

Your soul also implants within you qualities of determination, strength, courage, and forcefulness. When these capacities are recognized and valued by you, and when you act upon them day by day in the physical world, the result will be *success* in all of the areas of human life that you decide are important to you. Such success will fill your life with joy and love, which will help stimulate healthy influences in your life, and in your physical body.

There are so many complex energies that your soul has woven together in your personality matrix in its attempt to guide you toward fulfillment and health in this lifetime that it would take many volumes to fully explore all of them. Instead of describing each complex thread, we will portray all of them with a simple vision that will help you *feel* the interaction between *soul energies* and *personality choices*. It is this interaction, and the way you *manage* it day by day throughout your life, that will determine whether or not you have the fullest possible health in this lifetime.

Imagine that you have come to a mountain top with a large group of friends. You all have come to sing some beautiful songs together. However, as you arrive at the mountain top, there comes to be a general argument about where each one of you should sit. Soon, many ones are angry, and they are shouting at one another. Then, there is a large fight, in which all ones are striking one another. There is a wounding, and bleeding, and a great deal of pain. Finally, all of you go home without singing. Thus, even though you had a great *intention* to sing, the *manifestation* did not come about because you chose to focus upon *differences* and *disagreements*, rather than upon your intention.

In the same way, the souls of you ones, by placing all of the magnificent eternal energies into the personality matrix of each of you, *intended* for you to come forth into earth to rejoice together, to love all human beings, and to fulfill yourselves individually. And, in the early stages of earth life, human beings were able to do this for a number of generations. However, gradually, rather than focusing upon the intentions of the souls, which are the tendencies within you toward goodness and love, you ones *chose* to give more attention to human *differences*. Eventually, you became very frightened about those differences. Then, through many generations of human life, instead of following the impulses toward love placed into you by the souls, you began to choose to follow your fears. Eventually, that led you ones to fight with one another, rather than to love one another.

In this process of *choosing* to focus upon fear more than love, you ones created the seeds of all human discord, including the personal strife among individuals, and the larger struggles that end in wars between groups and countries. This is the fight on the mountain top, *created* by human beings, even though the souls' *intentions* were for you ones to sing together in love. In this disharmony, caused by human beings following fears about differences, you have the beginning of *disease* and *illness* within the human bodies.

Yet, all of the discord on the mountain top does not change the fact that you were intended to come together and sing with your friends. It does not prevent you and your friends from *returning* to the mountain top, and, this time, not giving your attention to differences, you can follow your *intentions*. You can place your emphasis upon the desire to sing. Then you will sing beautifully together.

The potent eternal energies that were aligned with the perfect intentions of the souls in the beginning of human life still live in all of you. They have lived in all of your various human personalities throughout your many lifetimes on earth. You can *choose* to place your attention upon those potent energies as they now live within you. You can emphasize them, and you can live them fully day by day. If *all* human beings did this, then you would all come together in understanding, and you would sing together, and you would rejoice in love. From this, you would gradually begin to make changes in the way that your human personalities stand between the eternal energies and your physical bodies. As a result of these changes, most of you would heal *from within*, and the magnificent and complete health that was intended for you by the eternal souls would be manifested fully in human life.

Chapter 2

Your Personality

And Your Soul

*—To create a healthy life, it is not necessary to be a perfect human being, in your eyes. It is only necessary for you to be an **honest** one. If you are consistently honest about your present qualities as a human being, then you will eventually come to know yourself so well that you can discover which personality patterns help you to heal, and which ones block your abilities.*

A s we have pointed out, in a simple way of speaking, your personality stands between the perfect energies of your soul and your physical body—your personality is the magnifying glass through which the soul energies must pass in order to reach your body. Thus, the human energies of thought, feeling, desire, memory, belief, and so forth that you create within your personality day after day will determine whether the glass will be clean or dirty, and that will dictate how much of the perfect energies of your soul will reach your body, or how much of them will be distorted or blocked.

This means that much of what determines whether you live your present life in health or illness lies within the many different energies that live inside your human personality. Therefore, in order to create full health in your life, you will need to find a way to discover the disruptive energies that you create in your personality that can interfere with the perfect forces of your soul, and you will need a way to heal those energies and free yourself from their limitation.

There are many different kinds of human personality energies that can trigger various tendencies toward illness and abnormal manifestations in your physical body. These include energies of confused thinking, feeling, desiring, willing, remembering, imagining, and so forth. Throughout these teachings, we will show you ways to learn about such human energies. But, for now, we will begin by giving you a principle that applies to all of the complexities of the many different thoughts, feelings, and attitudes that you could have about life. When clearly understood and acted upon, this profound principle can lead to full and complete health for most human beings. We will present the principle now. In later portions of these teachings we will expand upon specific ways to use it in your day to day life.

Concerning the relationship between your human personality energies and your health, we can say:

When there are emotional and mental

turmoils in your personality, experiences of badness, wrongness, fear, doubt, and all of the disturbances that are quite negative in human life, and when, persistently, *over a long period of time, you do not allow your personality to directly experience and heal those negative areas*—you either consciously or unconsciously push them aside—then, the unhealed negative personality experiences become the disruptive forces that can stir up inherent tendencies in your body toward a certain weakness or illness, or, they become forces that can inwardly cause malfunctioning in your body.

This is a very important principle that you can use to guide yourself, once you have thoroughly absorbed it and understood it. We will elaborate upon this principle in a later chapter. For now, we must look at certain areas of knowledge that are necessary for effectively using the principle.

YOUR RESERVOIR OF WISDOM

First of all, it is important to understand that all human beings have a vast reservoir of wisdom about life, and health, that lives within their present personality matrix. Yet, for most ones, there is not a conscious awareness of the existence of this store of knowledge. Thus, you have a great treasure within you that you are usually not aware of.

To feel how this lives inside you, imagine that you own a large field. Beneath the ground of that field there is much gold. At first, you do not know that the gold exists, and you believe that your land is worth-less. Thus, your first step in using your treasure is to discover that the gold is there.

Then, when you come to your field after discovering that the gold is there, you would not stand and hope that the gold would simply leap from the ground into your hand. You understand that the nature of this realm is that you must *dig* for the gold. Yet, as many of you attempt to draw healing knowledge to yourselves, particularly knowledge concerning the relationship between your physical body and your eternal soul, there is often the expectation that the knowledge will magically appear in the mind of yourself without any adjustment or work on your part. When the knowledge does not appear, then it is often assumed that such knowledge is not present inside you. This leads to a belief that many of you now hold, that the healing knowledge is *separate* from yourself, that you must go forth and find it outside of yourself, and then feed it into your human personality.

Gradually, many of you are beginning to realize that the true understandings of the eternal world, the physical world, and your personal place in both—particularly the place of your human personality and your physical body in human life—are already held *unconsciously* within your being. The gold already exists within the ground. *You* are the ground. Therefore, after you learn that the treasure is there, then your challenge is to uncover it—to bring to your *conscious* awareness, that which already exists within you unconsciously.

Even the willingness to simply *think about* this reservoir of wisdom that lives in you can cause a different kind of feeling to stir inside you. Instead of feelings of ignorance, emptiness, and impatience to rush out and try to fill yourself with knowledge from *beyond* you, there can come the realization that your task is to find a way to penetrate deeply beneath your own conscious awareness into the reservoir of hidden wisdom that presently lives *within* you.

THE NEED FOR NEWNESS AND CHANGE

To create a deeper understanding of the health of your human body, its relationship to your eternal soul, and, the "place" of your human personality between your body and your soul, you would also need to understand what we would call in human words, *newness* and *change*. If you would come forth into this lifetime only drawing upon what you have accumulated in other times of earth as a human being in your own past lifetimes, there might be a great deal of understanding and manifestation in many areas, but there would be a kind of *misalignment* with the *present* earth reality. That is because, often, *that which was true of human life in the past is not true in the present.*

The knowledge that you would draw forth from past stores of human wisdom—particularly that which was formalized and written down by human beings in the past, and which has been brought into the present time as ancient teachings—those areas can be quite interesting, *but they are not always ap-*

plicable to your present human existence. They often need to be *changed* in light of what your human personality is living in the present time.

Many of you who have attempted to draw upon ancient wisdom in order to fulfill yourselves and create health in the present time have often found disappointment. Therefore, in your desire to gain healing knowledge, even though you do need to encourage your ability to draw ancient wisdom from the past when it serves you, there is also the need to play your part as a *creator* of wisdom in this lifetime.

You are the one inside your human personality who must take your present base of knowledge about health and healing, and, in creativity, bring *new* understandings into the present time that are uniquely yours, that go beyond the old wisdom, and that fit your present earth reality. For example, many individuals have drawn upon older teachings that advise human beings to eat only vegetables, and to avoid eating the meat of animals. You need to understand that such teachings were created for circumstances and times that were much simpler than the present. You are living in a complex world that makes more demands upon your physical body, requiring more nutrients for your body to have the physical strength to meet those demands. Therefore, eating meat might be very beneficial for your particular body, even though some old teachings may warn against it.

At times, you will need to build upon the past wisdom and *change* it in order to create new knowledge for yourself as it is needed in the present. This is particularly true in the area of health, where there are now manifestations of certain diseases and other complexities that have never before existed in human life. You must learn to look inside yourself for the wisdom and understanding that will enable you to address all of your present complex human situations—particularly challenges to your health—with the creativity that is needed to discover *new* solutions that will work in the present.

As you work for newness, also be aware of the importance of *honesty* and *clarity* about what you are, temporarily, as a human being. It is not beneficial for you to say to yourself, "There are certain ways that I *must* be in order to be the *perfect* personality, in order to draw upon the eternal forces to create health in new ways in the present." To create a healthy life, it is not necessary to be a perfect human being, in your eyes. It is only necessary for you to be an *honest* one. If you are consistently honest about your present qualities as a human being, then you will eventually come to know yourself so well that you can discover which personality patterns help you to heal, and which ones block your abilities.

YOUR HEALTH, YOUR SOUL, AND GOD

Let us begin our understanding of the complex interactions between your human personality, your soul, your body, and the forces of God by focussing upon this thought: *All human beings leave earth through death. Your death will naturally bring about a dramatic change in the way you experience yourself.* However, *if you wait for death to bring about that change, you will rob your present personality in this lifetime.* Let us clarify this.

During the period between your birth and your death, which is your present human life, you are living a *temporary* physical existence in which your focus is intentionally narrowed in order to allow you to *intensify* your experience of the *physical* world. Therefore, you do not usually have conscious awareness of eternal realities. Yet, *before* your birth, your present human personality was aware of the energies of your soul and of God that sustain you. Then, at the physical birth of your present body, your human personality brought a kind of "veil of opaqueness" over this awareness. Your personality lost conscious knowledge of all of the divine energies that are woven into your being. You began to live the human illusion of being *separate* from such divine energies. This illusion will continue until the death of your physical body eventually releases you from your narrow human focus.

However, if you desire, while you are still alive in your present body, you can expand your human experience by bringing forth a conscious awareness of the divine energies that are woven with your human personality and your physical body. To accomplish this, you will need to make certain openings within your personality, which we will explore throughout these teachings.

You can begin to take a step toward such openings simply by creating *ideas* about the connections between yourself and the eternal energies that sustain you. To begin with a simple idea of the way in which the life of your human personality is organized around the energies of your soul and of God, we will use an image to communicate more directly to your feelings. Imagine a goldsmith who has brought forth a bar of gold to be made into a crown for a king. There is also a diamond merchant who has brought forth loose diamonds to put into the crown. *You* are the artist who must now create the crown. The gold and diamonds have been *given* to you. The crown itself must be *created* by you.

In your present personality matrix, the gold represents the *energy of your eternal existence*, the forces of perfection that have been given to you as an eternal soul by God itself. The diamonds are the many individual *abilities* and *capacities* that have been fashioned by your soul from the forces of God and given to your human personality by your soul. The crown that you will make from the gold and diamonds of magnificent energies is *your present personal experience of earth life*.

You can shape the energies of perfection, given to you by God, in any way that you decide, according to your personal desires, beliefs, attitudes, and so forth. You can use the many abilities of your personality, given to you by your soul, in any way that you desire. You are free to *create* your personal experience of human life in any way that pleases you.

You make your crown—your experience of human life—by constantly weaving together the abilities of thought, feeling, sensing, willing, desiring, acting, and so forth. The way that you weave all of the energies of your personality matrix that have been given to you by your soul, and by God, will determine how beautiful your crown will be in this lifetime.

It is through your *will*, and your *choice*, that you create your crown of personal experience. You can choose what to emphasize in your personality and your life, and you can choose what to ignore. Throughout your life, moment by moment, day by day, you can choose what to do, what not to do; what to feel, what not to feel; what to think, what not to think. You can choose how to *live* as a human being.

The way in which you make your personal choices each day will not only determine how happy you will be throughout your life, but it will affect the health of your human personality and your physical body. The more you are able to align your choices with your eternal being, the less will you create blockages to the health-giving and rejuvenating energies of God and your soul that constantly feed your personality matrix, and each cell of your physical body.

As you work with yourself to create your life day after day, in order to monitor how your choices are affecting your health, it is beneficial to often ask yourself:

"How am I choosing now, in this moment? How have I been choosing throughout my life? Do my choices fulfill me, or do they bring me pain? Am I being swept away by the various negative energies in my life? If so, do I desire to continue to be swept away, or do I desire to change my choices?"

By working honestly with yourself in this way, and in ways that we will suggest in later portions of these teachings, you can build your crown of experience of human life in a manner that will please and fulfill you, and that will move you toward a greater manifestation of health. And, if you would do this in *love*, then, most certainly, the healthy life that you create for yourself will be a portion of the fulfillment of all of those about you. You will feel that your life is not only a gift to you, but that you are creating a beauty and goodness in your life that is your contribution to others, and to the unfoldment of the forces of God on earth.

Chapter 3

The Cause Of
Human Illness

*—When you hide your negative thoughts and
feelings, and you avoid bringing them to your attention, then you do not gain enough experience
with them to recognize that human negativity is
temporary. You do not learn from direct experience that negative thoughts and feelings cannot
damage your being. But, you do begin to set up
the conditions by which your inner negative experience may damage your physical body.*

So far, we have only touched briefly upon some of
the ways that your personality can be involved in
creating blockages to your health. In order to go
deeper into the area of the *cause* of human illness,
we will now create a simple understanding that can
bring together the many different and divergent
ideas and beliefs that human beings have concerning
illness—the cause of illness, and the healing of it.

Let us begin with a vision of that which does *not* need to be healed—the *healthy* human expression. Then, we will show you what disrupts that health.

In looking at that which is the healthy human being, you would see, of course, a physical body that is free of any abnormal symptoms—a fully functioning body that has no disease or malfunction. Now, it is important to realize that in such a body, there are not necessarily *perfect* human personality energies. In fact, at this time, *there are many healthy human bodies on the face of the earth within which there are quite negative personality energies*. Thus, within normal, healthy bodies, there can exist negative human energies that have the *potential* to disrupt health. There are a number of factors, which we shall now explore, that will determine whether or not the negative personality energies will actually disrupt the health of the physical body.

THOUGHTS, FEELINGS, AND YOUR BODY

Among the many different human personality energies that affect the physical bodies of human beings, those that will most determine whether the body remains healthy or not are the energies of human *thought* and *feeling*. We could say that, in most cases, the healthy physical body will remain healthy if the thoughts and feelings are worked with in certain ways—ways that we will examine later. However, before you can work in those ways, you will need a clear understanding of how your thoughts, your feelings, and your physical body interact.

Although some of you already understand that

you are not your physical body, nevertheless, at least while you temporarily live in the physical world, your body is extremely important to you. In a way, it is natural to identify with your body, and that helps you value your day to day physical existence. However, identifying with your body does lead to some confused attitudes about who *you* really are.

Because you identify yourself with your physical body, in everyday experience you do not usually separate your body from your thoughts and feelings, or from your sense of yourself. When your body is damaged, you feel damaged. When your body is threatened, you feel threatened. When there is a thought of your body being destroyed, you have a feeling of fear that *you* will be destroyed. Your body and its physical condition can also trigger many different thoughts and feelings that all become mixed together inside of you as an experience that you usually accept as the *reality* of your being.

To go beyond this ordinary human sense of entanglement of body, thoughts, and feelings, we now ask you to balance it with a larger awareness of your *real* being. In this larger awareness, you would see that the truth is that you have come into earth in many different human bodies, and, *you have left every one of those bodies through death.* Still, *you* are not diminished or damaged. You continue to exist as a magnificent eternal being. And, once again, as a *human* being, you are now temporarily housed in a physical body—a body that you will eventually leave through death.

As we have pointed out earlier, in order to maintain the fullest health in your physical body, you will need to feel, or at least try to imagine, your eternal existence, which is not dependent upon your physical body. On the other hand, to remain committed to your present earth life, and to find purpose and meaning in it, you will need to acknowledge and respect the temporary fact that your present body is extremely important to you.

Now, while balancing these two aspects of you in your mind, return your thoughts to the principle that we have given in a previous chapter: When you hold negative thoughts and feelings within yourself for a long period of time without working honestly with them, they can cause a disruption of your health. From this you can begin to see that the relationship between your thoughts, your feelings, and your physical body, and, the way that relationship affects your health, can be simply stated in this way: *Human negative thoughts and feelings can create the distorted energies within your personality that are the beginning of illness and disease that manifest in your physical body.* The human personality energies of doubt, fear, pain, and other negative personal experiences, in interaction with your body, are the seeds of disruption of the health of the body. They are the energies that can cause your personality to become a barrier between the perfect eternal energies of your soul, and your physical body. They can become the dirt on the magnifying glass that temporarily prevents the full force of the eternal energies from passing through to your body.

We must extend this a bit further. It is not the

fear, doubt, pain, and negative personality experiences themselves that can cause illness in your physical body. *It is the swallowing, or suppressing of those experiences* without honesty, without clarity, without enough opportunity to bring those experiences to the surface in order to live through them, to share them, to express them, and to realize that they are *only* thoughts and feelings.

To elaborate upon this, let us imagine a female one who is deeply in love with a male one, but the male one is quite cruel and insensitive. The male one rejects the female, and she begins to fall into despair. She has feelings of depression and great pain. However, let us say that instead of allowing those negative feelings to come fully to the surface, she says to herself, "I must be strong and independent now. I do not need him. I will not allow him to cause me pain." She tightens her feelings and refuses to allow herself to feel any pain. She pretends that she does not care. She hardens her heart to the male one. In this response, she is swallowing and suppressing her negative patterns instead of expressing them, and she is setting the stage for future challenge to her health.

Now, imagine a male one who often has angry feelings toward his female mating-one. But, he is afraid that if he shows her his anger, she will stop loving him, and he will lose her. So, he continually pushes away his feelings of anger, and he pretends that he is calm and happy when he is with her. He too is swallowing strong negative feelings that need to come to the surface, and he is inviting the challenge of illness into his life.

When you hide your negative thoughts and feelings, and you avoid bringing them to your attention, then you do not gain enough experience with them to recognize that human negativity is *temporary*. You do not learn from direct experience that negative thoughts and feelings cannot damage your *being*. But, you do begin to set up the conditions by which your inner negative experience may damage your *physical body*.

THE CAUSE OF ILLNESS

Looking more closely now at the cause of human illness, we would say that illness is caused in a healthy body when the personality inside that body, over a period of time, has not been able to bring negative thoughts and feeling to the surface in order to live them, communicate about them, and heal them. To express this as a general guideline for your mind, we could say: *The process that is most illness-causing, that is most debilitating to the human physical body, is set into motion by constantly swallowing negativity, by holding fears and negative thoughts and feelings within the personality over a period of time without healing them.*

Let us call this illness-causing process, *personality disruption*. When the negative inner experiences of life are constantly swallowed, then personality disruption occurs. This process of personality disruption usually comes about because the personality has not had enough experience with life to know that it needs to bring the inner negativity to the surface and heal it. When the personality disruption occurs, *it generates the negative human energies that can eventually manifest as illness and disease in the physical body.*

When individuals are creating personality disruption by swallowing negativity instead of healing it, even though they may at times be consciously aware of some of the fear and other negative human experiences that are associated with the disruption, the actual process of swallowing the negativity is usually *unconscious.* The individuals are usually not aware that they have developed a habit of suppressing much of their negative inner experience, so they continue to do it without realizing what they are doing. In such cases, before steps can be taken toward healing, the person will need to do some inner work in order to become aware of the habit of swallowing the negativity.

For example, let us imagine a male one who is miserable in his work because his supervisor is constantly criticizing him. The male one becomes very angry with his supervisor, and he begins to hate him. Yet, he believes that if he shows his anger and hatred, he will be dismissed. Thus, he constantly swallows those strong feelings, without noticing, and he convinces himself that he actually likes his supervisor. In this response, the male one might preserve his job, but he unknowingly sets up a habit of suppressing strong negative feelings that need his attention. In order to heal such feelings, he would first need to become aware that he is swallowing them. Then, he would need to find a way to bring them to the surface, express them, and heal them.

HOW ILLNESS HAPPENS

We have spoken of the eternal energies of your soul that constantly feed your personality and body. To understand how illness actually manifests in the human body, you could begin by holding in your mind the fact that your present physical body is sustained by many different kinds of non-physical, spiritual energies. Considered all together, these different energies can be understood, in a general way, as the energies of God itself. Such energies would include the energies of your own eternal soul, energies of guiding souls to you, energies of certain magnificent beings beyond earth that would be difficult to describe for you at this time, and the extraordinary, creative, loving energies of life that you might consider to be God itself. Thus, when we speak of your human personality being a magnifying glass through which a light must pass in order to shine on your body, you could consider that the light entering the glass represents the combined energies from all of these sources. When your personality disruption dirties the glass, then you are temporarily interfering with all of these eternal energies as they attempt to infuse themselves into your physical body.

These eternal energies are quite different than anything that you know of in the physical world. For the moment, we will not attempt to enter into a description of the nature of these energies. We will simply remind you that these energies constantly flow into and sustain your personality matrix. They also attempt to pass through your human personality in order to enter into the actual *matter* of your physical body itself, by entering into the blood, and by diffusing into all of the cells of your body.

With this in mind, let us return to the healthy human body. In a healthy infant, you would understand that the eternal energies that we have described enter into the child's body and animate the blood and all cells of the body. When there is no interference, the eternal energies perfectly feed each cell of the infant body with a kind of reality that we can only describe as *a certainty that there is only good, that there is no danger, that there is nothing that can destroy your being. This is the truth of all life, outside of the human subjective experience of negativity,* and the eternal energies feed this truth into every cell of the infant body.

As this human infant would grow, and as the fears of the present lifetime are stimulated, and then exaggerated by unconscious fear patterns brought from past lifetimes on earth, there is created within the personality the disruption that generates the kind of energy that we have called negative mental and emotional energy. Such negative human energies are quite *temporary*. They exist *only* within the inner experience—within the human personality—of human beings. Essentially, these negative mental and emotional energies cease after the death of the physical body.

Even though these negative human energies have only a temporary existence, in terms of human experience within physical reality, negative mental and emotional energies are usually *experienced* by you as

being much stronger than the perfect eternal energies that constantly feed your personality matrix.
And, even though the eternal energies have *created*
the physical reality, and actually sustain the physical
body, since the nature of human existence is built
upon human free will within the physical world, the
souls allow human thought and emotional energies
to *temporarily* have a much stronger impact upon
physical bodies than the eternal energies, in the
physical sense. In other words, the energies of human thought and emotion are temporarily allowed to
override the perfection of the eternal energies that
feed the physical body. That is why your negative
personality energies can become the dirt on the
magnifying glass—the barrier that stands between
the perfect eternal energies and your physical body.

When the growing child begins to swallow and
suppress fears and negative experiences, not being
able to bring them to the surface, fully experience
them, communicate them, and heal them day after
day, and this is continued over a period of time, then
the personality disruption occurs, generating those
strong negative mental and emotional energies that
temporarily override the eternal energies as they attempt to feed the cells of the body. In this way, the
negative human energies begin to impinge upon the
perfect functioning of the cells within the physical
body, creating an unintended distortion.

To describe this distortion in a simple way, we
would say that, before the distortion, the perfect
eternal energies were constantly feeding the cells of
the body in a way that would say to each cell, in ef-

fect, "All is good," and, "You are safe." The distortion created by the unhealed negative mental and emotional energies overrides that influence, and it says to the cells, *"There is danger here."*

Under the pressure of this "danger warning" from the negative human energies, the cellular structures begin to respond in ways that you would understand as *abnormal*. The cells begin a kind of an *emergency* response, in which factors that were not intended for ordinary cellular life and growth are stirred into action. For example, the disease that you call "cancer" is one of the abnormal cellular responses set up by this kind of emergency response within the cells.

This is a very simple way to hold in your mind how it is that human negative thoughts and feelings can begin to disrupt the perfect functioning of the physical body, even when the body is constantly being fed by the eternal energies of God. We will explore this in greater depth in a later section.

INFLUENCE OF THE SOUL

Now, you must add to all that we have described, the understanding that we have previously mentioned, which is, that present human beings, earlier, as eternal souls, standing beyond earth before your present human birth, did actually create your own fetus forms. Wielding the complex and unlimited eternal energies, you as souls chose the kind of physical bodies you would inhabit in this lifetime. And, many souls, for reasons that we will speak of later, chose to impinge upon the perfect functioning of their fetus form, even before its birth.

Thus, there would be infant bodies that at birth come forth into life with less than perfect physical functioning. This could manifest as an obvious deformity, illness, or abnormality of physical functioning, or, it might manifest as *tendencies* toward disease or ill health that will arise later in the child's life. Thus, there will be children who do *not* create the kind of negative, disruptive human energies that we have described, yet, there will still be an overriding of the perfect eternal forces that feed each cell of their body, because the soul has chosen for the personality to live in a body that is less than perfect. Clearly, in such cases, limitations to the health of the individual are *not* caused by the negative mental and emotional energies that we have described. We will expand upon this in the following chapter.

Chapter 4

Soul Choices
And Health

*—You can generate certain "healing energies"...
that can accelerate the eternal energies that constantly feed the cells of your body. ... the creative, positive human energies of your thoughts
and feelings can **amplify** the forces of God by
inviting them more fully through the threshold of
matter to become more active in the stimulation
of the cells of your physical body.*

A s we have indicated, there are many complex
relationships between yourself as a human personality, and you as an eternal soul, particularly in the
factors that can affect your health. We shall now attempt to further clarify this area for you by examining the relationship between the *choices* of your
eternal soul, and the choices of your human personality.

First of all, let us look at the human desire for

health. You need to recognize that all of your desires in human personality are, for the most part, rooted in a desire for *pleasure*. When you say, "I desire health," usually, you are not choosing health out of a strong idealistic, spiritual impulse, but out of the quite natural desire for the *pleasure*, the human satisfaction and joy, that you have when you are healthy and free from the pain of illness. This tendency to choose for the pleasure of health can often be woven with confused and distorted patterns of thought and feeling within an individual.

For example, let us imagine a male one who is of the age of thirty years. Let us say that he has an unusually intense, over-exaggerated focus upon sexual pleasure that has caused a lack of interest in a deep, sensitive relationship with a female. Let us say that it has even caused in him a lack of interest in understanding the females that he is intimate with, to the extent that he would have little caring for them personally. Thus, you would see in this one a kind of roughness and insensitivity. The result is that with the many female ones with whom he would make sexual union, he would be concerned only with his own pleasure. This would cause a great deal of challenge and pain for the females who would come toward him desiring deeper love, desiring more than a superficial sexual engagement.

Imagine that in this male one, as he comes to be forty years old, he has not balanced these exaggerated tendencies, and he becomes obsessed with health in order to maintain his seductive charm, in order to satisfy his sexual needs. The result of this would be that he would adopt a perfect regime of diet, exercise, rest, and all that is important to the health of the physical body. At the same time, you would see, deep within him, an impulse of his own soul gently prodding him toward learning about his fearful personality patterns that cause him to over-emphasize sexual pleasure, and to, thereby, miss the deeper aspects of love relationships that his soul has intended for his personality.

Now, in a way—and this is a bit difficult for words because of the human tendency to see his soul and his personality as *different* entities—we could say that in spite of the work that he is *consciously* doing to create perfect health, there are deep *unconscious* energies of wisdom within his personality matrix that would essentially "give permission" for the soul to begin to stimulate latent patterns and tendencies toward illness in his physical body. Such tendencies toward illness would have been placed into the fetus form of his body by his soul before his birth.

Let us say that this tendency toward illness would be a tendency toward the disease of *diabetes*. This tendency would be associated with his hunger for emotional sweetness and love in his life, and with his fearful unwillingness to allow his heart to be touched. Even though he would have many sexual unions, there would be no real love and sweetness in his life.

Therefore, the soul of himself would set into motion the latent tendency toward diabetes which has been *chosen* by unconscious wisdom energies within his personality matrix. The result would be the manifestation of the disease of diabetes within his body, even though his conscious personality had chosen perfect health. The disease comes about because of an "agreement" made with his soul.

AGREEMENTS WITH THE SOUL

All human beings have their own particular agreements with their soul. Some of these agreements would say, "This human lifetime will be led relatively free of physical challenge to the body." So, for such human beings, even when they go forth in their choices to create negative thoughts and feelings for long periods without healing them, and even if they engage in eating, drinking, and living activities that, in general, would tend to damage most bodies, because of the agreement with their soul, the strong potent energies of the soul are not held back from the cells of the body by the negative human personality energies. Because the soul, for many reasons, desired health for a lifetime for the physical body, the negative human energies that would ordinarily be detrimental to the health of the physical body are simply "brushed aside" by the eternal energies.

For those human beings who create negative human energies that *do* cause detriment to the physical body, you must assume that there is a kind of "giving way" of the soul energies to the human choices in order to allow the human energies to hold full sway over the body. At times, this is done to bring forth a kind of revelation, to the human personality, of certain things that the personality refuses to pay attention to and understand.

For example, if a female one would constantly ignore that part of her personality that wishes to love others and nurture them, and she has fears to open that part of herself, and she does not heal the fears, then, it is possible that the negative human energies that she generates by the unhealed fears may eventually lead to a disease that manifests in her breasts. Such a disease would turn her attention, consciously or unconsciously, to the area of her life that has to do with nurturing others, or being nurtured. In the course of grappling with the disease, she may reveal to herself the underlying fear patterns that need to be healed.

When the soul decides that there is no important personality learning to be gained by creating a tendency toward illness in the physical body, then the body is left rather "neutral." The soul does not set any particular strong direction for the physical body, and the body is left to the influences of the *personality choices* throughout the lifetime. This allows the human personality to learn about the consequences of its choices by seeing them demonstrated upon the body, according to the laws of physical matter.

To clarify this, imagine a male one who has smoked cigarettes for many years. The soul of himself has *not* created an oversensitivity in his lungs—in his body there would be no inherent tendency toward lung disease. Thus, the state of his lungs is left neutral, and those lungs will respond to the impact of the cigarette smoke in accordance with the laws of physical matter. In such a case, the lung tissues would be irritated, scarred, and damaged by the smoking. The result could be a negative over-stimulation of the cellular structures that could cause a cancerous response in the lungs.

WHEN THE SOUL CHOOSES ILLNESS

One of the most difficult soul choices for human beings to understand is when the soul chooses illness and disease for the physical body. To help you in this understanding, we would ask that you would now imagine that you are one of great and vast wealth. There is no need in your life to ever make any kind of work, or effort. Yet, you are youthful. You are vigorous. You are passionate about life. Therefore, you decide to go forth and climb a large mountain. You would toil and strain for many days to climb this mountain. There would be a great deal of pain, stress, cold, and fear. And a one would say to you, "Why would you make such a choice that is so painful?"

Such a question is asked by ones who are looking only at the challenge and pain involved in your mountain climbing. They expect you to follow the natural human tendency to withdraw from negativity and avoid it. They cannot see the purpose and meaning, the joy, and the deep sense of accomplishment that are involved in your climb up the mountain. They cannot see through the pain and negativity to the truth that lies beneath it.

In human life, *if you look only at challenge and pain, and you withdraw from it, you will never see the truth of life, or understand the choices of your soul.* Often, the important choices of your soul will lead you into situations that involve some challenge and pain for you. If you run from the situation because of the pain in it, you will never become aware of the soul choice that you needed to understand and make a part of your life.

For example, let us imagine that you have an exaggerated fear of anger and hostility in your human relationships. And, let us say that one of your important soul desires in this lifetime is for you to heal that fear. Thus, your soul begins to strongly guide you to come into contact with people who tend to be angry and hostile toward you, so that you can have your fear stirred up, can experience it, communicate about it, and heal it. However, as you come into contact with those people, instead of allowing the beneficial angry interactions to occur, you decide that those people cause you too much pain, and you simply turn away from them and avoid them. In turning away from the pain, you are missing the deeper truth, and you are passing by important learning that could be very beneficial to you in your life.

Many humans are so frightened of negativity and pain that, at times, they will make their choices and decisions in life primarily on the basis of *avoiding that which is painful*. It would be extremely difficult for them, with those kinds of personality patterns, to even imagine that it could be an extraordinary accomplishment for a soul to bring forth strength, courage, and creativity into a body that, from your point of view, is not considered perfect—that is diseased, malformed, or limited in some way. You would simply see negativity, not the deeper purposes and meaningful reasons why the soul chose a body with such physical challenges.

To fully understand why the souls would choose to bring forth physical human bodies that you would see as imperfect, you will need to grapple with your own feelings of *badness* about negativity. You will need to work through your own fears and doubts in those areas and heal them.

Until you can feel the extraordinary sense of accomplishment, mastery, and satisfaction that can come from overcoming challenges in earth, it will be difficult for you to understand why, and to *feel* why, an eternal soul, with all of the universes to choose from, and with all possibilities at its command, would choose, for example, a badly deformed infant body that would necessitate the experiencing of the pain of crippling arthritis for an entire lifetime. Why a soul would choose for the child to begin life with severe facial and bodily deformities that would cause others to shrink back at the sight of such grotesqueness. Why there would come a sudden disease that would end the life of an innocent child after only a short period of time in life, causing grief and pain to the ones around the child.

These are extremely difficult areas to understand when you stand in the midst of an extraordinary world seeing only the negativity, and saying and believing, "Negativity is bad." Therefore, you will need to bring your feelings of badness about such areas to the surface, *experience* them, *communicate* them, and *heal* them. By doing that, you can make the adjustments within your attitudes and beliefs that will open the door for you to eventually come to know the extraordinary joy that an eternal soul—and we remind you that *you* are that soul—can experience from having mastered an earth life under difficult circumstances.

To help you more fully understand the way in which certain soul choices bring forth a lack of perfection in the health of some human bodies, we can generalize about certain "categories" of soul choices. Let us say that the first category includes soul choices in which it is very important to the soul that there be imperfections or disease that either manifest at the birth of the human body, or that manifest at a later time in the life of the person. In these cases, for the most part—and here it is not accurate to generalize for *all* human beings—we can say that no matter what the human beings choose to do in their life, mentally, emotionally, and physically, the influencing soul energies will still manifest the challenge to health. Thus, if a soul would choose a cancerous growth in the breast of its physical body, no matter how loving and nurturing the human personality would be, by the soul's choice, the cells in that part of the body would be so over-sensitive that there would be the manifestation of the disease in the breast area.

In this category, there are not a great number of instances of such soul choices, but they do exist. In such cases, the challenge to the individual is not so much to heal the physical body, but to heal the mind and the emotions—to bring forth the courage and strength that are necessary to joyfully live the magnificence of God in each day, even under the great pressure of disease, illness, or other limit to the body.

Of more common occurrence is the category in which the soul chooses to leave the unfoldment of the human body to be tied directly to the *choices* of the human personality.

LETTING THE PERSONALITY CHOOSE

When the soul does not deliberately choose illness, then the human personality itself will determine the health of the physical body. Any malfunctioning of the body, excluding those caused by environmental factors, will be brought about by the various choices that the human being makes in life, day after day. In such cases, as we have stressed, the primary causative forces upon the health of the body will be the thought and emotional energies that come from personality choices.

This can be a complex area because there are certain principles, or "laws" that will determine *how* the human personality choices affect the body. These laws have been created by the souls in the beginning of human time, and they live in the physiological structure of all human bodies. In the human brain itself, there is, to put it simply, a capacity for "dealing out" to the whole body the negative influences that are created by the personality choices. This is quite simplified, but we can say that, under the brain's direction, there are certain physiological, "animal" structures in the body that respond in particular ways to different types of fear and negativity, under different situations. Thus, a certain kind of human negativity can produce a certain disruption in a particular part of the body.

For most humans, these are not hard and fast principles, but, for example, those who squeeze the joy out of their lives for many years would find that the disruptive energies that they create will usually result in physical challenges in the lungs. Most who would swallow their truth, and would fear to speak the truth out loud for many years, would find that the disruptive energies would tend to be directed toward a challenge to the health of the throat. The feeling of carrying tremendous burdens in life for many years, without healing those feelings, would generally result in some kind of difficulty in the shoulders of the body. Constant unhealed fear that there will be badness in the future can stir up a fear to walk toward the future, which can bring about challenges to the legs and feet. A persistent feeling, that goes unhealed for a long period of time, that there is too much pain in life to take in—that you cannot digest life because it is too painful—can lead to challenges in the digestive system of the body. Similar feelings of fear that painful emotions cannot pass through you without damaging you can lead to challenges in the area of the kidneys.

There are many principles such as these that you can learn to use as guidelines to understand how your body will respond to different kinds of negative mental and emotional energies. You can also use your intuitive capacities to draw upon your own inner wisdom to discover such principles. However, you must remind yourself that such principles are not absolute. There is much variation and difference of patterns within all human beings. Thus, you will need to be flexible as you use such principles to guide yourself in your own life, and in your attempts to help others.

As you work with your own human personality choices in your attempt to guide yourself in healing, and in the process of maintaining health, you must be aware that you can generate certain "healing energies"—and we are speaking now of certain *human* energies related to your thoughts and emotions—that can actually accelerate the eternal energies that constantly feed the cells of your body. In terms of physical reality, the creative, positive human energies of your thoughts and feelings can *amplify* the forces of God by inviting them more fully through the threshold of matter to become more active in the stimulation of the cells of your physical body. In other words, when your magnifying glass of personality patterns is clear, it will *intensify* the light of eternal energies passing through it to your body. In a later chapter, we will look more closely at these human healing energies and the way that you can work with them in your own healing.

These kinds of human healing energies also are directed in certain complex ways by the physical brain, and by certain physiological functionings similar to what we have described as the animal functioning of the body that responds to the way that the brain deals out energies. Thus, if you have caused illness in the lung areas of your body by many years of squeezing the joy out of life, and you begin a deep, loving kind of trusting and opening that creates joy, and you begin to stimulate your human healing energies, then, crudely speaking, in a manner similar to the way in which your brain would have directed your negative thought and feeling energies into your lungs to cause the illness, the brain will now direct your creative human energies—aligned with eternal energies that you have chosen to bring through the threshold of matter in a more intense way—into the afflicted area of the lungs.

By healing your fears and negative personality patterns, you stimulate the human healing energies, and then your brain directs those energies to the appropriate part of your body. Thus, as you learn more about your negative personality patterns that can be involved in specific kinds of illness, you become more prepared to create the appropriate healing energies within yourself that will dissolve the illness and bring about a healing.

GENETIC MAKEUP AND HEALTH

Another area that must be considered in understanding how your health is related to the choices of your soul is the area that you would call heredity, or the *genetic makeup* of the physical body. In truth, human genetic makeup is simply an extension of the soul's choices into the physiological structure of the human body. In other words, the souls have created physical bodies to respond to the influence of the human genes, and, the souls' actually control those genes. Therefore, the impact of heredity upon the physical body will be similar to what we have looked at earlier, in terms of the soul making choices that will influence the body.

For example, if there is a strong soul desire that a particular human being will struggle with cancer and die of it in this lifetime, and that is a soul choice that is relatively certain, then, the *tendency* to manifest cancer would be present in the child's body at birth. In such a case, there would be certain cellular patterns created in the child's body, by the soul of the child, that would be linked to the fetus growth in the womb of the mother. To accomplish this, the soul might choose for the child to be born to a mother who would have what you would call the "genetic" tendencies toward cancer. The body of the mother would then be the avenue whereby the soul of the child would create the tendency to cancerous responses in the body of the child.

All of this would be controlled by the soul of the child, the soul of the mother, and the soul of the father, through the manipulation of the genes within each of the human bodies involved. Scientifically, you would consider the child's "inheritance" of the cancerous tendency to be the result of certain actions within the genes, having little understanding of what *causes* human genes to form the particular structures that they do. Being unable to perceive the energies of the souls at work upon the genes of the father, the mother, and the child, and not realizing that *soul choices* cause the genes to do what they do, many humans would attribute the formation of genetic structures to a kind of random chance.

In another human being who has no soul tendency toward cancerous growth in the body, there could be a mother with even more of a cancerous tendency in her genes, but the soul does not choose for the child to "inherit" the tendency. In this case, the genetic structure of the child would not be affected by the tendency to cancer, and there would not be any hereditary link involving cancer. As long as the child maintained healthy choices, it would never be challenged by cancer throughout its lifetime.

What you call genetic structure and heredity can be seen as the *context* created by the souls as a means of carrying out the intentions of the souls for the physical bodies of earth. The genes are the structure *created* by eternal souls in the beginning of human life, through which human procreation can be more efficiently controlled by the souls.

As a crude example to show you the feeling of this, imagine that you would go forth to play the sport of *bowling*. You are free to set the bowling pins in the street and to throw your ball at them. You would be playing the sport of bowling in that way. However, the *context* is not perfect. You would need to chase the ball down the street. It is much more efficient to go to a bowling alley where the ball will be contained. Thus, the bowling alley is the perfect context for the sport of bowling. In a similar way, the perfect physical context for the soul who wishes its human body to die of cancer is for the child to be born into a family with a genetic structure that includes a tendency toward cancer. The genetic structure of the family thereby contributes the physical factors to the makeup of the child's body that will accomplish the purpose of the soul, which is to have the body of the personality die of cancer.

HEREDITY, ENVIRONMENT, AND HEALTH

Many times, the choices of a soul are exercised in ways that, from your perspective, appear to be heredity. Thus, if you would come into earth with a tendency toward weakened eyesight that is intended to manifest later in your life, you would need to understand that you will have weakened eyesight, in spite of your own personality growth and accomplishment, because your soul has desired a certain diminishment of your eyesight for important purposes. There are some influences that are "hereditary," in the sense that it has been agreed that they will be a part of the human life, and, in most cases, they will manifest, regardless of the choices that the human beings make.

In such cases, you must remind yourself that *you* are the soul. *You* have decided to bring about such influences upon your physical body. As a soul, you made the choice to *create* the hereditary tendency. Thus, you have created the reality that you must live with. As you learn more and more about how you create your own reality, you will come to realize that although most of your present reality is created by you as a human being through your thoughts and feelings, much of it is created by you as an eternal soul.

As you come forth as a newborn infant, if there

are inherited abnormalities that manifest immediately as physical limitations, then, of course, your child personality will begin life with these limitations. In such cases, the limitations simply need to be *accepted*—you will not usually change those factors. The inherited characteristics chosen by your soul will shape your physical life. Your area of choice, as a human being, will be how you *respond* to the inherited qualities.

Then, as a growing child, your human *environment*—meaning all of the people, places, and things about you—will begin to trigger certain responses in you. Here again, you would need to understand that the environment in which you find yourself will also reflect *choices* made by you as an eternal soul.

For example, a certain soul might say, "The personality that I now project into human form will come forth to an angry father. As a small child, the child will most likely be beaten physically. This will of course be painful for a while, but it will have many important purposes of learning and healing for the child, for the father, and for the entire family." In such a case, the soul's choices will bring the child into an environment that will have a strong negative impact upon the life of the child. The child may appear to have no choice, in terms of the creation of its environment, but, as always, the personality of the child does have a choice in how to *respond* to the environmental factors chosen by the soul.

You must assume that your soul has an understanding of all of the possibilities that you can unfold in this lifetime. Your soul would have a knowledge that certain difficult and dramatic environmental factors will strongly affect your personality in ways that will eventually benefit you. Thus, your soul will have many important, positive purposes for sending you into environmental factors that may appear negative or difficult to you.

In terms of how heredity and environment can affect your health, it might appear that the choice is out of your hands. However, you must remember that you are always free to use the magnificent energies within you to create health for yourself, no matter what hereditary or environmental factors you might be working with in your life.

You also have the capacity to *unintentionally* create a *lack* of health by the way you work with your thoughts and feelings about heredity and environment. For example, let us say that your father suffered from severe mental illness. If you have a strong belief that you are, due to heredity, susceptible to mental illness, then, you can create fears and distortions within your personality that might eventually manifest mental illness, even though it was *not* a part of your soul's choices. In such a case, the mental illness would not be inherited. It would be *created* by your human fears, and your distortions of thought and feeling.

There are certain environmental factors that can affect your health, regardless of what you might do in your thoughts and feelings. These include the *physical* forces in life that impinge upon your animal nature—your physical body. Thus, if you drink a strong poison, you will die, whether you know you have drunk the poison or not, and even if you *believe* that your body cannot be damaged by the poison. If you breathe toxic fumes, your respiratory system will suffer, no matter what you are thinking or feeling at the time. Such physical forces in the environment will act upon your body in a way that must conform to the laws of physical matter.

You ones do live within a physical environment that at times might challenge your health. However, you must assume that your soul understood that this would be the case. You must assume that your soul had full knowledge of all of the environmental conditions that human beings might create on earth, and that your soul anticipated all that you must work with in the environment, and, indeed, gave you the capacity to work with and master your environment.

Chapter 5

Your Health
And Your Inner Life

*—No matter what happens to you in the outside
physical world in this lifetime, you have the wisdom and the strength to inwardly **respond** to all
that takes place with total freedom, and you have
the wisdom and the power to **choose** your responses in any moment.*

One of the most wonderful gifts that your human
personality has been given by your soul is the rich-
ness, intensity, and variety of your inner life. Your
human ability to think, feel, remember, desire, and
imagine, and your capacity to have all of your other
marvelous inner experiences that you have in each
day of your life is made possible by the most extraordinary creative accomplishments of the eternal
souls.

Yet, many human beings do not appreciate the

miraculous nature of their inner life, and they tend to take it for granted. Some are even dissatisfied with it, or feel that it is bad. Not only do you ones often fail to appreciate your inner life, but, many of you do not realize that in living your day to day existence, what you decide to do with your inner life—the way that you manage it—will determine whether or not you manifest the fullness of health that your soul intends for you in this lifetime.

Even though we have said earlier that your health depends upon your awareness of your eternal nature as a soul, the accomplishment of *full* health requires more than the knowledge about your soul and the eternal realities that we have been exploring with you. It is not your soul that comes down into the physical earth life to make the many daily human choices that will result either in health or illness for you. It is your *human personality* that has been sent to make those choices. And, to make sound choices, you will need knowledge about how you as a personality create your inner life, moment by moment.

For the most part, the important energies in your inner life that are involved in maintaining health and in healing illness are the ones that are under your *conscious* control. They are your own personality patterns that we have been speaking about, including your thoughts, feelings, desires, beliefs, attitudes, memories, and so forth. All of these make up the *inner patterns* that you will need to learn to work with in an intelligent and loving way if you wish to manifest the fullest health possible in your earth life.

YOUR COMPLEX INNER PATTERNS

Each human personality is extremely complex, in terms of the various conscious and unconscious patterns that make up your inner life. You can easily realize your complexity by contemplating the extraordinary number and variety of thoughts and feelings that you have been aware of up to this point in your life. Then, you would need to greatly multiply that number of conscious experiences to account for your many *un*conscious patterns. Added to this are the vastly complex eternal energies that constantly interact with your human personality patterns during this lifetime. Then, of course, all of this is multiplied by thousands, in terms of the many lifetimes that you have lived as a human being on earth. Also, your complexity includes the extraordinary energies that have to do with your continuing life as a soul in vast eternal realms of existence.

We are not suggesting that you must fully understand all of this complexity in order to create health. Only *allow* for it, by not demanding simple and immediate answers to the questions that you have about yourself and your inner patterns. Because you are so complex, you will need to have patience as you work to learn about your inner life. Yet, even without complete understanding of your complexity, you can still learn to create your inner life day by day in ways that can bring forth health for you in this lifetime.

Let us begin our understanding of the complex personality patterns of your inner life by creating a simple vision to help you feel this area. Looking with you now at yourself as a human being who has come forth as an extension of an eternal soul, you are much as a small child who has been given a wonderful *package*, a beautiful present. Imagine the child holding the large box, wrapped beautifully in papers quite colorful. Within the child, there is a great feeling of excitement. This present could be *anything*. The entire world of *possibilities* is open. You as an eternal soul have prepared such a package for you as a human personality. As a soul standing beyond earth, you are joined to *all* realities, including those that are physical, and those that are not physical in form. You are joined to all universes. And, you are commanding many realms. When it is time for you as a soul to create a new human personality, you have the possibilities of all of those vast realities from which to choose energies. Just as if you are choosing some gifts to put in a box for a child, you as a soul are choosing certain traits and characteristics to put into the personality matrix and the physical body that will be your next human form. As you make your soul choices, you have all universes to draw upon. This is the way your own soul would have made *its* choices before your present birth.

This "box" of traits and characteristics that you have been given as a present by your soul includes *tendencies* for you to think in a certain way, to respond emotionally in a certain way, to have certain ideas and attitudes, and to create in a particular way the many different inner patterns that live in your human personality. As you are born into your human life, you open this box of human traits and qualities, and there can be a great deal of joy in this as you discover all of the wonderful gifts that you have been given by your soul.

However, as you develop your personality traits and begin to grow, it comes to be *your* time to choose. Your soul has made its choices by narrowing the field of eternal possibilities to those that are most important to place into your package of personality and bodily qualities. Now, it is up to you as a human being to *choose* what to do in the *physical* world with all of those gifts given to you by your soul. You are free to ignore them and do nothing—to become passive and lazy, and live a life of flatness and lack of fulfillment. Or, you might push yourself harshly, you might force yourself, you might be unintelligent and misuse some of your abilities. You are also free to choose to unfold all of your abilities with great creativity, strength, and love, thereby fulfilling the purposes for which your soul gave you the gifts.

For most of you who have now come to adulthood in human life, you tend to be relatively stabilized in certain human personality patterns. You have already made some choices that have become *habits* of thinking, feeling, believing, choosing, willing, remembering, and all of the other inner activities. At the present moment, those habits *are* your inner life.

The way that you have created the complexity of your inner life in the past now influences your health in one way or another. Harmonious patterns are stirring beneficial and healthful influences, while disharmonious ones that you are not healing are creating a blockage of some kind. In this sense, you could view the many complex human personality patterns of your inner life as though they are a large orchestra that you must conduct. If you give each member of your orchestra different music to play, you will have disharmony, you will have noise. In the same way, if you feed your inner abilities of thought, feeling, desiring, and so forth with constant negative choices, you will create an inner life that is filled with chaos and disharmony, which can gradually cause a disturbance of the cellular structures of your physical body, eventually breaking down the health of the body.

When you as the conductor are able to work with all of the various instruments of the orchestra until they can all play the same music, and you train them to make the timing quite perfect, then you have a wonderful symphony. Within your inner life, when you are able to bring the choices of love and wisdom to all of your different, complex personality patterns, then your inner life can become extraordinarily beautiful. Your inner life will not become the dirty magnifying glass that creates a barrier between your soul energies and your body. Instead, it will be the clean glass that will *amplify* the eternal energies. Consequently, your body will receive the perfection of all of the soul energies that were intended for it—energies of harmony, rejuvenation, and healthy growth.

Even though you may have already created habits of thinking and feeling that are now bringing negativity into your inner life, with some understanding and patience, you can learn about those patterns, and you can begin to heal them. To help you in this, we will now speak about some important areas of experience that make up your inner life, and we will show you how they work within your personality. As we do so, try to feel that each area that we examine is brought forth as a *seed*. You would not expect a seed to blossom the moment you put it into the ground. You understand that there are certain cycles of growth that seeds go through. But, eventually, they come forth and blossom quite beautifully and wonderfully. So, we will now plant some seeds with you, and you can nurture them and eventually bring them to full growth.

YOUR ATTITUDE TOWARD YOURSELF

One of the most potent influences upon your inner life is the set of energy patterns that you create in your personality by the *attitude* that you consistently take toward *yourself*—the way that you see yourself, think about yourself, and feel about yourself. What you believe to be true or false about your own personality and being, over a period of time, can either cause disease, or it can bring you health.

For example, if you constantly say to yourself, "I am bad for this reason, I am inferior for that reason, I am wrong for this reason," then your human personality becomes the dirty magnifying glass standing between the eternal energies of your soul and your physical body. When you continue to create such negative attitudes toward yourself over a period of time, you generate what we have described earlier as personality disruption, and that creates the distorted human energies that can disturb your health. When the distorted energies caused by negative attitudes toward yourself are carried through many years without healing, they can cause a great deal of damage to your physical body. They can also begin to undermine your emotional and mental health.

On the other hand, if you consistently try to believe that you are a valuable, lovable person who is rooted in goodness, then you will encourage a fuller inflowing of the eternal energies through the threshold of matter into your physical body. The *human* energies created by such a positive attitude toward yourself will not create the heaviness that distorts the perfection of the eternal energies that are constantly flowing into you. Instead, a consistent positive attitude toward yourself creates human energies that are closer to the perfection of the soul's energies, and those positive human energies can actually enhance and magnify the way the soul energies enter your physical body. A positive attitude toward yourself creates a clean magnifying glass that increases the potency of the eternal energies as they pass through on their way to the cells of your physical body.

However, we are not suggesting that your attitude toward yourself must always be *perfect* in every moment in order to maintain health. There are challenges in all human lives, and those challenges can cause you to feel less than perfect about yourself. Occasional feelings of inadequacy do not threaten your health. But, if, over a period of time, you do not bring feelings of negativity about yourself to the surface, and you *constantly* believe that you are inadequate, inferior, or bad, then you can cause the detrimental impact upon your health that we have described.

With the importance of your attitude toward yourself in mind, we can now give you a very effective principle to guide you in assessing your attitude toward yourself day by day: *When you assume something negative about your being, then you are confused, you are wrong.*

We are not denying that there might be personality patterns in you that you can experience as negative. There can be aspects of your personality that you do not like, and, from your viewpoint, they are negative. However, if you see those negative qualities and assume that *you* are negative or bad because of them, then you can rest assured that you are confused. You are not seeing the truth. You are seeing your own human personality *creations* of thinking and feeling. Negative thoughts and feelings about yourself are *temporary* manifestations. They are not a reflection of your permanent, *true* being, which is a continuing goodness and magnificence within you. Understanding this fully will be a very important aspect of your healing work.

For most human beings, in working with your attitudes about yourself and your being, it is usually beneficial to *over-estimate* yourself, in terms of how you feel about your inherent goodness and your true inner capacities. In fact, most individuals would never see themselves as large as they truly are, no matter how much they over-estimate.

This does not mean that you will pretend that you have no challenges, or that you will turn away from the facts about your life and pretend that you are a perfect personality. It simply means that when you are thinking about yourself and your *true* nature, *you can always assume that there is more goodness within you than you are consciously aware of*. This larger attitude toward your inherent goodness as a human being will establish a sound base for healing and health.

To help you to see this more clearly, we would say that you live within what we can speak of, symbolically, as a large *sphere* of personality. This sphere represents what we have called your *personality matrix*. In the center of the large sphere of your overall personality matrix is a smaller sphere that represents your *human personality*. In the center part of your human personality sphere—and this center part is very small—there is your *conscious*, moment to moment, awareness of yourself as a human being. In the other parts of this human personality sphere are your *un*conscious human patterns, a few of which can be negative, from your viewpoint. However, the largest parts of the human personality sphere are filled with magnificent human qualities that you have brought from your many past lifetimes on earth.

All of the *negative* human energies within your human personality sphere are "heavy" energies that are *temporary* earth realities. All of the harmonious, loving, and *positive* human energies within your human personality sphere are of a different, *permanent* "wavelength" that is aligned with the eternal energies of your soul, and of God.

Those eternal energies constantly fill your larger *personality matrix* sphere, as well as your smaller *human personality* sphere that is contained *within* the personality matrix. The eternal energies merge with the positive human energies that you create, thereby filling your personality matrix with powerful positive energies, both human, and eternal. Thus, when you make *positive* assumptions about what exists within your personality matrix sphere, you are moving toward truth. When you assume that your personality matrix is *negative*, you are moving away from truth.

If you take this kind of attitude toward yourself, you can see that the only negativity that exists within you are the small, temporary areas that are consciously *experienced* as negative by your human personality. These would be the experiences within your human personality sphere that come to your small conscious center of human awareness and frighten you, trouble you, or bring you pain and suffering. If you assume that these negative experiences are coming from the truth of you, or that they are the truth about life, then, in time, you can make yourself ill by such assumptions. If you recognize that such painful experiences are coming into your conscious center of awareness from negative thoughts, feelings, and other *human* patterns that *you* have set into motion, and that they can be changed by you, then you open the door to health and to healing.

No matter what attitude you take toward yourself, you will still need to work intelligently with your negative human experiences in order to bring them to the surface, experience them, understand them, and heal them. However, while you are working with such negative experiences, the *assumptions* that you make about yourself and your life will be all important in determining whether you are healthy or ill.

Again, we must emphasize: To be healthy, it is not that you must strive to always be perfect, or to never have negativity in your inner life. You simply need to honestly and patiently *live* your negativity as best you can in any moment, without believing that the negativity is the truth about you, about other human beings, or about life. Also, while you are working with your negativity, you will need to find a way to consciously remind yourself each day of what the truth of you actually is. At times, you will need to *create* attitudes toward yourself that reflect the truth of your being. In these teachings, we will suggest many ways to do this. For now, you can use the simple vision of the sphere that we have given. You can say to yourself:

> **"I stand in my small inner point of conscious human awareness working with temporary negativity, but, inside my sphere of *human personality*, and the larger sphere of my *personality matrix*, there are positive *human* energies, and there are the perfect *eternal* energies that bring wisdom, goodness, and love into my life."**

Always, in your healing work with yourself and others, when you wish to attune to that which is truth, you can say to yourself, silently or out loud:

"Within my personality matrix sphere, there are extraordinary qualities and energies. They are in my personality matrix because they have been placed there by me, as an eternal soul. They are there because I, as a soul, desire them to be there, because I desire to manifest them through my human personality."

This will always be the truth, no matter what your human mind or heart might say in any moment.

This leads to a similar attitude toward yourself that you must cultivate in order to facilitate your healing. You will need to feel that there is a *perfection* in you that is *never* diminished by anything that you think, or feel, or do in this lifetime. This does not mean that you are always perfectly pleased with yourself or your experiences. But, at all times, you need to strive to feel a kind of unending perfection like that which lives within the flower. If you do not crush the seeds, they will grow a flower, and that flower will grow and produce new seeds, and those new seeds will grow a new flower, on and on in a continual cycle of perfection. In you there is a perfection that grows goodness, love, wisdom, and truth in constantly unfolding new cycles, as long as you do not crush the seeds by harshness, cruelty, or constant fault finding toward yourself and others. If you feed yourself love, the seeds of perfection will constantly grow flowers of goodness in this lifetime, almost without effort.

In creating attitudes toward yourself that are aligned with truth, you can remind yourself that the seed, or *energy* of perfection within you is never diminished, as long as you live in your physical body. When your body eventually comes to its death, the energy of perfection simply changes its *form*, and it then shows itself as what it has always been—an eternal being standing beyond the physical world. It shows itself as the perfection that is your eternal soul.

With this in mind, we could say that the key to health and healing is: *To bring the conscious awareness of the true perfection of you into such an intense relationship with your human mind, emotions, and body that your human personality becomes infused with a conviction that, in spite of any challenge or illness that might occur in your life, your perfection is undiminished.* If you can accomplish this, it will give you the faith and the courage to strive for manifesting perfection in your mind, your emotions, and your physical body, even when you are ill, or when you are challenged in any way.

UNDERSTANDING YOUR INNER LIFE

As we now look more deeply into your inner life as a human being, let us return to the vision of the small point of conscious human awareness at the center of the sphere of your human personality. Your ordinary feeling of yourself is that you view the world from this small point of awareness. This feels as if it is where you live inside your physical body. In fact, this center of awareness feels like it *is* you.

Within this center of awareness inside your human personality, you are constantly aware of many different personality patterns that are continually shifting and changing. These many patterns include your own thoughts, feelings, desires, memories, images, ideas, and so forth, as well as all of your physical sense perceptions—what you see, hear, touch, smell, and taste—of the outer world and other human beings. Although you are aware of a vast number of different individual patterns inside of you, to you they feel as if they are all woven into a whole that you experience simply as *yourself*. All of your inner experiences add up to the feeling, "This is *me*, and I am inside of my body."

From moment to moment, throughout your entire human lifetime, all of the complex patterns that make up your inner experience feel as if they are you. Thus, as a human being, you take all of the extraordinary complexity of life, and you reduce it to a simple feeling of an inner experience of *you*.

It is as if you are standing in a large field filled with beautiful flowers. There are unending varieties of flowers as far as you can see. However, you have found one particular rose that is most beautiful to you. You bend over to it, and you examine it closely. In that moment, you are aware of only that one single rose. All of the vast complexity and beauty of the other flowers is temporarily lost to you. In the same way, as an eternal soul, you are aware of the whole field of flowers—the infinite complexity of all universes. However, as you now stand as an individual human personality, you are bending over to look at one flower—your awareness of yourself as one individual inside a human body. Temporarily, for you as a human being, the entire universe consists only of what you are consciously aware of, moment by moment, within your small point of awareness inside your human personality.

The result of this *narrowing of focus* is: *extreme intensity of individual experience.* This is an intensity that the souls intended to create in the human experience. In fact, in a way, it would be appropriate to say that one of the purposes of human life on earth is to gain this kind of intensity of personal experience.

Thus, within your own personal intensity, from your point of view, your inner experience of a single moment can become *all* of reality. This is particularly true of experiences that involve health and illness. If there is illness within your body, you feel, "*I* am ill." With health in your body, you feel, "*I* am healthy."

It is very important for you to be aware of this personal intensity that is a characteristic of your inner life, and to remember that you are *creating* it within your inner experience, moment by moment. It is also important to remember that, in any moment of your life, you can freely choose whether you wish to remain focused upon your personal intensity, or, whether you desire to temporarily *step back from it.*

You have the freedom to direct all of your conscious attention toward the intensity of a single moment of your personal inner experience, to the extent that you become lost in that experience. In other words, you can choose to bend down and lose yourself in the experience of a single rose. Or, in any moment, you can *choose* to try to focus upon the *whole* of your experience of yourself, which is much larger than the one single experience. You can stand up and become aware of the whole field of flowers.

For example, in a certain moment, if you are feeling very frightened that you might die of cancer in this lifetime, you have the ability to lose yourself in that feeling until you are convinced that it is the truth. However, you also have the ability to *shift your attention* to the larger reality of yourself so that the feeling about cancer is put into perspective as simply *a temporary feeling of fear*.

Learning how to shift your attention at will from individual inner patterns (from the single rose) to your wholeness as a human being, as well as an eternal soul (to the whole field of flowers) will be a part of the work that we will help you do to gain mastery over your inner life. As a starting point for this work, it will be necessary to understand how the different human personality patterns of your inner life work inside of you.

As we have touched upon, there are many streams of *conscious* patterns that make up your inner life, including your thoughts, feelings, beliefs, images, physical sense perceptions, and so forth. All of them are influenced *unconsciously* by impulses that flow forth into you, but of which you are unaware. These hidden forces come from different sources, including your own personal unconscious thoughts and feelings from this lifetime, unconscious influences from other human beings around you, unconscious memories that you have from past times that you have lived on earth, and, always, the magnificent eternal energies that are constantly flowing into your personality matrix from your own soul, the souls of others, and the forces of God itself.

All of these unconscious influences will affect your conscious thoughts and feelings. They will also affect the images and ideas that you may have. They will affect your responses to other human beings in your environment.

However, throughout your lifetime, the influence of the unconscious aspects of your life will always have *less* impact upon you than will your conscious choices and creations. Although it can be helpful to remind yourself that you have all of these unconscious influences, since they are so difficult to become aware of and understand, you will benefit by giving most of your attention to your *conscious* life. You can assume that the creation of an honest, loving, and joyful conscious life will harmonize all of the unconscious influences. You can also assume that, as long as you are honest with yourself and others, the unconscious influences will somehow be brought to your attention whenever there is a need to address them and work with them.

Again, we remind you: *The degree of health that you manifest throughout this lifetime will depend upon the way you create your inner experience day by day.* And, the way you create your inner experience depends upon whether you believe your experience is caused by *you,* or whether you believe it is caused by forces beyond your control. To understand how your inner experience is caused by you, we must look at the way you exercise your *choice* in your life.

THE IMPORTANCE OF CHOICE

That which determines whether your thoughts, emotions, and all of the other patterns of your inner life will be experienced by you as chaotic and painful, or whether they will feel joyful and fulfilling, will be the way in which you exercise your human choice day after day. All of your inner personality patterns are affected by the daily choices that you make in your life. What you choose to dwell upon will dictate how your thoughts and feelings are used, and that will determine whether or not you build the foundation for a healthy life.

For example, if you constantly choose to find fault with the people around you, then you will create an atmosphere of criticalness and negativity through which you will look at all of life. Through this dark veil, your life will appear to be limited, negative, and unsatisfying. On the other hand, if you dwell upon joy, creativity, honesty, and love, you will find that your life will usually appear quite beautiful, satisfying, and meaningful.

In working with your daily choices of what to focus upon, remember that what *feeds* you is often so much greater than what *comes out of you* as your day to day experience. As we have emphasized, what is constantly being fed into you are the most extraordinary and beautiful eternal energies. Yet, when you make daily choices that are rooted in negative attitudes about life, what comes out of you is a cloud of negativity that, from your viewpoint, turns all of the magnificent eternal influences, temporarily, into a dark kind of human experience that involves suffering and pain.

Sometimes it is easy for you to be aware that you are actually choosing your thoughts, your feelings, and other aspects of your inner experience. If you decide, "I will now think about being wealthy, and I will think about the many things I will buy with money," then you are aware that you are causing your moment of imagining wealth. However, at other times, your inner experience can seem to spring forth on it's own, unfolding in ways that seem to have nothing to do with your choices. If you are sitting alone feeling that no one loves you, then you are not usually aware that you have *caused* that feeling of loneliness by the way that you have chosen to work with your thoughts and feelings in the past.

Thus, at times, you may need to remind yourself that your inner experiences are caused by the choices that you make each day, and that you can control and master your reality by learning to choose in an enlightened way. This will be particularly important when the physical circumstances of your life seem to be creating negative experiences for you. When this occurs, you may need to remind yourself of this truth: No matter what happens to you in this lifetime in the outside physical world of other people, places, and things, you have the wisdom and the strength to inwardly *respond* to all that takes place with total freedom, and you have the wisdom and the power to *choose* your responses in any moment.

YOUR INNER LIFE AND YOUR BODY

To help you more clearly understand how your inner life can affect the health of your physical body, we will need to look again at the way in which your emotional and mental energies interact with the cells of your body. Here, we will expand upon what was discussed in an earlier section concerning the cause of human illness.

We would ask you to imagine that each cell of your body has a certain *non*-physical *atmosphere* around it, and *within* it. This atmosphere is composed of a non-physical energy that is not perceived by human beings. (In some ways, this energy is vaguely similar to the human conception of electro-magnetic energy.) This atmospheric energy about and within the cells in your body is quite close in "vibration rate" to the perfect divine energy of your soul. As this cell atmosphere energy presently exists within your body, it is a very *subtle* energy.

Now, imagine the energy of your own thoughts and feelings that we have described earlier. This too is a non-physical energy, but, in *earth* reality, it is a strong energy. This energy is "thrown off" when you think and feel. Its vibration rate can vary, depending upon whether your thoughts and feelings are positive or negative to you.

When you think and feel, this strong human mental-emotional energy "flows through" your physical body where it mingles and interacts with the more subtle energy atmosphere of each cell. The subtle energy atmospheres of the cells are *fed* by the thrust of your stronger mental-emotional energies.

In the personality of a healthy, balanced human being, there is usually a preponderance of energy coming from thoughts and feelings of love, creativity, joy, and fulfillment. This does not mean that there is a complete absence of negativity, challenge, and pain. But, such a healthy human being would usually be able to create experiences of joy and fulfillment, even when there were challenges in life.

Using a healthy female one as a beginning example, we would say that the influence of her mental-emotional energies upon the atmosphere energies of each cell in her body would be *neutral* to *positive*. The mental-emotional energies produced by her experiences of love and joy create a vibration rate that harmonizes well with the perfect vibration rate of the atmosphere energy of each cell. Thus, the thoughts and feelings of such a person would generally *enhance* the healthy unfoldment of the cells of her body. In such a person, there would usually be physical health and strength. (We point out that this is a very generalized statement. Each individual will have different degrees of manifestation of health, according to the individual personality patterns.)

Now, imagine a female person who is mostly filled with *fear*. She is one who has experienced pain and negativity for many years, and has not been able to heal it. Of particular challenge is her constant *struggling* with her own fear, and an unwillingness to experience the fear. The result of this is a certain "distortion" of the energies being thrown off by her thoughts and emotions. This creates an energy frequency, or wavelength, that does *not* match the perfect atmosphere energy of a cell. The result of this interaction is that the stronger mental-emotional energies become a negative *pressure* upon the cell. These distorted mental-emotional energies temporarily fill the atmospheres about each cell, causing, as described earlier, a certain *alarm* to be set off within each cell. This alarm prompts the cell to make the "emergency" response, because the perfect vibration of the subtle atmosphere energy of the cell has been disrupted by the stronger distorted mental-emotional energy.

The nature of this emergency response will vary, depending upon the kinds of negative thoughts and emotions being generated, where the cells are located in the body, and the personality and soul patterns in each individual. In one person, perhaps the emergency response of the cells would cause the cells to enter into an uncontrolled growth cycle that you would speak of as cancer. In another person, the emergency response could lead to various other diseases or malfunctions of the body.

In addition to the general negative pressures placed upon the atmospheres of the cells throughout the physical body, the distorted mental-emotional energies have a particularly strong influence on the *blood* of the physical body. In certain ways, the cells that have to do with the propagation of the blood of the human body are much more sensitive and more responsive to human mental-emotional energies than are the other cells throughout the body. (You would call these sensitive cellular processes in the blood, the human immune system.) Because of this sensitivity, the blood of your body is the first physical aspect of you to receive the impact of your mental and emotional energies.

The cells of your blood also stand as a *transition point* between the non-physical energies of your soul, and your entire physical body. In a very simple way of speaking, we could say that the blood in your body is the first physical *receiver* of the impulses from your soul. As your soul pours forth energies of the eternal stream of perfection and love into your personality, the blood receives the first *physical* impact of those eternal forces. The blood then becomes a "distributor" of the perfect forces of growth and health that are received from your soul.

When the cells of your blood receive the impact of negative mental-emotional energies that you create within your personality, the pressure of the negative energy can interfere with the forces of health and growth coming forth from your soul into the cells. This sets up the emergency response in the cells of the blood, which can in turn negatively influence the cells in various parts of your body, causing those cells to respond in abnormal ways. The negative mental-emotional energies create the dirty magnifying glass through which the rays of soul energy must pass.

This gives you a clearer picture of how disease and illness can be traced directly to your inner life of thought and emotion. It is in this way that your thoughts and emotions can either stimulate the cells in your body toward health and growth, or they can set up the blockage in the cells that turns the body toward illness and malfunction. However, we must again remind you that all human beings will not respond to inner negative creations in the same way. As we have pointed out earlier, all human beings have unique patterns in their personalities that can cause one person to be more prone to illness from certain emotional and mental pressures, while others can create similar negative inner experiences and still not manifest illness or disease. Thus, it is not of benefit to generalize too broadly here.

To simplify your understanding of how your own thoughts and feelings are directly connected to the health of your physical body, and to manage your inner patterns in ways that will be most beneficial to your health, you could say to yourself each day:

> **"In this moment, and in all moments that I live in this physical body, I am *creating* this body by my thoughts and my emotions. To the best of my ability, I now set my intention and my will to create as much love, beauty, and harmony in this day as I can. If I go forth to the best of my ability to do this, then I will assume that the effect that my inner life will have on my body in this day will be very beneficial. I trust this to be true, and I release all fear that it is not."**

However, when you notice that you are struggling with inner negativity, do not feel that you are damaging your body. In your confusion you might believe: "Not only am I feeling quite negative in my inner life, but now I am frightened that my negative feelings are harming my body." Such an attitude will unnecessarily complicate the flow of the healthful, stimulating energies that come from your soul into your physical body.

When you are feeling negativity, remind yourself that it is fear, and fear cannot harm you. If you are willing to experience the fear, and then release it, then you would not expect it to have a detrimental effect upon your body. However, if you fear your own fear, and you continually fight with it, or ignore it and hide it away over a period of time, then, it can possibly have a disruptive effect on the health of your body.

To create the most beneficial interaction between your inner life and your body, remind yourself each day that as you love, and as you heal fears that arise within your personality, you are creating the most harmonious mental-emotional energies to merge with the eternal energies of health and growth that pour forth into you from your soul, and from God itself. If you constantly work in this way, then the perfect eternal energies will be allowed to penetrate to the depths of the physical structures of your body and animate them to bring about strength and health in all areas.

Chapter 6

Observing Your
Inner Patterns

*—You always have the option of losing yourself in your inner experience, or stepping outside of it. What is most important is to learn **which choice serves you best in any moment**, and to learn how to joyfully balance the two ways of experiencing.*

As you work to create health in your life, some of your time will need to be spent *changing* certain personality patterns that create blockages to your health. In later sections, we will examine ways to make such changes. However, before you can begin to work to change your personality patterns, you will first need to learn how to *observe* those patterns in order to fully understand them. You will need to take some time each day to temporarily disengage from your ordinary fascination with your own personality experience in order to study your personality patterns without being caught up in them.

When you set out to work with the many personality patterns that make up your inner experience of life, one of the first obstacles that you will face is the natural *intensity* of your human experience. Because the souls have created human personality life as such a strong and powerful experience, the tendency is for human beings to become lost in their moment to moment thoughts, feelings, ideas, and all of the other patterns that make up the inner life of a human being.

LOSING YOURSELF IN YOUR EXPERIENCE

Often, your personality patterns are like a large snake that is beginning to coil and wind in ways that show you that it is preparing to attack you. Yet, even though you have warning that the attack is about to come, you are so fascinated with the process of this snake that you forget to step backward, and the snake leaps forth and strikes you.

So it is with your own personality patterns at times. You will unintentionally create inner experiences that are quite challenging, frightening, and painful. Then, you become so engrossed in those negative patterns, so immersed in the intense experience of them, that you forget that you can step backward from them. You forget how to see your negative personality experiences for what they are: *projections of your own fear.* If you remain constantly caught up in those negative personality patterns and do not occasionally step back from them, they can strike you with their confusion and their turmoil, and the result is pain, and often, loss of health.

Let us give you another vision to help expand this area. Imagine that you are a small hog feeding at a trough. There are many brother and sister hogs with you who are eating quite fast. Therefore, you frantically come forth to eat, concerned only with eating as much as possible before the other hogs get all of the food. You launch yourself into eating with complete abandon. You become so caught up in your experience of the first bites that while you are chewing away, you bite the nose of your brother hog. And let us say that this brother hog is much larger than you. The brother hog becomes very angry, he bites you quite severely, and chases you away from the food.

Because you were so *caught up* in your experience of eating, the end result is that you do not get to eat at all. In the same way, many of you ones, *because you have become so obsessed with striving for certain inner experiences, have actually created the situation in which you cannot have those experiences.*

For example, let us say that you are desperately desiring the experience of a deep romantic love. Because of your desperation, you become obsessed with romantic relationships, and you begin such a relationship with many people at the same time. Then, because of the complexity of carrying out so many relationships at the same time, you feel confused, frustrated, and not loved at all. But, you are so busy frantically seeking the romantic fulfillment in more and more relationships that you do not notice that your desperate striving is creating the frustration that blocks the fulfillment you are seeking. Because you are so *caught up* in your experience of frantically pursuing fulfillment in love, you have blocked your experience of the actual fulfillment.

Many of you on earth at this time have chosen extremely passionate personalities. And, this is a period in which many of you are turning your passion more and more toward your own *personal fulfillments*. In general, this can be seen as a positive situation. Present human beings now have the opportunity of fulfilling themselves more deeply than past human generations, because of your intensity. Because you have a healthy appetite, you are more likely to eat a great deal at the trough.

However, if an appetite is all that you have, you run the risk of becoming caught up in that appetite. You might forget that, from time to time, you need to carefully examine what you are doing as you try to satisfy your appetite. You need to watch out for other hogs feeding at the trough. In other words, each of you, in order to maintain your path toward health, and toward fulfillment in your life, will need to learn the balance between deeply, intensely, and joyfully experiencing what you are attempting to create for yourself in your day to day life, and, recognizing when you have become lost in your own private experience—knowing when you have gone too far in self-involvement.

You cannot take command and mastery over your life when you are totally caught up in your own inner experience. When you are caught up in your experience you can only *live* it. You might be able to make *some* choices, but, full mastery, in terms of aligning all of the complexities of your being, is not possible when you are lost in your private experience. You cannot refrain from biting the nose of your brother hog when you are not willing to step back from your own frantic eating long enough to realize that his nose is in the way. In the same way, you cannot bring forth the magnificent idealistic qualities in you—your capacity to love others and give to them, and all of the other more altruistic manifestations of human life—that are larger than personal desire and ordinary human self involvement, when you are caught up in your own intense personal experience.

STEPPING BACK FROM YOUR EXPERIENCE

To master your inner life in a manner that will enable you to manifest full health, you will need to learn to step back from the intensity of your personal experience on a periodic basis. This is particularly important when you desire to heal a challenge to your health. When you are first approaching a health challenge, trying to determine why you have manifested it, you need to be able to disengage from your various personality patterns that have caused your illness so that you can see what those patterns are. By stepping back from the patterns, you can gain the deeper insight and wisdom that are needed to connect your personality patterns to the health challenge.

When it is time to heal that which troubles you, if you have not developed the capacity of stepping back from your inner experience, then you will be so caught up in the intense negative experiences that can come with illness—feelings of discouragement, helplessness, and hopelessness—that you might even begin to feel, "I can never heal. I will always be ill until my death." When you are ill, and you become lost in the negative inner experiences that can come with lack of health, then it is even more difficult to heal the health challenge itself. At such times, it is particularly important to be able to step back from the negative inner experience of that which has gone wrong in your body, your mind, or your emotions. You need to *already* have learned, before the illness occurs, how to take periods of time to make an inner connection with your deeper self in order to temporarily put aside the intensity of your own personal experience, to be able to step outside of the intense reality that is your ordinary inner life.

When we speak of learning to step back and observe your negative inner experiences, we are not suggesting that you will push your negative patterns away, hide them, or pretend that you have no negative thoughts or feelings. That would not serve you at all. In fact, it could bring you a great deal of pain in the future. As we have pointed out, swallowing your negativity can be quite disruptive to your health. Learning to step back from your personality patterns is not for the purpose of avoiding negative experiences. It is for the purpose of *establishing a small period of time in each day that is dedicated to seeing yourself more clearly.*

If you are willing to establish a daily period of withdrawal from the intensity of your personality experience, it can help you create a greater understanding of your inner patterns by temporarily freeing you from their strong hold on you. By learning to create a loving, objective, temporary separation from the intensity of your inner patterns, you can gain the ability to *observe* them in a way that can eventually lead to a full understanding of the patterns and their causes. This will prepare the way for *changing* any patterns that might be standing between you and a healthy life.

OBSERVING YOUR INNER PATTERNS

We will now suggest a way for you to step back from your personality patterns and observe them in an intelligent, objective way. This method involves making a daily *attunement* to your own inner life.

When you make your daily attunement, you will not approach it as one trapped inside of your personality. During your period of attunement, you will work with your personality as an *observer* of your patterns, looking from *outside* of them, just as you would observe another human being from outside. You will need to use your imagination and creativity to create this objective view of yourself.

At first, it is best not to use your attunement period to strive for intellectual understanding of yourself, or for factual knowledge about your personality patterns. The initial purpose will be to simply gain *a feeling of freedom* from the intense inner experiences of your personality life.

Now, ordinarily in your daily life, *it is not beneficial to create a feeling of distance from yourself and your inner experience.* During your day, it is quite important for you to live intensely *within* your personality experience. However, for this special period of attunement with your personality patterns, you will step back from yourself, and you will create a gentle, loving separation from your inner experience.

As you work patiently and persistently with the following method of attunement day after day, you will begin to clearly understand areas of confusion and distortion that you may have unintentionally created in your inner patterns of thought, feeling, belief, attitude, and so forth. During these attunements, you can also bring forth a deep intuitive wisdom that will help you understand how those patterns affect your health, and you will gain an insight into how to work with those patterns to heal and dissolve them.

We will now suggest a simple way to begin to observe your personality patterns so that you can eventually *choose* which patterns you will continue and which ones you will change. We would suggest that you do the following attunement in each day, for a period of at least ten minutes—longer if you desire.

You would begin the inner work by finding a quiet place where you will not be disturbed. Taking a comfortable position, you would carry out the following steps.

Step One. First, begin by completely relaxing your physical body. Do this for a moment or two. Breathe deeply and relax.

Step Two. Using your imagination, feelings, and thoughts, *create* within yourself a deep feeling of comfort, warmth, and love. Make this as real as you can, but do it in a calm, relaxed way without straining. It is important to feel peaceful and calm during your attunement.

Step Three. Gently begin to speak to yourself in your own mind. Say to yourself:

"In this moment, I release all of the thoughts and emotions, and all of the cares, confusions, and disturbances that I have grown inside my personality. In this moment, I am willing to put aside all of my earth life so that I may feel the true magnificence and beauty of the deeper realities of me."

These are the kinds of thoughts and feelings to generate within your own heart as deeply as you can. You may also wish to create other similar thoughts to help you maintain this loving focus.

Step Four. Using your imagination, create a feeling of lifting up and floating away from your ordinary personality patterns. Imagine yourself floating above earth, and let your thoughts and emotions, and all that is of earth, gently slip away.

Step Five. After you have created a feeling of floating for a moment or two, and you have begun to feel at least a beginning sense of release, then turn your attention to any area of your personality that you desire to understand more clearly. Create a thought to focus your attention upon your chosen area in an expanded way.

For example, let us say that you are struggling with a lingering illness in your body, and you desire to look at any underlying mental or emotional patterns that might be connected to your illness. Thus, in this step of the attunement, you would begin to invite any such patterns to the surface so that you may become aware of them. You could say to yourself:

"Now that I have stepped back from my personality, I begin to look at myself as if I am a guiding-one to myself. In this moment, I have an expanded wisdom and understanding of my own personality patterns. I now turn this new expanded wisdom upon any confused thoughts and feelings that I have about my health."

Step Six. With this kind of feeling of vast wisdom being created by you, imagine that you are standing *outside* of your human personality, and you are looking at your own inner patterns, not with criticism or judgment, but with a sense of deep understanding and great love. Then, begin to recall the troubling patterns, situations, feelings, or thoughts that are associated with the area of your personality that you have chosen to focus upon—in this example, your physical health.

Let the troubling areas float gently into your

awareness. Do not become caught up in the feelings, thoughts, or images that might arise. Simply let them pass through you. You need not attempt to solve great problems, or do psychological work with yourself. All that is necessary is to let your inner realities—your thoughts, feelings, and beliefs that your personality has created about your chosen area of work—float into your expanded awareness during this period of the attunement. You will simply *observe* all of this. You do not need to do any work with it.

By doing this from a detached, objective, and loving point of view, you can begin to understand and feel that your challenging patterns in this area are not really as troubling or threatening as they seemed to be at first. You can learn that these inner personal creations that you are observing are *temporary* personality patterns, not the truth about you or your life. Also, you will realize that they are neither good nor bad. They are simply what your personality has created. All that you need to do during this deep period of the attunement is to become aware of these creations of your personality, experience them, and lovingly observe them. You do not need to approve of them, or reject them. There is no response needed from you.

Try to remember what you observe about your patterns during the above experience. Later, when the attunement is over, you may wish to review your memories of the experience.

Step Seven. When you desire to end the period of

attunement, slowly and gently imagine yourself floating back into your personality and into your body. Give yourself plenty of time to do this. Gradually begin to notice yourself again experiencing the ordinary intensity of your personality life. Do this with joy and love. Gently guide yourself back to your ordinary alert awareness of your earth life. It is important to do this *slowly*, without rushing yourself.

When you are fully alert again, it is quite beneficial at that point to take several moments to write on paper any understandings, thoughts, and feelings that have come from your attunement period. This practice can eventually lead you to a great understanding of the inner patterns that you bring to the surface during your attunement.

Do not become discouraged if at first your attunement is confusing and difficult to understand, or if you feel that there is nothing to write about. With persistence and patience, you will dissolve the confusion, and you will bring back a deep understanding about your personality patterns, giving you many things to pursue in writing.

If you practice this attunement daily, you can eventually become quite proficient at taking a larger, expanded attitude toward your personality patterns, particularly the challenging ones. Gradually, as you carry out this attunement each day, you will notice that there will come a new understanding that will help you find the fears that lie within the personality patterns that have caused the feelings or the situations that seem so negative in your life. Eventually, you will be able to use this attunement period to learn about any inner patterns that may create blockages to your health.

The purpose of this attunement is to help you make an *intuitive* opening in your conscious awareness that will bring you clarity about your inner patterns that ordinarily trap you in their temporary realities. During the attunement, by distancing yourself from the intensity of your experience, you will gradually begin to open a deep intuitive knowing that springs from the stream of wisdom that flows into you from your own soul. Eventually, by drawing upon this wisdom daily, you can become so clear in your understanding of yourself that you can bring any of your personality patterns into this period of attunement, even the most troubling ones.

As you work to observe your personality patterns using the attunement that we have suggested, we must again stress that it is important not to overbalance toward insensitivity and detachment from your feelings outside of your attunement period. Do not use this method to numb yourself and shut off your feelings in order to avoid painful experiences. That would only create confusion and challenge for you. To truly manifest health, you will need to continue to work in your ordinary experience each day to *deepen* your capacity to feel, and to appreciate the intensity of your inner life. You will only use this method of objective observation in special attunement periods, or in brief moments when you wish to temporarily step back from your thoughts and feelings so that you can understand them. When the attunement period is over, you can return to a passionate involvement with your human experience.

EXERCISING YOUR CHOICE

Gaining an objective understanding of your personality patterns is a process that you can *choose* to set into motion in any moment in which you are willing to momentarily disengage from the intense involvement that you normally have with the experiences of your inner life. When you learn to lovingly step outside of your experiencing at the right time, then you will gain a valuable new perspective on your inner patterns. However, it is you who must decide *when* it is beneficial to step back from your experiencing, and when it is more important to remain within your thoughts and feelings in order to live them and work with them from inside the experience. Learning to wisely make this distinction will come with persistent and patient use of the suggested attunement in your own day to day life.

To help you feel the freedom that you always have to choose to either stay within your personal experience, or to step outside of it, imagine that you are sitting in a great symphony hall. There is music of extraordinary beauty being played that thrills you. You are caught up in the *emotional* intensity of the experience of enjoyment of the music. You can choose to remain absorbed in that experience, and by so doing, you are intensifying the joy and the beauty of the moment. However, in that moment, you could also choose to say to yourself, "I desire to step back from my intense emotional involvement with this musical experience and learn more about the science of sound by analyzing how it is that my ears can register sound and imprint it upon my brain." By making that choice, you have stepped *outside* of the emotional experience of the music.

Neither choice is good or bad. They simply bring you different *results*—different kinds of experience. In this example, by choosing to step outside of your emotional experience of the music, you gain new intellectual understanding, but you give up the emotional intensity that was possible by remaining within the experience.

What you need to keep in mind is that, *you are free to make this kind of choice in any moment of your life.* You always have the option of losing yourself in your inner experience, or stepping outside of it. What is most important is to learn *which choice serves you best in any moment,* and to learn how to joyfully balance the two ways of experiencing. By practicing with yourself, you will learn to monitor your choices, and you will establish your own personal cycles and rhythms. If you notice that you are *always* choosing to lose yourself in your experience, then you may decide that you need to step back from time to time. If you notice that you are always stepping back and analyzing everything that you experience, then, you may decide that you need to balance yourself by moving toward greater intensity of living within your experience. *You are the only one who can make the choice that is perfect for you in any moment.*

To look at another example, imagine that you are with a person that you love in a romantic way. This person is extremely important to you, and you wish to make a mating with them for the rest of your life. Imagine that this person begins to complain to you that you are not physically attractive enough for them. You begin to feel a deep sadness, a painfulness. You have a dreadful feeling that since this person finds you unattractive, they will leave you, and you will lose love for the rest of your life. Imagine that in that moment you say to yourself: "I now choose to step back from the intensity of my negative inner experience so that I will not suffer the pain of this moment." Such a choice may help you to harden yourself and numb your feelings so that you can escape a painful experience, but it would make it very difficult for you to lovingly deal with the real issues involved. In a situation such as this, you might wish to remain intensely involved in your emotional pain so that you could communicate it clearly in order to establish an honesty of communication that would help you resolve the relationship in a way that would please both of you.

We are attempting to emphasize for you that, as master of your personal world, *you* can decide when it is time to step back from your human experience and gain the distance to see your personality from a point of view that is not enmeshed in your inner creation, or, when it is more beneficial to live intensely within your experience in order to learn from it, to grow from it, and to rejoice in it. By reminding yourself each day that you have this freedom, you will remember that you are the one who creates your inner experience moment by moment. If that experience is leading to challenge and lack of health, you have the freedom to *re*-create it in ways that are more beautiful, fulfilling, and healthful.

Chapter 7

Your Desires

—The reason that human desire is so strong is that the energy of desire is intimately woven with the creative power of the eternal soul. Within your personality matrix, your desire, as well as your creativity, strength, will, and other capacities, are all springing forth from the eternal energies that flow from your soul into your personality.

When you come into physical form as a human being, even though you are infused with the strong and potent energies of your eternal soul, if there is not human *desire* in your personality, all of those eternal energies will be like seeds scattered upon hard packed earth. They will not take root and grow. If you, *as a soul*, place the most extraordinary abilities to create beauty, goodness, joyfulness, and healthfulness into a human personality matrix, and you, *as a human personality*, come forth and grow without any desire, there will be stagnation in your personality. There will be little activity for your physical body. There will be passiveness and flatness in your experience of life. The result of all of this can be an impairment of your health.

Many human beings have unintentionally created such conditions of passiveness and stagnation within their personality. Because of the pain and suffering they have experienced that is associated with certain ways they have acted on their desires in the past, many have come to limit their desires, or to smother them completely. Thus, many of the potent energies of the soul that were planted in the personality, and that need to be stimulated by desire, remain dormant and tend to stagnate.

As you come forth in each day to work with your inner life to create full health, you would need to remind yourself that your desires are the fuel for the engine that will drive the vehicle of human personality. If you smother your desires, there will be little power for the personality. Frequently, the smothering of desire is the cause of those illnesses that have to do with a loss of stamina and energy within the physical body—what you would call *chronic fatigue*, and other related kinds of responses.

Other ways in which the limiting of your desire can impact upon your body have to do with the depletion of certain energies that ordinarily, when there is full desiring, go forth to stimulate the brain, stir activity in the thoughts, and feed the emotions with a great deal of enthusiasm, excitement, and curiosity. By inhibiting your desire, you limit those energies that could stir up vigor and movement within your personality and your physical body. When you have healthy desiring, those energies will feed you joy and fulfillment, which will stimulate strength and health within your body.

The harmonious *fulfillment* of desire creates the experience of human *accomplishment*. The experience of accomplishment leads you to feel greater *purpose* and *meaning* in your life. When you feel purpose and meaning, those feelings feed back into the harmony of your personality, thereby accelerating the eternal energies that feed health into your body.

As we stress the importance of desire, this does not mean that *all* of your desires are beneficial to you, or that they should all be acted upon. Some of your desires might be associated with your human confusion, turmoil, and fear, and if you act upon them, they can bring negative experiences to you that do not benefit you, or the health of your body.

You would need to work with your desires to, first, bring them forth so that you can fully experience them and understand them. Then, you must use your human wisdom, intelligence, and sensitivity to try to find out which desires, if acted upon, would bring goodness, joy, and benefit to you, and to the ones about you in your life.

For full health in this lifetime, you will need to *respect* your human desires. You will also need to feel that you are *worthy* of having your desires fulfilled, particularly your desire for health. Further, you will need to understand your own particular desire patterns as you have created them within your human personality. Thus, we will now look at ways that you can clarify your desires. Then, we will speak about how to fulfill your desires more completely.

ASSESSING YOUR DESIRES

One of the first questions to ask in coming to an understanding of your desires would be: "What *are* my desires?" This would appear to be a simple question to answer. However, you ones often confuse yourselves with such inner criticisms of your desires that many times you are not sure what your important desires are. For example, many people will feel: "What I truly desire is probably not the best thing for me. I should desire something more noble and more ideal. I need to teach myself to desire better things in order to be a better person." These kinds of feelings can confuse you, and they can create a mistrust of the desires of your own personality, which can undermine your desire for health.

We are not suggesting that you should ignore impulses of idealism when you work with your desires. Such impulses will need to be felt, along with your other feelings. And, at times, your impulses toward idealism will be more important than your desires. However, in order to fulfill yourself, *you must be willing to desire*, to have your desires and *experience* them fully, even when they may seem less than perfect. By being willing to have your desires without restricting them, at least you come to know what your desires are. Then, you can decide for yourself, according to your ideals, which desires should be acted upon, and which ones should be ignored or changed.

There are many different reasons why you ones prevent yourselves from desiring. Some of you limit your desiring out of a feeling that you are not wise enough to know what is good for you to desire in your life. You would feel that another human being, or your soul, or God, should choose for you.

Others fear to let themselves desire because they believe their desires can never be fulfilled. They usually have conscious or unconscious feelings of: "What is the use of desiring? I will only be disappointed when I cannot fulfill my desire. The disappointment will bring me pain. I can avoid pain simply by not desiring."

Some human beings unintentionally limit their desires out of a fear that they will become selfish if they follow their own desires. They feel that if they are selfish, then other people will not approve of them or love them.

Others smother their desires because they have come to believe that human desires are not spiritual. They believe that if they fill themselves with their human personality desires, then they will somehow lose God in their lives.

For some, there is a fear that their desires will become so strong that they will become addicted to the pleasure of desire fulfillment. This is often associated with intense desires for such things as food, or sexual pleasure.

You will need to be quite honest with yourself and look into your heart to see how you presently limit your own desires. What are the ways in which you unintentionally smother your desires because of your own fears? All of the squeezing of human desire is done out of fear, of one kind or another.

The first step in assessing your desire patterns is to take a period of silence with yourself in order to look deeply into your personality and to ask of yourself: "Do I allow myself to desire, or, have I learned to limit and smother my desires for one reason or another?" You could begin this by creating a "scale" of desiring in your mind, and then placing yourself on the scale. Imagine that on the left side of this scale there is a *total* willingness to feel *all* desires with *maximum intensity*. On the right side of this scale, there is a *complete refusal* to feel any desire. In a deep attunement period with yourself, imaginatively place your own willingness to desire on this scale. Do not judge yourself or criticize. Simply notice whether you are desiring to the degree *that satisfies and pleases you.*

All of the fears that human beings create about their desires are based upon human confusion and misunderstanding, which leads you to feel that personal desires are bad, for one reason or another. You must remember that the *energy* of your desires is actually *energies of God that rise up within you.* Even if you would desire to go forth and take a negative action in earth, the *energy*, or *force*, that enables you to desire is the energy of God. However, your choice to point that desire energy toward negative action is a *human* choice, made by you out of confusion and fear.

Again, we must emphasize that it is important to create the feeling of freedom to desire whatever you want to desire. It is not beneficial to smother your desires, or prohibit yourself from *feeling* your desires. You may not wish to *act* on some of your desires, but you can let yourself at least feel all of them so that you can become aware of them, in order to decide which ones align with your ideals, and which ones do not. After you have allowed yourself to feel a desire and become aware of what it is, then you can remind yourself:

"I am free to do what I want to do with this desire that I have just experienced. If this desire seems to me to be rooted in fear and ignorance inside of me, or, if I believe that acting upon this desire would bring pain to myself or to another person, then, most certainly, I now can choose not to act upon the desire. But, I need not be frightened of the desire itself. It is simply a *feeling* that I have created inside of me. Just as I have the power to *act* upon my desires, I also have the power to *dissolve* and *release* the desires that I decide are not good and honorable in my life."

By creating this sense of freedom to desire and to choose your desires, you will begin to gain a certain authority over your personality in an area that is extremely important to your health. As we have emphasized, if you do not open yourself in the area of desires, then you may eventually find yourself withering within, becoming weak and lifeless. Your capacity to be excited and passionate about life can temporarily slip from your conscious life, and there can come a feeling of dryness and emptiness. This can all create negative mental and emotional pressures that can in time lead to various blockages to your health.

On the other hand, *if you become too caught up in your own desires, to the extent that you allow your desires to manipulate you, then you may find yourself clogged emotionally*. In other words, if you immediately rush out to indiscriminately satisfy every desire that you feel, then you will become so caught up in your own desiring that you will begin to restrict the range of feelings you have about yourself, other people, and life. You will tend to turn inward in self-preoccupation. This will create patterns of confusion and insensitivity that can eventually be detrimental to your health.

MANAGING AND MANIFESTING DESIRES

In order to truly master your desires, you will need to develop the capacity to first enter into your desires, to feel them, and experience them. Then, you will need to be able to step back from your desires, gently and lovingly, as master of your own personality, reminding yourself of your wisdom, strength, and courage to intelligently choose what you will do in life in response to your desires.

You ones have already learned, to some extent from trial and error, which of your desires bring temporary pleasure, and which bring you a more long-term sense of fulfillment, purpose, and meaning, as well as health to your body. What we will now suggest is intended to help you bring forth a greater conscious mastery over the process of desiring, and over the actions you take to fulfill your desires—a mastery based upon a *choice* that you will exercise in accordance with your highest ideals.

We will now focus upon the most important attitudes and thoughts that you will need to hold as guidelines for yourself in your work with desire. If you wish to intelligently manage the area of desire, and totally fulfill the desires that are important to you, then we suggest that you work with these attitudes and thoughts each day, thinking them to yourself quite often, and even writing about them occasionally.

As you work with the following thought patterns, first say them to yourself out loud, or silently. Then, try to let the truth of them sink into your feelings. Gently let yourself feel that your consciousness is being saturated with these thoughts. Let them fill you with a sense of goodness.

At first, it may seem that you are not penetrating very deep into your consciousness with these thoughts. However, if you work each day with what we suggest, you will begin to feel the changes inside yourself. Your thoughts and feelings are very powerful, and if you consistently choose to focus them upon the following areas, then you will begin to notice many positive changes in the way you work with, and experience, your own desire patterns.

The first thought to create for yourself is this:

"As a physical human being, I am expressing the energies of life that have created this universe. I am expressing these energies through

my human personality and through my physical body. They are the energies of God, and they express as my thoughts and my feelings, and, especially my *desires*. In this moment I remind myself to respect my desires, and to encourage them throughout this day."

Next, remind yourself to *experience* all of your desires as they arise within you. *After* you have experienced each desire, then you can decide what you wish to do about it.

Then, remind yourself that you have the freedom and the power to desire with a great *intensity*. You have the capacity to bring a passion to your desires.

Next, remind yourself:

"I am free to *act* upon any of my desires that please me, and, I am free to *release* any desires that do not please me. I am master of these desires."

Then, to the best of your ability, align your desires with your ideals, with love and wisdom, and with your human experience of life that tells you what is good and not good. Test the desires inwardly to see if there are any strong conflicts with any of your other important inner patterns.

After you have assessed a desire in this way, the final step is to *choose* whether or not to act on the desire. This choice will be based upon your feeling about whether the action would bring goodness into your life, or into the life of others. In this case, you are the one who would decide what is goodness and what is beneficial for yourself and others. You may seek the advice and wisdom of others, but, ultimately, you are the one who must decide whether or not it is good to act upon your desire.

These are some simple, but important steps to follow in making your choices about your desires. You would need to balance these steps with what you have learned in this lifetime about the *consequences* of acting on desires in earth. For example, imagine that you go forth into your working arena and you encounter a fellow worker who is quite angry with you. You begin to argue with one another, and you feel a rising desire to strike this person. You could say to yourself: "I am free to choose to *act* on my desire to hit this one. But, what would be the consequences of my action? Do I desire those consequences?" You may decide *not* to act upon the desire because you do not like the consequences of your action. Instead of striking the person, you may decide to learn and grow from the experience by noticing the *fear* in you that caused you to become angry.

On the other hand, imagine this same fellow worker on another day being quite sad. Imagine that there has been the death of a loved one to the fellow worker. As you talk to this worker, you feel a compassion pulling at your heart, but you do not know this one intimately. You have a desire to hold, and embrace, and comfort this person. But, you are frightened that if you act on that desire, the person will reject you. You are free to *ignore* your desire to express your warmth and comfort to the person.

However, as you learn from experience that the consequences of your acting on your desire to embrace your fellow worker could be beneficial to that one in need, then you might decide to push yourself a bit and overcome your resistance to acting on your desire.

Each of your desires can be quite different. Thus, you will need to work intelligently with all of them. If you can carry out this kind of questioning process with yourself as you work with your desires, you can more clearly choose the desires that you believe are important to act upon. The more you work in this way, the clearer your desire patterns will become, and the more you will be able to integrate your desires into your unfoldment of health.

ALIGNING WITH YOUR SOUL'S DESIRES

The next area that we would look at is the matter of aligning your human desires with the impulses of your soul that we will call the "desires" of your soul. (As we have mentioned earlier, these soul impulses are quite different than human desires, but there is no human word for such soul energies.) This area is a bit unclear for most human beings. The lack of clarity is due to the fact that you have not yet fully developed the capacity to understand that you are not really human beings.

In truth, from an eternal perspective, the human portion of you can be considered to be a "temporary illusion." However, it is quite a powerful and *valuable* illusion for you, and one that you must try to live fully while you continue within your present physical body. To inwardly withdraw from the human illusion before your physical death would not serve you well. You will find greater fulfillment in life if you rejoice in the human experience, and live it passionately, intensely, and with conviction. In fact, in a certain manner of speaking, fully living the human "illusion" with great intensity is one of your important purposes in this lifetime.

Part of the human illusion is the personal *intensity* that you feel in your own private experience. Because of this intensity, your desire patterns are constantly changing. At one moment, you feel an extremely intense desire to do a certain thing. Later, after you have done it, you might have no interest at all in that desire. Because of this fluctuating intensity, it is often difficult for you to know what are your *true* desires—the desires that are aligned with the truth of you as an eternal soul.

To begin to understand how your personality desires are aligned with the desires of your soul, we would ask you to imagine your human desire patterns as a *mirror*. However, this is a mirror in which the image that you see continually changes, according to the angle from which you view the mirror. In this example, the "angle" that you take to view your desire pattern, is *your attitude toward yourself.* It is always difficult to see the truth of yourself because you have so many angles from which you view your personality—you have so many different attitudes toward yourself. Furthermore, when you look at yourself, you see your *human* being, and that is the temporary illusion. It is not the truth of you. Therefore, you will need to remind yourself: "It is difficult to experience the truth of my being while I temporarily live inside the illusion of a human personality, particularly when my vision of myself is constantly changing with the different attitudes that I take toward myself."

However, it is not difficult to *imagine* the truth. Thus, to begin to understand the relationship between your human desires and your soul's desires, you could say to yourself each day:

"Regardless of what my human earth experience might tempt me to believe about myself, I insist upon believing the truth. I insist upon *imagining* the truth until I can feel it and live it. And the truth is that I am only temporarily a human being in a physical body. In my true being, I am an eternal soul. Even as I continually value and rejoice in the experience of my humanity, I remind myself that I am eternal."

Imagining yourself as an eternal being immediately begins to eliminate the necessary veil that is in place about your conscious awareness as a human personality. Whether you believe you know the truth about yourself or not, when you try to imagine yourself as an eternal soul, you are at least moving in the direction of truth. Then, when it is time to assess your soul's desires, you could say to yourself:

"In order to assess what my soul's desires would be for me in this lifetime, I must first be willing to imagine that *I am my soul*. That is the first step in my assessment process,

and that is the truth of me."

Imagining that you are your soul can be done during daily periods of attunement with yourself. If you truly desire to understand what your soul would wish for you to accomplish in this lifetime, you will need to take a period of time to imaginatively *become* your soul.

Here is a simple process for making such an attunement to your soul's desires.

Step One. Relax your physical body and create a calmness and a peacefulness within yourself.

Step Two. In your own unique way, create a deep feeling of love within yourself.

Step Three. Using your imagination and creativity, begin a process of releasing yourself from your human personality. Do this, not out of a sense of criticism or dissatisfaction with your personality, but out of a sense of drawing yourself toward a truth that is larger than your personality. Step back from your personality and create a feeling of expansion, a feeling of gently floating into that larger truth, knowing that your personality will be safe until you return to it.

Step Four. Open yourself completely and attune to the energies of God, as best you can. Using your imagination, create a feeling of an eternal love so large that you can give yourself freely and completely to it. Feel a goodness, a strength, and a perfection so large that you understand that it cannot be diminished. Feel a sense of the eternal magnificence living within you as the energies of God. Attempt to use your thoughts and your feelings to create this truth in any way that you can, whether it is a feeling, a thought, or a vision.

Step Five. Imagine this as deeply as you can: You are standing beyond earth with a vision that can see all life and all universes. You have a vast heart that can feel all human existence, and all other life in all other realms. You are a soul that is eternal. You can feel that you are *always* woven with the energies of life, the perfection and love of God.

Step Six. Attempt to identify the desires of your soul. Begin to imagine yourself as your soul, seeing with the eyes of God. See your present personality quite clearly, and in total love. As your soul, see all of the human desires that you learned to identify by working within your personality, and, in the present moment, understand those desires clearly. As your soul, also begin to see all of the *ideals* that you can possibly imagine. For example, you may begin to see peace throughout earth, and love to all human beings. When you identify one ideal that seems to stand out for you, then as you see it, try to feel it swelling up within you. Then, say to yourself:

"I believe that one of the desires of my soul is that my human personality take this ideal that I have identified and find some way in my human creativity and love to be a portion

of the creation of such an ideal in my day to day earth life."

Sit for a while in the feeling of this and explore what you imagine to be your highest manifestation of the ideal. Consider that the ideal might be one of the desires of your soul for you in this lifetime.

Step Seven: After you have spent as much time as you desire in this inner work, *slowly* and gently bring yourself back to a full and complete awareness in the present moment. You might wish to write on paper what you learned during your attunement to your soul.

This is the kind of inner work that you can do in each day to align your personality desires with the ideals that can represent the desires of your soul. However, you will need to work steadily and persistently with these attunements in order to gain a feeling of clarity about the ideals that you identify. At first, you may feel uncertain about whether or not those ideals actually are your soul's desires. Do not expect *certainty*. Simply remain flexible and honest with yourself as you do the work. In time, after you gain enough experience with your inner energies, you can feel more sure about the ideal impulses that you experience within you, and you will be able to tell if they originate within your personality, your soul, or both.

Always, after you have done the inner work that we have suggested, when you return to your ordinary personality awareness, remind yourself:

"Let me not judge myself if I seem to be working on this ideal in small ways in my daily life. I am the one who will decide how I will act upon the soul impulses that I feel. I may work in very small ways throughout my entire lifetime. If I choose to do this, then I rejoice in it. I may also work in large ways, if it pleases me. I may even dedicate myself totally to certain ideals that I decide are *desires of my soul*."

You as a human personality are the one who must decide what you will do with your soul impulses, and how you will do it. Your soul does not walk on earth, except as the eternal energy that lives within, and expresses through your personality. You are your soul's representative in earth life as you live your human personality. In order to manifest your soul's desires most fully on earth, you must take mastery over your own humanity, just as you will imaginatively take mastery as the soul during these periods of attunement.

Once you have learned this kind of attunement to your soul's desires—and perhaps it will take a period of time to learn—you will gain abilities that will help you create health for yourself throughout this lifetime. The soul impulse that we are calling the soul's "desire" is so much larger, so much broader, and so much more magnificent than human desire. There is an *unlimited* quality to that soul impulse. By learning to feel that unlimitedness within you, you can come to the place in this lifetime where you can create more confidence, strength, joy, and love in all of your work toward health and fulfillment.

HEALING ADDICTIVE DESIRES

As you are aware, there are certain desires that, when acted upon, tend to interfere with the health of your body. For example, the desire to continually take alcohol into your body will eventually work against the strength and health of your physical form. Such desires can be even more disruptive to your health when they become *addictive desires*.

We will look now at desire patterns in the human personality that become so persistent that you begin to experience them as fixations, or obsessions, or addictions. To begin, we would remind you that the *energy* of desire is a very potent energy. The power of desire energy within the human personality is quite extraordinary.

The reason that human desires are so strong is that *the energy of desire is intimately woven with the creative power of the eternal soul.* Within your personality matrix, your desire, as well as your creativity, strength, will, and other capacities, are all springing forth from the eternal energies that flow from your soul into your personality. When you desire a thing quite intensely, that feeling of desire stirs up the very powerful soul energies within you that have been given to you so that you can create, act, and accomplish in order to *fulfill* yourself in the physical world.

At this time on earth, *there are many people who have a great fear that they will not have fulfillment in human life.* Because of that fear, whenever a powerful desire arises within them, they begin to frantically strive to fulfill the desire *immediately*. They feel that if they do not fulfill their desire quickly, then all of the disappointment, frustration, and limits that they imagine to exist in earth life will become so strong that those will block the fulfillment of the desire. Essentially, such people feel that if the desire is not satisfied immediately, then they will be miserable and unfulfilled.

This impatient and fearful attitude causes ones to attempt to grasp fulfillment as soon as they feel desire. Thus, there are many who have now developed a certain need for *immediate gratification* of desires.

In the present society of the United States, in which there are many people who have a great deal of prosperity, as well as creativity, cleverness, and other powerful human capacities that are associated with fulfillment of desire, there are many who are able to very quickly satisfy their human desires. They are particularly adept at satisfying the desires for physical possessions, and for pleasurable sensual experiences. From these kinds of influences, there has been created a social climate that encourages the immediate fulfillment of physical desires.

In such a climate, when your intense desires are focused upon physical sensual fulfillments, such as eating, ingesting alcohol and drugs, various pleasures of the body, and sexual fulfillment, and you have the capacity to create that fulfillment immediately, eventually, there arises a certain capacity for *numbing yourself* through continual fulfillment. For example, if you go forth each day seeking only to fulfill the desire to eat food, to fill yourself with the pleasure of taste and the other pleasant sensations of eating, and that is all you do each day, then, after a while, the intense experience of the joy of eating begins to diminish. Then, you attempt to eat more, or you may try to have more intense experiences by eating foods with different tastes. Unintentionally, *you set up a cycle in which your search for fulfillment is based upon an experience of satiation, or jadedness, or numbness in your present fulfillment.*

There are many on earth who have very strong desires in an area in which they have been continually pursuing satisfaction, usually with a deep need for immediate gratification. Yet, at times, no matter how hard they work toward new fulfillment, they feel that they are not able to get enough pleasure or satisfaction of their desire.

This pattern exists in many human beings who have extremely strong, and often "uncontrollable" desires for food, alcohol, nicotine, drugs, or sexual pleasure. However, what you would need to understand here is that the *true* underlying desire that is prompting such people is not the desire for physical gratification. That desire has come about as a result of deep confusion within their personalities. In truth, the real desire that is stirring within their personalities is *a desire to be emotionally fulfilled in profound inner ways that involve love, and that bring about the experience of purpose and meaning in life.*

For such people, the sensual fulfillment that they come to seek, whether it involves food, alcohol, or other physical areas, becomes the substitute for the *emotional* fulfillment that they truly desire, but have been unable to achieve. Due to the training of their personalities during childhood and growth, which is influenced by their society, and by their inner personality patterns of confusion and fear, they come to believe that attaining *emotional* fulfillment is difficult or impossible, while gratifying *physical* desires can usually be done immediately. Thus, feeling that their emotional desires cannot be fulfilled, or, *that they take too much time and effort to fulfill,* all of their tremendously strong power of desire unintentionally becomes wrapped up in that particular physical area of pleasure that is *easy* to attain, which has *immediate* satisfaction, and which comforts them a bit in their emotional emptiness.

When such a confused pattern of desire for physical pleasure as a substitute for emotional fulfillment has been firmly established within the personality over a period of time, then it can become an obsession or addiction, particularly with those who choose such things as nicotine, alcohol, or drugs. After a while, ordinary emotional fulfillment and other pleasures that lie outside of the addiction area become less and less satisfying to the personality. For example, if you are a one *craving* alcohol and the temporary relief that it brings you, then you will not be so fulfilled by a small gesture of kindness that another human being may make toward you during the day. You are not so interested in the more subtle pleasure of artistic creation. You are craving the *immediate, intense* experience that the alcohol brings to your personality.

Gradually, by intensifying and exaggerating their satisfaction with experiences in the addiction area, and by diminishing the joy that they feel in other areas of their lives, the persons who are "addicted" begin a process of *splitting apart* their personalities. All of their thoughts and feelings become focused on the narrow range of fulfillment in the addiction area, while the great capacity of their personalities to find joy in *all* areas of life becomes temporarily dormant, waiting to be invited back into the *conscious* experience of the personality. Eventually, such persons may so exaggerate the pleasure of their addiction that it seems that *nothing* but that particular activity or experience can satisfy them.

This kind of addictive process begins with a lack of emotional fulfillment that results in a temporary inability to appreciate the beauty of love, creativity, harmony, and joy in day to day life. In essence, there is an inability to extract deep pleasure from the *ordinary* human experience.

Since addictive patterns are caused by a lack of emotional fulfillment, when attempting to heal addictive patterns, it is very disruptive to *condemn* the personality for its addiction, since that brings about even more emotional turmoil. If you continually berate yourself for any addictive patterns that you might have, this will cause you to feel more frustrated and more unhappy, making it even less likely that you will find joy in areas outside of the addictive area. The emotional pain of your own condemning will make it feel even more important for you to satisfy yourself through the addictive activity.

Assuming that there is not a distortion of your thought and emotional processes by chemicals, the key to healing most areas of addictive desire is, *the expansion of your joyful appreciation of the rest of your life outside of the addictive area.* Thus, the first step in healing will be to work diligently to find greater joy and emotional fulfillment in relationships with others, creativity, purposeful life activities, and all of the other important areas of your life.

The next step is to learn about the experiences of emotional frustration, sadness, and pain that have caused your life to seem so lacking in fulfillment, that have caused you to be so dissatisfied with your ordinary life experience. You will need to identify those old patterns, enter into them, discover the fears beneath them, and then heal the fears. (In a later section, we will suggest a method for healing fear.) If you carry a great deal of sadness and pain within you, and you are *not* working honestly and lovingly to heal it, you may find that you will continue to engage in addictive pleasures in order to numb your feelings of sadness and pain.

Whether you are working in a troubling area of addiction, or whether you simply have a pattern of desire in your personality that does not please you, as you begin to work with the desire pattern to heal it, it is important to continue to work to increase the opportunities for *joy* and *fulfillment* in all areas of your life. This can be particularly effective if there are beloved ones near you to help you. You can focus upon friendship and love relationships as a very fulfilling inward experience that eventually you can use to *replace* your addictive experience.

What we have suggested here is *general* guidance. All human beings will have unique, individual factors to work with in their challenges of addictive desire patterns. For many, there will be a need for assistance from other human beings, because the intensity of the desire for the addictive experience has become greater than the person's belief that they can create joy without that thing to which they feel addicted. At times, the feeling of being trapped in the addictive desires can become so great that the healing *requires* the assistance of other human beings—loved ones, counselling ones, or teaching ones.

To summarize, we could say, in general, for most areas of addictive desires where the behavior has not become too extreme, and assuming that there is not a chemical distortion of the personality, addictive desire patterns can be healed by working in the following three areas: (1) learning to bring magnificence and joy into all other areas of your life outside of the addictive experience; (2) learning to open your heart to love yourself and those around you; and (3) healing your fears in the ways that we are suggesting in working with your inner life. Doing these things will bring you the confidence and trust in your own great capacities of strength, creativity, and love that will help you release the desire to substitute addictive behaviors for the true joy and majesty of life.

In looking specifically at those who are addicted to alcohol and drugs, there is a question of heightened *emotional sensitivity* within the individual.

Those who choose to numb their feelings by using alcohol and drugs are usually ones who are very sensitive in their feelings. They experience their emotions to a deep degree. They feel more intensely their own pain, the pain of other human beings, and the sadness and despair of negative earth events. From their past experiences of emotional sadness and pain, they come to believe that their emotional sensitivity is the *cause* of the pain. Thus, in order to decrease their sensitivity, such ones will often use alcohol and drugs because those substances tend to have a temporary numbing effect upon the inner pain. Usually, such individuals are not consciously aware that they are attempting to numb their sensitivity.

For such ones to heal your addiction, the key would be to work to heal the fear that causes you to believe that negative experiences can harm you, and to heal your attitudes that cause you to believe that pain is a reality, and negativity is the truth of life. Then, you would need to actually celebrate your sensitivity, learning that your ability to feel so deeply is brought forth in your personality in order that you may feel joy and love more intensely. Once you have healed your own fear patterns, then you will allow your sensitivity to come forth without the desire to numb your deep feelings.

Again, we would emphasize: Ones who find themselves desiring to heal and dissolve addictive patterns of any kind will eventually need to find ways to fill their personality with love, beauty, and joy. This will be done by creating truth and fulfillment within your thoughts and feelings, and by creating relationships with other human beings that are marked by trust, honesty, and love. If you accomplish this, you will bring such joy into your day to day life that the pleasure of *all* areas of your life will be far greater than any pleasure that comes from addictive patterns. This will leave you free to use the energies of God within you to create health for your mind, your heart, and your physical body, without interference from negative personality patterns associated with addictive activities.

Chapter 8

Your Thoughts

—At this particular time on earth, given some of the powerful and pervasive means of communication that influence your human societies and shape your thinking, it is very important for you to gain the confidence to choose your thoughts, particularly thoughts that are in alignment with your own ideals, so that you can develop an attitude that you are the master of your own thoughts.

Some of the strongest energies that influence your present inner experience and your health are the powerful *mental* energies that you build inside of you through your thoughts. Your thoughts are extremely potent energies that can be either random and chaotic, or focussed and powerful.

We would compare your thoughts to a large herd of horses contained within a fenced area. At times, the horses run about and scurry to and fro without any pattern or discipline. At other times, you as the owner of those horses, if you choose, can come forth and herd them, ride them, or even harness them to wagons and put them to work. In the same way, your thoughts, if you do not pay attention to them, can be of great volatility and unpredictability. Or, you, as the owner of your mind, can learn to organize and discipline your thoughts to accomplish what you desire in your life. It will be particularly important to learn to master your thought patterns as you work toward health and healing.

YOUR THOUGHTS AND YOUR HEALTH

Looking with you now to the way in which your thought patterns are related to your health, we would begin by pointing out a certain sense of *disturbance* that occurs inside you when your thoughts are negative, or when they frighten you. This disturbance could occur for many reasons, since you ones are able to create negative and frightening thoughts about so many different things in life. You could have fearful thoughts about poverty, about loneliness, about your own body making death, and about many other troubling areas. Although there are many different things that you could think frightening thoughts about, let us generalize and speak of this disturbance in your thinking as one large area, and let us call it simply, *fearful thoughts.*

We must say here that fearful thoughts were not *intended* by your soul. The souls did not create the magnificent human capacity of thinking in order for you to create fearful thoughts that bring you pain and cause disruption between yourself and others. Your soul created your capacity to think in order to bring you greater joy, to help you master earth, to enable you to understand your existence, to solve complexities, and to accomplish many different purposes in human life.

To simplify all of this, we could say that the primary *purpose* for your ability to think is to enable you to have *greater fulfillment* in this lifetime. So, to begin moving toward a deeper understanding of your thoughts, you could say to yourself, at least once each day:

"When my thinking is moving me toward greater fulfillment, then it is being used in the way that it was intended by my soul. And when my thinking is moving in that direction, it is moving me toward health, harmony, and full functioning in my life. When I am constantly filled with fearful thoughts, then I am moving toward suffering and pain. I must clearly understand that those fearful thoughts are created by my *human distortion*. My challenge is to discover, through my intelligence, how I have distorted my thoughts, and then to decide how I will heal them."

By taking this attitude, you avoid the human temptation to blame other people, or life, for your painful negative thoughts.

As a general guideline for working with all of your thoughts, just as with some of the other areas that we have looked at with you, we could say: The more that you can think of the *truth* of you—which is that you are an eternal being, temporarily expressing in human form, and that you are constantly filled with forces of goodness, creativity, and love—then the more your thoughts will perform their intended function of moving you toward fulfillment. Such thoughts will also begin to stimulate many of the beneficial forces of health that live within your physical body.

CHOOSING YOUR THOUGHTS

An important step in working with your thoughts is to convince yourself that *you can choose your own thought patterns*. At times, this might be difficult to believe. You might feel, "I do not have a choice about what I am thinking. If I am troubled by poverty, then naturally I will think dark thoughts about the bad things that will come from this poverty." You will need to teach yourself that you *do* have a choice about what you think, and, you can learn to exercise that choice.

In order to exercise your choice about what you are thinking, you will need to build upon the work that we have suggested earlier concerning the loving *observation* of your personality patterns. You can learn to take periods of time each day to observe your thoughts, using the kind of attunement that we have suggested for observing your inner patterns.

By taking periods of time in each day to sit in silence with yourself and lovingly observe your thoughts, you can discover all of the various thought patterns that you have created that could possibly interfere with your health. Then, you will be able to change any fearful thought patterns that are leading you away from health.

During your periods of silent inner work, you can also learn to organize your thinking so that your thoughts do not overpower you. It is not beneficial for you to be *constantly* preoccupied with your thinking every moment of your day—to be totally lost in your own thoughts. You need at least a small period of time each day in which you can step back from your thoughts to discover your persistent *habits* of thinking. After you have gained enough experience with this kind of observation of your thinking patterns, you will be able to decide which ones need some work in order to be turned toward their intended purpose of helping you create fulfillment and health.

Another aspect of your work in learning to manage your thoughts is to occasionally take some periods of time to devote your thoughts to areas that are not so intensely colored by your own inner experience. All of you ones tend to be extremely passionate about your own life, but you are able to remain relatively objective about the lives of other human beings. Thus, if you will take small periods of time to step outside of your fascination with your own thought patterns to learn about the thoughts of others, this will make you healthier in your own thinking.

To help achieve this, you can sit in a period of silence imagining how another person would think about an area that troubles you. You could go to a friend or loved one and ask them to tell you what they think about those areas. By bringing the views and thoughts of others into your own thinking, the objective viewpoint gained from others will help you create a patience, calmness, and maturity in your own thinking. Then, your own fearful thoughts are less likely to create distortion in your life.

As you take periods of time in each day to work with your thoughts, you will begin to discover your fearful thought habits, and you will use the intelligence and wisdom given to you by your soul to change those patterns. Then, you can create new patterns of thought that will align your thinking capacity with its intended purpose of helping you create fulfillment and health in your life. This will result in healthy stimulations to your personality and to your physical body.

After you have done enough of this kind of work with yourself, you will develop a keen awareness of the thoughts that are in your mind at any moment. This will open the door to actually *choosing* which thoughts you will focus upon. For example, if you are totally absorbed in thoughts of losing your loved one, and you are not even noticing that you are caught up in this web of thought that produces painful emotion, you cannot exercise your choice to change those thoughts. Once you have developed the capacity to step back a bit and observe such thought patterns, you can say: "I notice that I have been totally lost in thoughts of losing my loved one. I am now free to choose to let these thoughts continue. I am also free in this moment to choose to turn my thoughts in a different direction."

After you have gained enough self-awareness to observe your thought patterns, then you will need to *practice* exercising your choice of what you wish to think about. You will need persistence in that practice, and you will need to trust that *the negative thoughts that you are changing are not bad*. Those negative thought patterns cannot harm you. Ideally, you will not be changing your patterns out of fear of the negative thoughts, but out of a desire to create more truth and love within your personality.

In your work to change your thoughts, as with your other inner work, there is also a need for honesty with yourself. You will need to ask yourself, "Why do I wish to change these thoughts?" Perhaps at times you will say, "I wish to change these thoughts because this is a frightening area to me, and I cannot stand the pain." Then, you clearly and honestly understand that your desire to work with your thoughts is motivated by a fear of pain. You are free to change your thoughts out of fear, if it pleases you, but, eventually, you may wish to say, "Let me enter directly into these areas of thought that frighten me, so that I may experience the fear beneath the negative thought patterns and heal the fear."

Always, you are the one who can decide which thoughts to have in any moment. You are the one who can decide whether a thought should be encouraged and delved into, or changed and put aside.

At this particular time on earth, given some of the powerful and pervasive means of communication that influence your human societies and shape your thinking, it is very important for you to gain the confidence to *choose* your thoughts, particularly thoughts that are in alignment with your own ideals, so that you can develop an attitude that *you* are the master of your own thoughts. As we look at the broad patterns of earth life at this time, we see that many human beings have deep confusion in their minds that comes from allowing their own creative, spontaneous choice of thoughts to be replaced by *teachings* that have been given by other human beings. Ordinarily, you do this out of a desire to improve yourself, or because you feel that your own thoughts and ideas are not as valuable as those that come from someone else.

Let us give a simple example of how teachings can become more important than your own thoughts. Let us imagine that you are feeling unloved, and you are taught by a person that you respect that if you will be more kind to others, they will love you. Thus, with a desire to *improve yourself*, a desire that is usually tied to a feeling of lack of confidence in your present personality, you begin to willfully *force* thoughts and attitudes of kindness upon your spontaneous thoughts. Even without this forcing, some of your thoughts would naturally be thoughts of kindness, and some of them might be of a negative nature. However, this forcing process that you set into motion creates within yourself a portion of your thoughts that will overwatch and censor all of your other thoughts. You artificially create a "watchdog" in your mind in order to eliminate everything that seems not to be kindness.

That overwatching portion of your mind would say: "You must think kind thoughts, or you will not be loved by others, and your life will be quite painful." However, that watchdog is aligned with *fear*, rather than being in alignment with your own free choice. Gradually, you learn to censor your thoughts out of fear, in order to force yourself to conform to a teaching of another person—that says you must be kind in order to be loved—rather than allowing the creativity and spontaneity of your own thought processes to unfold naturally, according to your particular personality needs. This often occurs with ones who are taught that their negative thoughts can cause illness. They begin to try to force away their negative thoughts because they are afraid that such thoughts will lead to illness.

You can understand that the limiting impact upon your personality, and that which can eventually disrupt your health, comes from attempting to *force* your thoughts in a particular direction because you have adopted the beliefs or attitudes of another person—expressed through their teaching—rather than *choosing* your thoughts according to your own beliefs about what is good in life. The result of forcing your thoughts to conform to teachings, especially when you do it with a self-critical attitude, is to cause a lack of confidence in your ability to create your own inner reality in joy and strength. This brings about a feeling that you cannot create strong health-giving forces within yourself. In other words, by continually forcing your thoughts to take a certain direction that has been taught to you by others, you weaken your confidence in your own ability to choose your thoughts in ways that will create goodness for yourself.

On the other hand, just as we have suggested for your work with desires, if you practice exercising your freedom to allow all of your thoughts to come forth spontaneously without suppressing any of them, then you gain a direct experience of the complex variety of your entire range of thought patterns. You come to *know* your thoughts clearly by becoming familiar with all of them. By such knowledge, you are more likely to understand which thoughts promote health and which ones interfere with health. However, if you do not allow all of your thoughts to first come into your conscious awareness, if you continually try to force yourself to avoid certain areas of thought, then you may begin to accumulate, in your unconscious patterns, thoughts that need your attention, but that remain hidden and are not available to be worked with.

After you have let all of your thoughts come forth freely to be experienced by you, then you can *choose* which thoughts align with your ideals and your truths about life and health, and which ones do not. You can decide for yourself what to do with each of your thoughts. You can choose to emphasize and expand upon the thoughts that you believe to be good for you, and you can begin to heal and dissolve the ones that do not fit with your ideals.

When we advise you not to force your thoughts according to the teachings of others, we are not suggesting that you avoid the teachings and wisdom of others. Those teachings that you find to be inspiring, and those that feel true to you can be freely *chosen* by you. They can be voluntarily taken into your own personality, and they can be made a part of your own beliefs. When you do this, then you can lovingly monitor your adopted thoughts and ideas in order to align them with your self-chosen ideals. In this case, even though you are following the teachings of others, you are *choosing* your thoughts rather than forcing them.

You can also learn to monitor your own thoughts in order to notice negative thoughts that grow out of old habits that you do not wish to continue. For example, imagine that your past experience has influenced you to dislike members of a certain racial grouping. And each time you see one of the individuals of that group you have thoughts of negativity and fear. You might have the thought, "I wish to avoid them. They are violent people. There is badness in them." To learn to lovingly monitor such patterns, you would need to say, while you are in the midst of these thoughts: "I do not choose to continue these kinds of mental patterns. I believe that they are not truth, and I wish to release them."

In that moment of self-created clarity, you would gently release the old thought patterns, simply letting them slip away, rather than forcing them away. Then, you could creatively replace the old thoughts with new ones that are more inspiring, and more closely aligned with your ideals. Perhaps you would say, "The ones of this racial grouping are souls linked to me in love. In this moment, I turn my thoughts toward goodness for them."

Even though it may take some time and practice to actually accomplish what we are describing, if you are persistent in such work, you will be extremely pleased with the way you will be able to choose your thoughts.

MASTERING YOUR THOUGHTS

As we have stressed, your ability to create health in your life depends a great deal upon how well you master your own thoughts. To gain such mastery, you will need to clearly understand some important areas of your mental capacities. To illuminate these areas for you, we will begin with this understanding: You as a human being have the ability to *respond* to your own thoughts, just as you have the ability to *create* them.

Your own thought patterns are self-created streams of human energy that *you* set into motion. However, from your subjective point of view, you also experience streams of thought within you that seem to arise spontaneously, without your choosing them. We can assure you that *all* of your thoughts come from some *choice* that you have made in the past, even if you do not remember making that choice.

For example, imagine that you, as a child, saw a loved one die of a heart attack. Over a period of years, you would choose to dwell upon the pain and fear that the experience stirred in you, but you choose not to take the time to heal your negative thoughts and feelings about the experience. Then, imagine that, as an adult, you are in the middle of a great feast with your friends and loved ones. You have not thought about your experience with death for a number of years, but, suddenly, this thought springs into your mind: "What if I should die of a heart attack in the middle of this feast?" You might feel that this thought has spontaneously come forth without your choice, but, in truth, it is an extension of the past choices that you made to focus on your fearful thoughts, and the choice not to work to heal such patterns.

This simple example will help you understand that your negative thought patterns can be given a certain *power* when you choose to propagate them. They can be infused with a negative *human* energy. It is not a strong energy. It usually cannot dominate your whole life, or overpower your own will. However, when you do not have a deep belief in your ability to choose your thoughts, to manage the way you respond to your thoughts, and to lovingly change them, then the persistent negative thought patterns within your personality can, at times, appear to have a life of their own. Some of those negative patterns can become so strong that you might feel that they are being fed to you by a source beyond your control. If you allow such patterns to go unhealed, they can cause you pain, and eventually they can challenge your health.

It is possible that as you work to master your thoughts, there will be persistent thought patterns that frequently trouble you, and which you seem to be unable to change. This can be particularly disturbing when the thoughts are about a present challenging situation in your earth life, such as ill health. When you notice that you are continually being bombarded by such thoughts, and you attempt to work in the inner ways that we have suggested, and you find that the thoughts will not change, then there are two likely possibilities. First, this could be a signal that you have created a *habit of worry* in that area of your life, and you need to spend some time examining your personality patterns in order to identify and heal the *fear* that caused the habit, rather than attempting to change your thought patterns. Or, it is possible that in the life situation about which you are having the troubling thoughts, there are *outer* matters that need your attention. You may need to go forth and deal with the situation, or with the people involved, working on those in a tangible earth way, rather than simply trying to change your thought patterns. At certain times, you might have fearful thoughts about situations that present physical danger in your life, in which case, you would certainly give the *situation* your attention, rather than trying to change your thoughts. You will decide which of these two signals you are being given by your persistent, troubling thought patterns.

If you decide that the persistent negative thought patterns are a signal that an outer earth situation needs your attention, then go forth in the very moment that you realize this, if it is appropriate, and deal with the situation as honestly and directly as you can. If the direct work cannot be done in that moment, then resolve that you will do it at a later time, and say to yourself:

"Since I cannot address the outer situation in this moment, then the challenge facing me

now is to rise up and master my troubling thoughts and put them aside until I can later deal with the situation. I now release these thought patterns, and I replace them now with thoughts of beauty, harmony, and love."

If, on the other hand, you decide that your troubling thought patterns are sending you the signal that worry has become a habit, then you would say to yourself: "All that I need do is heal these stubborn worry patterns that I myself have created. Since I created them, then I can heal and release them." What you would need to decide then is whether the present moment is the time to look for the fears that pervade your patterns of worry, or whether you will deal with that later. You would ask yourself: "Is this the proper moment to search within myself to discover the fear that underlies my worry, or do other areas of my life need my attention right now?"

If you feel that the present moment is the proper time to look for the fear that lies within your worry patterns, then begin in this way: Take a moment to reflect upon which aspect of your worry troubles you the most. For example, if you have been worried about a lack of money, then take some time to clearly define for yourself what is the most frightening thing about not having money. Is it that you are afraid that you will starve? Are you afraid that you will lose your home? Are you afraid that you will be disgraced in the eyes of your friends?

When you come across the most frightening area, remind yourself that the fear is a *feeling* inside of you. *It is not a reality.* Then, you can begin to work with your fear, using the method that we will suggest in a later portion of these teachings [Chapter Twelve].

If you feel that the present moment is *not* the time to delve deeply into the fearful thoughts that cause your worry, then say to yourself:

"At a later time, I will return to work with my patterns of worry. Right now, I draw forth my own strength and love, and I release these thought patterns of worry. I replace them with new thoughts of beauty and love. And now I go forth confidently to address the immediate situation in my life that needs my attention."

In this case, one effective way to temporarily dissolve thoughts of worry, particularly if they have become a strong habit, is to divert your attention by *distraction*. For example, you could say: "What could I find in this moment that is of creativity, beauty, and good that I can go forth to work in, to act in, or to speak to others about." The most effective diversion is to go forth to other human beings and to become concerned about them, and find ways to give to them, to be of service to them.

Working in the way that we have suggested to put aside your worry thoughts is a *temporary* measure. That is what you would do in the midst of a busy day when you do not have the time to work in a deeper way. However, if you have a habit of worry, eventually you will need to take the time to uncover and address the fears that underlie your worry patterns.

This addressing of your fears can most effectively be done in honest explorations of all of your personality patterns with the help of others—friends, loved ones, counselling ones. You will also need to work with yourself inwardly. In a later portion of these teachings, we will speak of the process of uncovering and healing fear in general. However, in working with worry specifically, you will usually be working with a *process* of fear, not so much with particular issues in your life.

With worry, many different fears can be involved, since worry is simply a pervasive *habit* of fearing. In one moment of worry you will fear one thing, and in another moment, a different fear will lie beneath your worrying. Persistent worry comes about when you have allowed the *habit* of fearing to grow strong. That habit can be triggered by many different things that frighten you from moment to moment. Therefore, in working with your worry patterns, you will need to engage in a *new* habit, which involves the constant revealing and releasing of the worry habit, no matter what fears are involved. You will learn to remind yourself:

"This thing that I am worrying about in this moment cannot harm my being. My worrying is a habit, and I can now release it, even as I enter into the fear that is triggering my worry in this moment. I accept this fear now, knowing that it is one of many fears, and knowing that none of my fears can harm me. I live the fear now. I dissolve and release it in love, and in the certainty that there is only

goodness within me."

If you continually work in this way with the many *small* fears that are associated with your worry, then, eventually, you will heal the habit of worry. Then, you can turn your attention to any deeper fear patterns in your personality that you believe need to be understood and healed.

HEALING PATTERNS OF CRITICISM

We will look now at a challenge of thinking that plagues many people in earth at the present time: the habit of using your thoughts to criticize, to find fault, and to make negative judgments against yourself, and against others.

We will begin this understanding by asking you to turn your thoughts toward a very strange event that takes place in the lives of many people each day. That event is: *the clouding over of the magnificence of life by the creation of human criticism.* To see this clearly, imagine that you are now looking at life from the vast eternal perspective of your own soul. First of all, you see all of the millions of earth years that it has taken for the souls of you ones to create the physical earth, to inhabit it, and to bring it to the present moment of existence, with all of the complexity that has been created by all of the human beings involved in unfolding the beauty and the majesty of earth life. You can see the unbounded beauty of nature, and the magnificent physical creations of human beings as they gain mastery over the earth environment. You can see all of the beautiful artistic creations of human beings in the painting, the music, all of the writing forms, and all of the other areas of human creative expression. You can see all of the charitable and altruistic enterprises of human beings. You can see vast areas of good and love constantly being poured forth into earth by billions of human beings day after day.

Now, looking at all of this magnificence of earth life with your soul vision, you notice the strange event of which we have spoken. You see a male human being in an earth morning, and, in the midst of all of the magnificence that we have just described, a magnificence that has taken millions of years to create, *this male one is using the unlimited divine creative capacity of God that lives within his personality to condemn his mating-one for not preparing his breakfast in the proper way.* You would see another person criticizing a loved one for saying the wrong words. Another might be actively involved in criticizing their bed for having caused a pain in their back, or they would criticize nature for pouring rain upon the streets, or they would criticize themselves for not being good enough in their lives.

This strange event is *the manifestation of the human ability to find fault, and to see badness, while living in the midst of the most extraordinary magnificence of God expressing into earth life.* This human ability to criticize springs forth primarily from *a lack of gratitude* for all of the goodness that abounds in life. The lack of gratitude comes about when human beings have so colored their vision with fear that they actually believe that there is no goodness in life.

They become so preoccupied with the areas of negativity that they have created that they come to feel that they are being oppressed, or cheated, or damaged by life. Certainly, when they are caught up in such negative feelings, they feel that there is nothing to be grateful for.

Habits of criticizing and finding fault are woven with many of the personal confusions that grow out of *fear*, and that have become negative patterns within the individual personality. You will usually need to do some intelligent and thorough inner work to reveal the fears that lie beneath your own criticisms.

For example, let us imagine that you are one who would continually criticize others for being very boisterous and vocally loud, and you feel that such persons are quite insensitive. As you work inwardly with this habit of criticism for a while, you may find that inside yourself you are very frightened of displaying yourself spontaneously to others because you are afraid of being criticized by them. You are afraid that you do not have admirable qualities to show off before other people. Because of this fear, you have adopted a habit of hiding yourself and drawing back. You have trained yourself to be quite calm, dignified, and polite. Although this *feels* appropriate to you, you have adopted such patterns out of *fear*—the fear of displaying the more spontaneous aspects of your personality. Thus, when you see a boisterous person, unconsciously, it reminds you of your fear that you do not have admirable qualities to draw attention to your personality in the way that the boisterous person is doing. However, rather than allowing the behavior of the boisterous person to trigger your fear, you unconsciously prefer to diminish the boisterous person and push that person away from you by condemning them and criticizing them. We use this example as a way of illustrating the kind of questioning and investigating that you can do as you work to identify the fears beneath your own particular habits of criticism.

Just as with worry, criticism is a process that can feed on many different things in your personality, and it can be triggered by any number of things in your environment. In other words, if you are in the habit of criticizing, you will criticize many things. If you are not in the habit of criticizing, you will not find so much to criticize in your life, and your life will seem much more positive to you.

However, there may always be some things in human life that displease you. You are free to feel that sense of displeasure, and you are free to do what you wish about the things that do not please you. You can choose to avoid them, or you can work with them to change them. You are also free to *refrain* from criticizing them. You can say to yourself:

"This thing does not please me. I do not like it. I can do whatever I choose about my feeling of displeasure. I can stay away from the thing and ignore it. I can come close to it and attempt to change it. I can change my *response* and find peace with the thing. But, whatever I do, I will *not* condemn this thing, label it as badness, and then habitually criticize it. I do

not desire to develop the habit of criticism."

We will now suggest a way of doing the inner work necessary to heal patterns of criticism. This can be very beneficial in most of the everyday, or "less-serious" areas of your life.

In healing habitual criticism, you do not need to work in great depth with *everything* that you criticize, although you may wish to do that. You can quickly heal the tendency to criticize and find fault by simply *refusing* to condemn a thing and label it as badness. To do this, you will need to honestly observe your feelings about things, people, and situations. When your feelings are negative, when you have a dislike for things, or when you feel the impulse to criticize and label them as bad, simply say to yourself:

> **"The feeling I have about this thing, this person, or this situation is *my dislike—my feelings*. The thing itself is not badness. Perhaps there are even other human beings who would find goodness and joy in this thing. I am quite clear about my feelings of dislike, and, for this moment, that is my truth. But, other human beings might have a different truth. I certainly shall not impose mine upon them. If I am asked my opinion about this thing, I may wish to share it honestly. I may wish to say that this does not please me, and that I find this and that negative about it. But, I refuse to condemn. I refuse to criticize."**

You must be very *flexible* with yourself as you work to heal habitual patterns of criticism and fault finding. If you become too rigid with yourself, you may attempt to *suppress* all feelings of negativity. As we have stressed, to continually suppress negative feelings can distort your personality and cause you great confusion. At times, there can even be some benefit in letting critical feelings arise within yourself, for the feelings communicate to you quite clearly what pleases and displeases your personality.

To work in a flexible way to heal your patterns of criticism and fault finding, you would first let your negative feelings come to the surface so that you can know what you feel about a certain thing in that moment. Then, decide what you wish to do with the feelings. You do not need to translate them into criticism and fault finding. There are many other choices that you have. For less serious criticisms, simply taking the time to observe your critical feelings, and reminding yourself that you wish to heal them, will usually lead to the healing.

However, when there are persistent troubling issues associated with your patterns of criticism, such as those that arise from challenges in your relationships of love and mating, or deep conflicts with people whom you must be near continually, there is a slightly different approach needed in your inner work. If the troubling situation involves another human being, you could first try the simple approach of noticing your critical response, then reminding yourself that the other person has a different viewpoint. Then, attempt to simply *release* your feeling of negativity and criticism.

If that is not successful, and you continue to feel

very critical and negative, then there is need for *communication*. First, the communication can be with yourself. You can say to yourself: "What is it *in this person* that so frightens me that I continue to make a negative feeling of criticism about them? What is it *in me* that is causing fear?" Perhaps your fear is of a certain action or personality pattern in the other person. If so, you would need to examine what it is about that pattern that frightens you, and why that pattern is so important to the other person that they continue engaging in the behavior that challenges you.

Perhaps you will need to understand their life from their point of view. In your imagination you may need to enter into their life in order to understand them and why they act as they do. If you are successful in seeing the situation from their point of view, then you will stimulate an understanding within yourself that will help you release your criticism.

If the inner communication with yourself is not successful, and if you truly wish to heal your criticism, then you will need to communicate with the other person. You will need to communicate your feelings to them, honestly and clearly. However, you must be careful not to *accuse* them of something negative simply because their behavior is irritating you. Rather, you would say: "Inside my own feelings, I am creating a great irritation to this portion of your behavior. I wish to heal the fear *in me* that is causing my irritation. Would you help me by communicating with me about it?"

In areas where you are persistently critical of situations, or events, or even objects of earth, and there is no individual with whom you can communicate, you would need to communicate with yourself and go through the same process. Say to yourself:

"What is my fear that has caused me to respond so negatively to this thing, situation, or event? How can I work with my fear? What do I wish to do about this thing? Do I wish to avoid it for a while? Do I wish to push myself a bit and go toward it, and learn to not criticize it, perhaps even learn to appreciate it? What goodness is there about this situation, event, or thing?"

As with the other areas of your personality, when you do your inner work on habits of criticism, after you have worked with the fear patterns, the next step is to turn your thoughts and feelings away from the negative illusions that you have created, and direct them toward the truth. In working with your criticism and fault finding, you can remind yourself of the truth by saying often:

"Each human being is imbued with the same forces of God that live within me. In that sense we are the same. Yet, each human being is infused with the uniqueness of their own soul's energies, and with their own particular human patterns. Thus, in some ways, we are all quite different. Each of us may see a different truth, and each of us may respond in different ways. The more patient I can be with others and their visions of truth, and the

more sensitive I can be to their desires, their fears, and their doubts, the less I will be tempted to find fault with them and criticize them. And, the more I can bring this same patience, love, and understanding to my own personality, the less I will criticize and find fault with myself."

By working toward this kind of attitude about yourself and others, you will learn to feel the love that joins you to others. This will help you recognize and heal the tendency to use your powerful mental capacities to criticize and find fault. And, the healing of criticism will free your energies so that they can be turned toward the creation of health in your life.

HEALING PAINFUL MEMORIES

There is another area of your thinking that you will need to master as you move toward a full manifestation of health. That area is *memory*, particularly the negative memory patterns that are disturbing, frightening, or painful for you.

For example, imagine a female one who has been sexually violated and severely beaten in the past. Even though the painful events occurred many years in the past, within her present personality, memories of those events spontaneously arise quite often in her mind, seemingly without her choice being involved. The feeling in herself is that in some way she is a *victim* to those memories, and she constantly responds to the memories with fear and pain.

In order to work with such negative memories,

and for most people they will not be as intensely negative as this example, it is effective to concentrate on *the present memory patterns*, and not so much on the past *negative experiences* that are being remembered. This is particularly true when the experiences are long past, and when you have done your best to heal the past situation, and your thoughts and feelings about it.

To heal persistent painful memory patterns in the present, you will attempt to *dissolve* them. First, it is very effective to take a period of time each day in which you release all *resistance* to the memories. Each day you can give five minutes of your time to this. As with your other inner work, you will always begin by creating a deep relaxation for yourself as you begin your period of silence. Then, you can work with these kinds of thoughts:

"My negative memories might be frightening and painful, but *they cannot harm me*. They are only inner experiences created by my own thoughts and feelings. I now turn my full attention to this persistent negative memory that is troubling me. I let it come forth now. In fact, I encourage it. I give it all of my attention. I now let these memories grow strong in me."

You could then use your imagination to actually *exaggerate* the memories, and take a few minutes to immerse yourself in them. Enter into the various negative thoughts and feelings that you have about the memories. This willingness to enter into the negativity of the memories will eventually convince you that the memories cannot harm you.

At times, expanding your painful memories in this way may cause you to feel sadness, or emotional pain, or fear. Monitor yourself lovingly as you do this inner work, and *only go as deep into the painful memories as you desire to go. Do not push yourself into painful, fearful memories if they disturb you greatly.*

After you have spent as much time experiencing the negative memories as you desire to spend, then turn to the final portion of your inner work period, which will be used to direct your attention back to the truth of your being. As with all of the other inner work that you will do, remind yourself that you are an eternal soul filled with love. Remind yourself that there is goodness and beauty in your life, and that none of your human experiences in earth can damage your true being.

If you do this inner work with painful memory patterns each day, gradually, over a period of time, you will learn that you can enter fully into all of your persistent negative memories without harming yourself. Even though you may stir up negative emotions within yourself, you will learn that those emotions cannot damage you. Eventually, you will be able to enter any memories that you desire to work with, no matter how frightening or disturbing those memories might be. You will enter into them, experience them, and then release and dissolve them in love.

You can also do this kind of work with friends, or loved ones, or with a counsellor. As you draw forth your troubling memory patterns, you can communicate them verbally to the person with whom you are working. Describe the memories in detail, and explore all that you can recall about the past situations. Do not become too involved in the past *experiences*. Keep the focus on *your present memories*, reminding yourself that memories cannot harm you. You would also allow any negative emotions about your memories to rise up to be experienced, communicated, and then released. At the end of the work period, turn your attention back to the truth of your being, and ask the person to love you and encourage you to see your own beauty and magnificence.

You can also *write* to yourself about your painful memory patterns, describing them in writing in a detailed way. Try to *live* the memories as you write about them. Then, at the end of the writing period, release the negativity and write about the beauty and goodness of yourself as a human personality, and as an eternal being. Remind yourself in writing that the negative memories have not diminished the truth about your being. This writing process can flush out and dissolve the pain and fear that have become woven with your memories of the past.

We suggest that you begin this inner work on the *less* painful memories that trouble you. Later, after you have gained confidence and trust, you can approach the painful memories that seem more disturbing.

In any of this work with your memories, *if you become too frightened, then stop the work and seek comfort and love from friends and family, or from counselling ones trained in human psychology.*

Gradually, as you do this inner work, you will come to understand that memory is one of the many energies within your personality matrix that can be brought under your conscious mastery. You can use your memory as *you* desire. You can freely choose *what* you remember, and *when* you remember it. However, as with the other areas that you will work with in your personality, in working to dissolve your negative memory patterns you will always need to guard against *suppressing* your painful memories and hiding them from yourself out of fear. Enter into the memories and explore them so that you may heal the fear. Then, you can move on to the step of dissolving and releasing the memory patterns. To cut short the healing process by jumping right to the dissolving step could possibly lead you to unintentionally push away painful memories because you are frightened to face them.

On the other hand, you will find that it is not of great benefit to give *too* much attention to, or to become preoccupied with, your painful memory patterns. It would not serve you well to exaggerate the importance of such memories, or to blow them out of proportion by feeling that they are large demons that will devour you. You would not wish to overdo the inner work periods during which you enter into your negative memories. This would simply bring an unnecessary morbidness into your feelings, or a preoccupation with negativity.

In working to heal your painful memory patterns, it is *balance* that is important. You will learn when it is beneficial to encourage those memories, to explore them, to fully re-live them, and then heal them. And, you will know when it is beneficial to simply turn your attention in a different direction and not be so concerned with your memories.

These are decisions that only you can make within yourself. You are the one who is having the memories. You have *created* them. You are the one who is *responding* to them. You are living them. You are the one who must decide the time for *analyzing* your memories, the time for *experiencing* them, the time for *releasing* them, and the time for turning your attention to the truth.

Remember that there is no *badness* in your memories, even if some of them do not please you. Even if some of them frighten you. The past negative *experiences* in your life are *over*, and your negative *memories* of those experiences are simply *present* inner patterns that do not bring you joy, or perhaps cause you fear and bring pain *in the present*. With calmness, patience, and gentle understanding, you will be able to heal your painful memory patterns in the present, just as you are able to heal any other areas of negativity that might arise within your inner experience as a human being.

Chapter 9

Your Emotions

—In order to gain the capacity to more intensely rejoice in the beauty of earth life, you ones who have come into earth as human beings have agreed to allow your emotional patterns to have a very strong say in your inner life. Therefore, the souls have created the human personality structure in a way that emphasizes emotions, and causes them to be extremely strong experiences in human life.

You can easily recognize that your day to day feelings—your emotions—have a very strong impact on your inner experience of life. Your emotions can produce powerful inner energies that are often quite intense and dramatic for you. As with your other personality energies, you can either learn to master the powerful emotional energies within you, or, you can allow them to run wild within your inner experience, a choice that often results in pain, suffering, and loss of health.

In your day to day life, your emotional patterns

will tend to be more volatile and more dramatic than your patterns of thought. When you think frightening thoughts, even though they might be disturbing, you can usually understand that they are only your thoughts. However, when you feel a frightening feeling, that feeling often seems so real to you that you can actually believe that your being is in danger. If you are *feeling* that life is hopeless, you can believe that life truly *is* hopeless. *You often believe that what you are feeling in a certain moment is actually the truth about life.* Mistaking your feelings for the truth about life is one of the tendencies you will need to adjust as you work with your emotional patterns.

Because of their intensity, your emotions can easily lead you to create confused beliefs about the nature of life. For example, in a moment of deep discouragement, you might begin to feel, "Life is terrible and hostile. It will destroy me." However, no matter how strong that feeling might be for you, we can assure you that it is just a feeling. It is not the truth about life. Life can *never* destroy you. Of course, it will eventually destroy your present physical body. But, you are not that body. You are an eternal being, and no matter what you may feel in any moment, you *cannot* be destroyed.

Since you ones have a tendency to mistake your feelings for the truth, working with your emotional patterns can often be more difficult than working with your thoughts. Thus, you will need patience and persistence in your day to day work with your emotions.

As a general guideline—and this is true for all areas of your inner life—the more you work toward *creating feelings of love for yourself and other human beings*, the greater will be the beneficial influence upon your emotional life, and, consequently, upon the health of your body. Choosing love as your ideal will be a major factor in mastering your emotions, and in learning to manifest full health in this lifetime.

On the other hand, if your ideal is simply *to collect pleasurable experiences for yourself*, then it will be more difficult for you to master your emotions. This is not to say that you must turn away from pleasurable experiences. We are simply pointing out that the larger your ideals, the more they involve other people, and the more they are rooted in love, the easier it will be to learn the truth about your emotions. When you are caught up in self-indulgence, you isolate yourself from others, and your emotions become confused and distorted. They become more difficult to manage in a healthy way.

ATTRACTIVE AND REPULSIVE FEELINGS

As you can readily observe in your own inner life, there are some emotional patterns that *attract* you, and others that *repulse* you. There are feelings that please you and that you will desire to increase within your inner experience. There are other feelings that are painful to you, and usually you will desire to decrease them, or avoid them entirely.

Thus, your emotional patterns can at times seem to be two different realities within your inner life, and you will usually have different responses to each of the two streams of feeling. You will generally rush to embrace the emotions that are in the pleasurable stream, and you will ordinarily strive to avoid the pain of the negative feelings.

This pattern of *attraction* and *repulsion* is a "natural" response, in terms of the *animal* nature of the physical body of the human being. The animal bodies of earth were given an instinctual capacity to draw toward pleasure and avoid pain, as part of the process of maintaining physical life on earth. This animal instinct lives within the *matter* of your physical body, and it can strongly influence your thoughts and feelings about life.

The animal instinct in your physical body is different than the eternal forces that have been placed into your personality matrix by your soul. Although your soul intended for you to learn to rejoice in your physical, animal nature, it did not intend for you to be *dominated* by such physical realities. Your soul intended for you to *master* the attraction and repulsion of human emotional energies that are related to your animal nature.

When you allow your emotional life to be dominated by the simple animal response of attraction and repulsion, which is dictated by pleasure and pain, you unintentionally "split" yourself between positive and negative feelings. If carried too far, you can begin to desperately long for a constant experience of positive emotions, while going to great lengths to avoid negative feelings. If you continually exaggerate your desire for pleasurable emotions, you can literally become "addicted" to the pleasure of positive feelings. This exaggeration causes the split between your positive and negative emotions to grow even larger. Eventually, it can stimulate confusion and turmoil that can begin the personality disruption that can negatively affect your health.

Yet, throughout your lifetime, there will always be a certain natural attraction and repulsion in your emotional life. You would not expect to eliminate this entirely. There will be a "normal" range of response in your particular personality that you will learn to live with and balance in your day to day affairs. But, if you begin to notice a large difference between your positive and negative emotional experiences, then you would need to bring more attention to your emotional life. The *extremes of difference* in emotional responses will cause you to inwardly fight with yourself and your feelings.

We are not saying that extremely intense emotions, either positive or negative, will challenge you. We are speaking of an exaggerated or obsessive preoccupation with pleasurable emotion, lived against a background of extreme fear of emotional pain.

If you develop the habit of obsessively seeking the pleasurable emotions and fearfully avoiding the painful ones, you can also become dependent upon the human beings who seem to spark pleasurable emotions in you, and you will tend to avoid individuals who trigger your negative feelings. In extreme cases, you can begin to cling desperately to people who stir your positive feelings, out of fear of losing them, and you can become terrified of people who bring you pain.

Thus, you can see that if the attraction-repulsion response in your emotions is not understood and managed intelligently, your emotions can become a tyrant in your life. If it becomes so important to you to always feel pleasurable emotions, and so frightening to feel negative ones, you will find yourself engaging in extreme actions and situations, either to gain more pleasure, or to avoid pain. If you notice this taking place, then you can say to yourself, "I am coming close to being tyrannized by my emotions, rather than mastering those emotions." In such cases, you will need to work lovingly with yourself to learn how to heal the different fears that are involved in your exaggerated emotional responses.

MASTERING YOUR EMOTIONS

Just as we have been suggesting for other areas of your inner life, in order to master your emotions, you will need to learn to *observe* your emotional patterns in a loving, objective manner. However, since there are so many different areas of emotional expression, you will need a simple starting point for your work.

As you begin to work to lovingly observe your emotional patterns, we suggest that you start with only the feelings that are most important to you. By working in the large, important emotional areas first, you can bring about some strong positive changes that can encourage you in all areas of your inner work.

Thus, your first task is to decide which emotional areas are most important to you. For some, it will be feelings of *love*. Others might focus upon feelings of *harmony*, or *power*, or *purpose in life*, or other kinds of feelings. Even though what you consider to be your important feeling areas will change over time, you can begin with your present important feelings as a starting point for your inner work.

As you learn more about your emotional patterns, you will discover that negative emotions are less likely to trouble you when you are willing to fully *experience* your emotions day by day, even when they are unpleasant or painful. As we have emphasized, the swallowing of emotions can lead to great challenges to your health. The willingness to experience your feelings when they arise, and your willingness to patiently work with them day by day, can eventually lead to a soundness of emotional and physical health.

However, you will need to work with honesty and courage to make certain that your emotions are allowed to come to the surface at the appropriate time. For this, you need to align your *intelligence* with your emotions. For example, imagine that you are in the middle of a very important test in a class, and you begin to feel frightened. Since you have a time limit for the test, it is not intelligent to say, "I will take some time now to bring my fears to the surface and work with my emotions." Instead, you would say, "I take note that this will need some work later, but for now, there are other more pressing issues than exploring my fears about this test."

In many ways, your emotions are tied to the actions and behavior of others. Therefore, you will often need to decide what to do with your emotions in light of how the ones around you are responding to you. For example, let us imagine that you have chosen to work to encourage feelings of *patience* in your inner life. Then, one day you find yourself with a person who is physically beating you. At that moment, it is not beneficial to say, "Now, I wish to work on patience. I will allow this beating to continue." In that case, you need to work on fast movement to take you away from the beating. Later, you can work on patience in forgiving the one who was beating you. There are certain times when it is appropriate for you to focus upon your work in the emotional area. At other times, responding appropriately to the actions of other human beings will be more important to you.

There are certain kinds of emotional experiences that are natural to your human existence. They will most likely arise throughout your lifetime, no matter how well you learn to work with your emotional patterns. For example, if there would be the death of a beloved one in your life, there would spring up within you feelings of sadness, loss, or despair. If you are faced with a certain physical danger, the feeling of fear for your safety will arise spontaneously. If a person would insult you, immediately, feelings of irritation, anger, or resentment could rise up. Positive emotions can also arise in this way. If a one does a large kindness for you, gratitude and love can well up within you immediately.

With these kinds of spontaneous emotional experiences, it would not benefit you to try to control them. Your choice in these areas would be to decide:

"How long do I wish to give in to these feelings? How long do I believe I need to experience them?" In other words, your freedom lies in your ability to continue the feelings that have spontaneously arisen, for as long as you decide they are desirable in your experience.

Eventually, you can train yourself to intentionally *create* the emotions that you desire to emphasize in your inner life. You can choose to create the feelings that foster health within you.

However, if you prematurely attempt to create certain emotions before you have learned enough about your personality patterns, there could be a temptation to create positive emotions in order to escape the painful negative feelings that frighten you. It is for this reason that we recommend that, at first, you let both your negative and positive emotions arise naturally. Do not attempt to interfere with this process while you are learning about your personality. Work patiently with all of your emotions, learning from them, growing from them. Then, as you learn to love yourself more, and as you bring forth more of the wisdom that lives within you, you will eventually find yourself in situations where you feel that you are quite honest, loving, and trusting with yourself, and you wish to manage and change certain emotions as they arise.

HEALING EMOTIONAL PAIN

We turn now to the area of *painful* emotions. Painful emotions are frequently experienced within the inner reality of present human beings. Such painful emotions are a common disruptive factor that adversely affects the health of many ones at the present time.

The *causes* of the various painful emotions that you experience in your life can be quite numerous—you can feel bad about many different things. However, your *response* to the painful emotional experiences occurs within a more narrow range.

For example, you could have a deep feeling of sadness brought about by the loss of a loved one, loss of your possessions, noticing the pain that others are experiencing, or by observing unpleasant consequences to people on earth caused by violence or war. Your "single" feeling of sadness can be caused by many *different* things in your earth life. Or, you can have a feeling of loneliness that is a simple, clear, single feeling, but it can be caused by a variety of complexities in your relationships with numerous human beings, and the feeling can be triggered by many different situations.

As you consider your own painful emotional experiences, you can remind yourself that there will be two primary areas of focus: (1) *the outer events* in your life that involve people, places, and things; and (2) *your inner response* to all of those factors, including your response to your own feelings and inner life. As we have mentioned earlier, the first area of outer events is varied and complex, and often it cannot be directly *controlled* by you. The second area of your inner response is a much simpler area to understand, and it is totally under your control, even though you may not always feel as if you have such control.

There is a certain range of outer events that most normal human beings will respond to in a similar manner. If there is a death of a beloved one, most human beings will experience sadness and emotional pain. Consciously and unconsciously, you ones in earth teach one another the generally accepted range of emotional responses, and you *learn* what is appropriate as an emotional response to a certain event.

For example, imagine an isolated tribal grouping of human beings who believe collectively that when there is the death of a beloved one, that beloved one has become perfect and has entered into a spiritual world in which they will have great joy, and from which they will bless those who still live on earth. In such a grouping, there would be children surrounded by adults who *celebrate* the death of beloved ones by laughing, singing, and dancing. When those children become adults, you would expect them to have the same emotional responses.

Even though your society and the outer events in your life do have a strong impact upon your emotional life, you would need to remember that your *response* to those outer events is *subjective*—it takes place inside you—and your response is influenced by many things other that the physical events of your outer life. Your response to outer events is related to certain inner energies that you have unconsciously drawn from your own soul. Those energies prompt you to intuitively and instinctively have certain emotional responses that are related to many personality patterns from your *past* lifetimes. In addition, your present emotional responses are also influenced by the state of your human body, your mind, and your long-standing emotional patterns from this lifetime.

Thus, in working to understand your painful emotional experiences, you would first remind yourself of all of these factors that can be involved in your emotional responses. To truly understand and heal your painful feelings, you will need to learn to observe and work with, quite alertly and lovingly, all of the different factors that affect your emotional experiences.

Over a period of time, if you continue to study all of these factors in a loving way, you will gain an understanding of the kinds of events and situations that are most challenging for you, and that are most likely to be associated with your painful emotional experiences. Eventually, you will learn to adjust your response to those events, or you will learn to act differently when the events are taking place. You will learn to make different kinds of adjustments that will help you respond without such intense negativity to some of the situations that persistently challenge you. This learning will come about from a steady, ongoing, day to day process of inner work with yourself in which you observe, identify, and understand your life events and your emotional responses to them. Then, instead of creating emotional pain, you will learn to consistently create beauty and love within your emotional patterns.

We will now look at ways to work within yourself

when you are experiencing painful emotional states, regardless of the causes. This work will help you heal the pain of those negative feelings, and that healing will open the door to full health for you in this lifetime.

First, you would need to work with yourself in a certain *general* way that would be effective no matter what the nature of your emotional pain might be, whether it is loneliness, despair, frustration, anger, depression, or any of the other painful human emotions. Here is a very simple way to work inwardly to bring about understanding, comfort, and, eventually, healing.

Step One. Begin by relaxing your physical body. Release all thoughts and feelings of earth. Then, create a gentle feeling of peace, harmony, and love within yourself.

Step Two. Identify the painful emotion that you wish to work with during this period. If you have only a vague feeling of emotional negativity, try to clarify it. For example, if you simply feel a great sense of heaviness in your emotions, ask yourself: "What is this feeling?" Keep questioning yourself until you gain some clarity. Perhaps you would decide that you are feeling a confused sort of *depression*. Thus, you would say to yourself: "I am feeling *depression*. Now I will heal it."

Identifying the negative feeling gives you a place to start in your healing process. It gives you a sense of understanding. Even if you may feel powerless to do anything about your negative emotion, at least you are able to identify that emotion and explain it to yourself.

Do not spend too much time with this step. Simply find a convenient label for your feeling, then go on with the inner work.

Step Three. *Enter directly into the painful emotion.* Using your imagination and your feelings, create the negative emotion as strongly as you can, and enter into the feeling of it. Cease resisting and struggling against your feeling. Let the feeling of emotional negativity saturate you inside. As you continue to do this, at the same time, attempt to create *relaxation* within yourself as best you can. Then, say to yourself:

"There is a negative feeling here inside me that *I have created*. I allow this feeling to fill me now so that I may experience it fully and come to know it."

Step Four. Deepen your experience of the painful emotion. Quite consciously encourage the negative feeling to grow stronger. Say to yourself:

"Let me now enter deeper into this painful emotional experience of (name the feeling you have identified) within me. I do this in patience and love. Let me feel the painful feelings more deeply to see what lies within them."

In our present example, you would enter more

deeply into the *depression* that you identified, still making a relaxation within you as much as possible as you do this. Whatever painful emotion you identify, give yourself totally to the feeling of it, and explore the feeling without hesitation. Let the feeling *fill* you from within. You can even try to exaggerate the painful feeling.

As the negative feeling fills you with its heaviness, perhaps there will be certain fears that will arise in you. Usually, you will fear that the painful emotions will bring *badness* of some kind into your life. For that reason, there will be a natural tendency to tense yourself and fight against the negative feeling. During this, simply be gentle with yourself, create more relaxation, and allow the painful feeling to flow through you easily, without restriction.

Step Five. From *within* the negative feeling, calmly and objectively examine the feeling, and your *response* to the feeling. As you do this, you will usually notice that the feeling of *badness* will gradually begin to diminish. You can help this process by gently questioning yourself about what you are feeling. For example, naming the feeling you have identified, you could say:

> **"What does this (depression) feel like? Where do I feel it in my body? Is it in my chest? Is it in my stomach? My head? What does it feel like in each part of me? How do my emotions, my body, and my mind respond to the feeling?"**

Mentally describe to yourself in detail the sensations of the painful feeling inside yourself. Carefully observe your responses to the painful emotion, and try to remember those reactions so that you can work with them later.

Do this step for as long as you feel is necessary—perhaps five or ten minutes.

As you are working with yourself in this way, if you find that the negative feelings become more intense, you can say to yourself: "What do these more intense feelings feel like?" Working in the same way, guide yourself through the experience of the more intense emotions.

Step Six. Begin to remind yourself that the painful emotion that you have been experiencing is not the truth about life. It is only a human *feeling* that you have created. Thus, again naming your painful emotion, say to yourself:

"Now it is time to remind myself that this feeling of (depression) that I have been experiencing is only a temporary emotional pattern. It is *my* feeling. I have created it. It is not truth. And, feelings cannot harm me. No matter how deep the emotional pain might be, it cannot damage my being. It can only disturb me temporarily, stirring up my fears. But, emotional pain cannot damage the magnificence of my being."

In this portion of your inner work, try to create as many thoughts and inner statements as you can that will help you feel that the negativity that you are experiencing is simply a self-created illusion that is caused by your fearful emotions. For example, imagine now that you have been working with feelings of depression, and you have been feeling that all of life is darkness and blackness, that you will never laugh and rejoice again. After you have entered into those feelings and explored them for as long as you feel is necessary, then you have come to the step of reminding yourself that the negative feelings are not truth. You would extend this step by saying to yourself:

"These feelings of (depression) are only my emotions, and my emotions cannot damage me. It is not true that all of life is darkness and blackness. That is *my own inner experience* that I have created for many complex reasons, due to confusions in my own human personality. I have created the *illusion* of depression and darkness in life, and now is the moment in which I wish to dissolve the illusion and heal it."

Step Seven. After you have finished reminding yourself that emotions cannot harm you, and that they are not the truth, then it is time to turn yourself toward the real truth. We remind you again that the truth of your being is: *you are eternal; you are always filled with an unending energy of love, whether you can feel it or not; and, you have great qualities of wisdom, strength, and many other capacities within you* *of which you are not usually consciously aware.* Thus, if you were doing this portion of your inner work with depression, to turn yourself toward the truth, you would say to yourself:

"The most effective way to dissolve the illusion that all of earth is bad and hopeless, and that my feelings of (depression) are the truth, is to turn myself toward the real truth. The truth is that there is good in all of life. There is good in me. I am filled with a love that never ends. My abilities to heal negativity are far greater than I have realized. I am eternal love, and nothing can change that."

In working with yourself in this way, you are aligning your thoughts and feelings with the truth. You are also stirring up the energies of love, strength, and beauty that lie within the personality matrix of you.

Step Eight. After you are satisfied that you have carried out your inner work for as long as is necessary, then slowly and gently bring yourself back to full alertness and awareness in the present moment. Take as much time as you need. Do not rush yourself.

In working with yourself to heal your emotional pain with this method that we have suggested, you will be working in a manner that is similar to your work with other aspects of your inner life. However, this area of emotional pain is a bit more complex because your emotions of negativity are usually extremely intense for you.

In order to gain the capacity to more intensely rejoice in the beauty of earth life, you ones who have come into earth as human beings have agreed to allow your emotional patterns to have a very strong say in your inner life. Therefore, the souls have created the human personality structure in a way that emphasizes emotions, and causes them to be extremely strong experiences in human life.

Thus, when you are working with your own *painful* emotions, whether they are feelings of depression, loneliness, frustration, no matter what they might be, do not be surprised to find it more difficult to understand and heal negative emotions than it is to heal other negative aspects of your human experience. With painful emotions, you must be more *patient* with yourself. You can expect the healing to take longer, and you can demand a bit more from yourself in terms of gentleness with yourself, creativity in your inner work, and love for your personality.

With long-term, persistent patterns of painful emotions, such as the grieving for a loved one who has been lost, in most cases, drawing love and comfort to yourself from other human beings will eventually, as time passes, help you heal the pain. If you work patiently and gently with others who are understanding and loving, your painful feelings will gradually dissolve.

You may have observed that each bout of emotional turmoil that arises within your human experience seems to be the *reality* of the moment. In working with your emotional pain, at times it can be of benefit to remind yourself of how many emotional turmoils you have lived through and *survived* in this lifetime. Each time, the emotional pain seemed like reality, and each time, you lived through it, and it disappeared. Remind yourself that those past painful experiences have not destroyed you. You are still sound, and whole, and magnificent. This kind of thinking could encourage your mind and your emotions to rise up and *expect* this present wave of painful emotional experience to be healed, just as all of the past ones were healed.

If you happen to believe that your *past* painful emotional experiences have somehow damaged you, or diminished you, or crippled you, then it will be more difficult for you to heal your *present* emotional pain. When you believe that you have been damaged by certain painful emotions in the past, then, when similar feelings arise in the present, you will believe that they can damage you again. This can cause you to be frightened of your own negative emotions.

The healing of emotional pain is a *process* that takes place over a period of time, and there are different stages to the process. At first, in the beginning of the cycle of pain, you may simply seek *comfort*. You will surround yourself with feelings of love and comfort in order to convince yourself that you are not being damaged by the emotional pain. You will draw friends and loved ones near to help you soothe and comfort your feelings of pain as you pass through them.

Eventually, however, there comes a time when it is necessary for you to rise up from your painful emotional experience and begin the active healing process. That is when the inner work with yourself truly begins. At that point, the first step is *encouragement*. You will need to convince yourself that you *can* heal yourself. To do this, you could work with your thoughts and feelings in the following way, saying to yourself:

"I rejoice in the comfort that I have received, and now that I am stronger, I rise up to love myself. As I love myself, I begin to reach forth into my own heart, and through my own creativity, strength, confidence, and love, I draw forth the inner energies of healing for myself. I also begin to look for ways in which I can attune to other human beings and draw forth inspiration for my healing from their kindness, generosity, and love."

You could also remind yourself that you do your healing in stages. First you *comfort* yourself. Then, you *encourage* yourself. Then, as we have described, you *enter into* your feelings of emotional pain in order to live them fully and discover what fears and responses in you caused the pain and made it so intense. Then, you *focus* upon how to re-spark love, and how to turn yourself toward the truth, as we have described.

By expecting the healing of your emotional pain to be a process that can take a period of time, you will not become concerned if you do not instantly heal yourself. You will continue to calmly and patiently comfort yourself throughout the entire healing process, saying to yourself:

"No harm can come to my being as I am healing myself of this emotional pain. I am eternal, and this challenge is temporary. I will let this emotional pain rise up to be expressed and experienced by me, to be understood, and eventually to be healed. Whatever step of the healing process this moment may be, I live it now, and I rejoice in being alive, and I bring as much love and trust to this moment of healing as I possibly can."

The kind of patient, gentle, persistent inner work with yourself that we have suggested, combined with your work with others who will stand by you and love you, ordinarily will be strong enough to help you heal *any* emotional pain that might arise in your life. However, at times, you might find yourself intensely exaggerating emotional pain to the point of continually feeling trapped in it. You may feel: "No matter how hard I try to heal these painful feelings, it seems that they always remain. They never heal. And I am left in pain and sorrow." At such times, even if you work in the ways that we have suggested, you may continue to feel depression, despondency, aloneness, or despair. If that is the case, we strongly suggest that you go forth to seek out the help of loving individuals who have knowledge of the psychological aspects of human life. Find wise counselling ones, and draw upon their wisdom and their love to help you locate the fears in your personality patterns that are causing your emotional turmoil. Together, you can heal your fears, and you can draw forth the love within yourself and themselves in order to dissolve the emotional pain and return your personality to the truth.

As you work day by day to heal your painful emotions, you will find that you are taking a great step toward the full manifestation of health in this lifetime. Since the negative emotional patterns within you are usually the most distorting of all of your inner patterns, then the healing of those negative emotions will be one of the largest factors in your healing work. If you persist in the steady healing of your negative emotions, you can expect to draw forth the forces of God within you in a most magnificent way that can result in strength and health in your life.

Chapter 10

Your Beliefs

—As you live each day, in a sense, you become a product of your moment to moment experiences of thinking, feeling, acting, and doing. Those experiences have led you to create your present beliefs about life, and they will mold your future beliefs. You are involved in a constant process of "creating" yourself through your beliefs, and this process will either feed your physical body healthy influences, or it will block the forces of health.

The next stream of inner personality energies that can affect your health is the energy of your *beliefs*. By continually responding to your own thoughts, emotions, perceptions, and the other inner streams of your experience, and by continually interacting with the world around you that is comprised of people, places, and things, you create your beliefs about life, moment by moment.

Beliefs and attitudes are similar, and, just as with your attitudes, your beliefs will determine whether you will see life as good or bad, happy or sad, nurturing or destructive. This will determine how your body responds. Thus, your beliefs will be an important factor in determining whether or not you are able to manifest health.

Your beliefs have to do with *conclusions* that you have drawn about life, or that have been taught to you by other human beings. If you would say, "I believe that life is harsh and painful," that is a conclusion that has either been influenced by pain that you have experienced yourself, or that you have learned about from others. If you would say, "I believe that life is quite magnificent and beautiful," that belief would be related to experiences of magnificence and beauty that you have had yourself, or that you have been taught about by others. From those influences, you have concluded that there is goodness in life.

BELIEFS AND YOUR EXPERIENCE

The beliefs that you have about your present life arise from the steady stream of inner experience that you live each day—your thoughts, feelings, ideas, memories, responses to others, and so forth. With some of your inner experiences, it will be easy to see how they are connected to your beliefs. For example, if you come to your school as a small child and you are constantly treated as one of stupidity and ignorance, then obviously that will have a strong impact on your beliefs about your own intelligence. Even though all of the influences on your beliefs may not be this clear-cut, most of the interactions of thought and emotion that make up your present belief structures can be brought to your conscious mind with patient and loving self-study.

Often, strong beliefs can be influenced by experiences that you have had in past lifetimes on earth that are different than your present experience. For example, there are many ones who have had quite painful experiences in this lifetime, but they still deeply believe that there is goodness in life. This belief in goodness can come from other times on earth in which they have strongly experienced that goodness, and have come to believe in it as reality, as truth.

In working with your beliefs and your human experience day by day, *flexibility* is the key. You will need to be able to have a belief about your experience of life, and then be quite flexible in going beyond the feeling that your belief is truth. You will need to say to yourself, "This is a *belief* that I have created, based upon *my personal experience* of life. It is not a *truth* about life."

You will also need to remember that you have formed your beliefs for some reason. That reason lives in you and your personality patterns. Or, it lies within your experience of your environment and the human beings about you.

As you live each day, in a sense, you become a product of your moment to moment experiences of thinking, feeling, acting, and doing. Those experiences have led you to create your present beliefs about life, and they will mold your future beliefs. You are involved in a constant process of "creating" yourself through your beliefs, and this process will either feed your physical body healthy influences, or it will block the forces of health. If your beliefs are aligned with the truth—which is that there is love and goodness in life, that negativity is human created, that it is temporary, beliefs such as these—then your thoughts and feelings will generate the beneficial energies that stimulate health in your body. If your beliefs are, "There is badness in me and in others; life is bad; there is evil; all is lost," then you are detracting from your health.

MASTERING YOUR BELIEFS

To learn to master your beliefs, you will need to set aside some time to work with them in each day, at least for a small period. If you wish, this work can be done at the end of the day, before sleep.

Take some time to sit quietly with yourself and briefly review your beliefs in that moment. As you do this, you will need to be patient, objective, and kind with yourself. Try to associate your beliefs with some of the experiences that are the reasons you have those beliefs. For example, you might say, "In this day, I believe that life is quite harsh, for I have lost my job." In another day, you might say, "I believe that life is wonderful, for I have spent a day with a beloved friend." In another day, "I believe that life is quite abundant, for I have made a great deal of money in this day." In another day, "I believe that life is filled with forces of God, for I have had in this day a deep experience of God."

On some days, your beliefs might be quite negative. You do not need to fret about that. Simply notice the reasons why you have the negative beliefs, and know that *your beliefs will always change in time*. You will always have the creativity to find a way out of negative beliefs. And, you can always find a way to enhance and augment your positive beliefs.

In order to make changes in your beliefs, you will need to work in the manner that we have described earlier to learn how to balance between living *inside* your inner experience, and stepping back from it to observe it from the *outside*. To remind you of the feeling of this, let us use a simple example. Imagine that you have a bowl of cereal with many different grains in it. You look at the cereal and say, "This looks quite delicious. I shall eat it." Another person looks at the same bowl of cereal and says, "This is an interesting mixture of substances. I believe I shall analyze it scientifically to determine the chemical components of it." In this situation, you would receive the pleasure of fulfilling your hunger, while the other person would receive the pleasure of satisfying intellectual curiosity. You would not say that one experience is good and the other is bad. They simply bring about different *results*, in terms of the impact upon the inner experience of each person.

Consider that your private inner experience is the bowl of cereal, and the grains represent the different *beliefs* that you hold about life. If you say, "I shall only *live* my life with intensity, according to my beliefs; I shall not analyze my beliefs or attempt to understand them," then, you are the one simply eating your cereal for pleasure. You can expect a fulfillment of your appetite for *intensity of inner experience*. You are also free to say, "I look at my inner experience and I wish to *understand* its makeup. What are the beliefs that create my reality? How do they work together to form what I experience?" In this case, you are the one wishing to know the chemical composition of the cereal. You will satisfy your curiosity and your desire for *knowledge* and *understanding*.

To live your life passionately without questioning your beliefs in order to gain intensity of experience, or to focus upon knowledge and understanding, are simply two choices that bring about different results, in terms of your inner experience. The important issue here is how you will balance *all* choices that you wish to make. Most people would desire to have the intensity of inner experience, along with knowledge about the beliefs that determine that experience; to have the *emotional* fulfillment of *living* certain beliefs, along with the *intellectual* satisfaction of *understanding* those beliefs.

To attain such a balance, you would need to cultivate an attitude that brings you the freedom to *choose* your beliefs, based upon your *experience*. You could encourage this by saying to yourself each day:

"I will *live* the intense beliefs that I have grown within my personality up to this point in my life. They are important to me. But, I will also take some time to lovingly *observe* those beliefs so that I may understand what they are made of, and how and why I have developed them? Then, I will decide if my beliefs please me, or if I wish to change them."

When working to understand how your beliefs directly affect your health, you have only to ask yourself: "Which belief troubles me? Which belief seems to limit me? Which belief is causing me challenge or pain?" For example, you might discover that you have a strong belief that other people are untrustworthy, that they will disappoint you and cause you pain. As a result of this belief, you have adopted the habit of hardening yourself against others, which results in loneliness and a lack of love. In such an example, your belief that others are untrustworthy has become a challenge in your life, and you can expect that if it is not healed, it may interfere with your health.

When you have clearly identified a troubling belief, you would need to sit in a period of silent attunement with yourself, during which you would draw forth memories of all of your experiences, thoughts, and feelings that are related to the troubling belief. By practicing this persistently, you will learn to identify the confused and fearful personality patterns that are woven into your belief. In time, you will understand the experiences in the past that led you to form the present troubling belief.

Then, it is a matter of deciding if you wish to continue to hold on to those patterns and the belief, or, if you wish to make some changes. You would need to remind yourself:

"This belief is not truth. It is a *subjective* reality that I have created inside me for the reasons that I have just discovered. I am free to change this belief if I desire to do so."

More difficult to work with are the *unconscious* forces that feed into your beliefs and attitudes about life. Yet, even though you may not always be able to gain conscious knowledge of such forces that are related to troubling belief patterns, you can still use your imagination and intelligence to work to heal them.

For example, imagine that you find that each time you enter a church, you have a strong feeling that religion is used by people to delude themselves into believing in a God that does not really exist. You have not been taught this by anyone in your *present* lifetime. Thus, you could assume that there are some unconscious factors that have influenced you in creating this belief. Those factors might be related to experiences of *other* lifetimes that unconsciously have led you to create a prejudice against those who worship God in religious contexts. Even if you did not know the specifics of the *causes* from those other lifetimes, you could still remind yourself: "In the past, at some time, I might have had very painful and frightening experiences to cause me to be so judgmental, and to have such a lack of understanding of the experiences of others that lead them to involve themselves with religious groupings. I now wish to examine my beliefs and see if I desire to delve deeper into what may have caused them in the past."

As you work to understand unconscious factors that affect your present beliefs and attitudes about your life, one of the most effective ways to gain clarity is to write your beliefs on paper, or to speak about them to other people. The process of communicating your beliefs and attitudes will force you to clarify them. Where before they were vague and only partially conscious, when you communicate about them, you bring more of them to light, and you bring out more possibilities for understanding. In the communication, you can use your imagination to explore *possible* past factors, *feeling* them to see if they feel accurate or not.

In all of your work with your beliefs, you will always need to come back to this question: "Are these beliefs that I am now observing in myself ones that I desire to continue and propagate in my inner experience, or, are they ones that I wish to change?" When you see clearly that there are negative patterns woven into your beliefs, then you will usually desire to change them. Most often, the greatest challenge will be that you are not aware of your own negative patterns. Thus, at times, you can mistakenly feel that your beliefs are woven with truth, when in fact they are actually aligned with your own fear.

In working to understand your beliefs, it can be very helpful to draw assistance from a loved one, from a friend, or from a counselling one. This would be particularly important to do if you find that your beliefs continually conflict with the beliefs of many people around you. In such a case, you may wish to say to your friend or loved one, "Help me define these beliefs that I have built. Help me understand how I have created them. Help me see what has convinced me that these beliefs are true."

Understanding and mastering your beliefs will

eventually result in a release from confusion and doubt about your life. You will find a clarity about your human personality that will bring you a great deal of joy. You will learn to create new beliefs that are rooted in a sensitive, loving understanding of yourself and others. This will help you make the kinds of inner openings that invite a full inflowing of health-giving forces into your emotions, your mind, and your body.

Chapter 11

Your Will

*—Your will is an extraordinary force that you
have available to you in this lifetime. The force of
your will is one of the most powerful expressions
of the force of God living within your human personality. It is your will that gives you power over
the physical world.*

One of the strongest inner streams of energy
within your personality matrix that can affect your
health is the force that is your *will*. Your ability to
intelligently make conscious and willful choices, and
to direct yourself through life by those choices, is a
powerful capacity within you that can not only enable you to create full health, but it can eventually
lead you to a complete mastery of the physical world.

The eternal souls, in their creation of physical reality, and in their intentions for the human personalities within physical bodies, have established
human will as the power that can gather the extraordinary spiritual energies from beyond earth, harness

them, and then pour them forth into the physical world as a *human*-created reality. The souls' intention is for human beings to create their part of reality as a reflection of the perfection of God itself. Thus, learning how to master your will can lead not only to a healthy life for you personally, but it can also help you to play your part in the magnificent unfoldment of life on earth.

UNDERSTANDING YOUR WILL

Your will is an extraordinary force that you have available to you in this lifetime. The force of your will is one of the most powerful expressions of the force of God living within your human personality. It is your will that gives you power over the physical world. You can draw freely upon the force of your human will in your quest for a full and healthy life.

For many of you ones, it is usually difficult to feel the power of your will in your day to day life. That is because you have had experiences in which you tried to will your life to unfold in a certain way, and it did not. The frustration of unfulfilled desire often causes you to feel weak, rather than powerful. Many of you have experienced this in the *love* area. You have desired a certain one to love you for a lifetime, and they have turned away from you. Others have desired great wealth, but have not achieved it. Some have desired health, but have manifested illness instead.

Most of you have important desires in various areas of your life that you have not been able to completely fulfill in this lifetime. For many of you, the painful and frustrating experience of deeply desiring something, and then seeing your path to fulfillment blocked, has convinced you that you do not have the power to create the things in life that you desire.

Within your *highest* potential, as eternal souls, you have the ability to actually *will* a thing into existence, without acting or doing. This is an ability that some of you were able to manifest in your human lives in ancient periods. However, because of certain changes in the way that human life now manifests, rather than simply willing a thing into existence, you have agreed to align with the human belief that you must *work* for what you desire. You must *act* and *do* in order to *manifest*. This brings the human will into the physical world in a way that is easier to manage. Even though you cannot now master the extraordinarily complex process of simply willing a thing into physical existence, you can will yourself to work in order to manifest what you desire in the physical world.

Most of you in your present lifetime will use your will in this "normal" way. However, some of you may choose to elevate the use of your will to a level that is closer to its intended purpose. This can be particularly effective in the area of health. If you can learn to will yourself to saturate your thoughts and feelings with the truth about life, which is that *you are the perfect forces of God living in human form*, then you can bring about changes in your personality that can give you the confidence to begin to infuse your will into your desires in a powerful new way. This can open strong energies within you that can begin to fully infuse your physical body with the eternal forces that were intended for it.

ALIGNING YOUR WILL

You can choose to align your will with any of your personality patterns, such as your thoughts, your feelings, your desires, your beliefs, and so forth. The greatest challenge to your health comes when you align your will with your negative thoughts and feelings.

For example, let us say that you have a friend who has shouted at you in an argument. Your *negative feeling* at that moment is, "This friend is now an enemy." In your confusion and hurt, you align your will with that negative feeling and you use your will to reject your friend. You decide that you will never see that friend again. The result is pain and turmoil for you and your friend. In that situation, you are just as free to say, "I am angry with this friend. I have a *feeling* that this friend wishes to damage me. I am having a *feeling* that this person is my enemy. But, I now will myself to create some patience and sensitivity so that I can work with these feelings and heal them. I wish to align my will with my desire to create further friendship and love with this one."

It is easy to forget about the power of your will when you are tossed about by the storms of your negative emotional and mental experiences, when you are frightened, or in pain. Yet, even when you are challenged, you can still *choose* to align your will with a belief in your own strength, and in the goodness of life. You can consciously create a *belief* that you do have control over your will, and that you can use your will to create what you desire in your life. By working in this way, eventually, you will learn to use your will in an enlightened manner.

Although your will is a powerful force, as it lives within your human personality, it is not a perfectly clear reflection of the true nature of eternal energies. That is because your will is colored by the entire range of your human personality patterns. Thus, if your personality is filled with negativity, you can expect your use of your will to be unintentionally distorted by the negativity. In such cases, your willful actions can often interfere with your health.

On the other hand, if your personality is filled primarily with honesty and love, you would expect your will to be aligned with those. Your will would be used in a creative and productive way that would eventually bring about the health and fulfillment that you desire. If you continually align your will with love, and you work steadily and patiently to heal your negative personality patterns, then, even if you do experience negativity from time to time, even if at certain times you do know great pain and are deeply challenged, you can still use your will to more fully invite the energies of God through the threshold of matter to infuse your body with greater health-giving influences.

MASTERING YOUR WILL

At times, your will might appear to be a mysterious force that seems difficult to master. Even though you may have such feelings, you can still understand your will as simply another one of the many forces within your personality that is intended to be used by you for your own fulfillment.

The fluctuations that you feel in your ability to master your will are due to the fact that your will, like all of your other inner energies, is always connected to your *thoughts* and your *emotions*, and your thoughts and emotions are highly volatile. They fluctuate dramatically throughout your lifetime. Thus, at times, you may feel weak and seem to have no will, while at other times you can feel strong and willful, depending upon your thoughts and emotions. Such fluctuations of feeling can be considered to be "natural" for human beings.

The important understanding for you to keep in mind as you work to master your will is that the effect of your will upon your daily life depends upon your entire inner experience—the way that you manage all of your personality patterns day after day. If you manage your inner life in ways that are aligned with the truth, then you align your will with the health giving forces of your soul that feed your body. Your will becomes a potent force that stimulates health and perfect functioning within your body.

We will now suggest some general steps for mastering your will. You can accomplish such mastery by intelligently and lovingly aligning your will with your desires. The following process can be used in any area of your life in which you wish to use your will to manifest health and fulfillment. To be effective, you will need to use this process daily.

Step One. Find a private place and begin by relaxing your physical body. Calm your thoughts, and create feelings of harmony and love.

Step Two. Clarify the desire that you wish to act upon. Think through what you desire, and specifically define it for yourself. You might say, "I desire to use my will to create health for my physical body." Whatever your desire might be, bring it clearly into focus in your mind.

Step Three. Concentrate your attention upon what you desire to will into being. In working to harness your will to your desire, one of the most effective tools is concentration of your attention through repetition of focus upon the result. Remind yourself of what you have willed yourself to do, using either verbal statements, thoughts, writings, or images. See the *results* of your desire. Clearly envision the results that will be accomplished when you fulfill your desire. If you are working for health, then you would see your body healthy and strong. This brings forth the power of your will into the area of your desire, and you begin to inwardly fuse your will with your desire.

Step Four. Remind yourself of your unlimited abilities to accomplish the results that you desire. Do this even when you have feelings of doubt about your abilities. You may wish to make affirmative verbal statements to yourself. For example, you could say:

"Within me I have a great, unlimited creativity. I have diligence and perseverance. I have strength and patience. I have ingenuity and cleverness. In this moment, I am *willing* these capacities to come forth strongly within my personality. I am now turning all of these abilities toward the fulfillment of my desire."

Step Five. Create a specific focus for the actual work that you will do in the physical reality of earth to use your will to accomplish your desire. Define for yourself the specific steps that you will take in the outer world toward the fulfillment of your desire. For example, if you are focusing on your physical health, you might decide that you need to act in the area of diet, or exercise, or the healing of certain inner personality patterns. Specifically identify the kind of work that you will do in your earth affairs. It is beneficial to write about these steps in great detail, examining what needs to be done in each step, and exploring any potential obstacles that will need to be removed from your path.

Step Six. Stimulate your will. Create deep feelings of desire within your personality for the goal you have established. Stir up great feelings of *determination* to succeed, *inspiration* to act brilliantly, and *perseverance* to pursue your desire without cease. Stir up any other deep feelings that can stimulate your will toward fulfillment of the desire.

As you learn to create these deep inner feelings to stimulate your will, you may begin to notice personality patterns in you that weaken your will. For example, you might notice a habit of procrastination that inhibits your actions on your desires. Or, you might discover patterns of laziness which make it difficult for you to work enough to accomplish what you desire. Even though you try to be willful and disciplined, you end up following your impulses of laziness. Or, you might wish to exercise your will to accomplish something important in your life, but are afraid that you will fail, so you never try. To fully exercise your will, you would need to take some time to heal such obstructive personality patterns one by one. You could accomplish this through loving inner work with yourself, using one of the methods that we are suggesting in these teachings. Eventually, you can heal any doubts, or fears, or inhibitions that stand in the way of your will.

Step Seven. Inwardly align your creativity and strength with your will. Creatively envision how you shall complete the earth tasks that are necessary to accomplish your goal. Learn to draw forth, in your imagination, various ways of accomplishing the tasks that you set for yourself. Then, attune to the eternal creative energies of your own soul and of God itself, and teach your personality the truth by *saying* it to yourself in this way:

> **"I have an unlimited capacity to maintain my will, and to align my will with all energies of life. I have an unlimited capacity to align my will with the energies of God so that I may accomplish what I desire in my earth life."**

Step Eight. After you have done this inner work with your will for as long as you desire, then *slowly* and gently bring yourself back to alert awareness in the present moment.

What we have suggested here is a simple way to understand your will, and to work toward utilizing the force of your will in the fulfillment of your desires. You shall decide in which direction the force of your will shall be turned, and you shall decide how long you wish to bring your will to bear on certain portions of your life. As a complex human being, you will find that there are many areas of your life toward which you shall desire to direct your will. The areas that are most important to you can receive the most intense force of your will, in terms of accomplishing and achieving in the outer earth world. As with the other streams of your inner energies, steady, persistent work with your will can result in a tremendous release of healing energy into all areas of your life.

Chapter 12

Your Whole

Personality Experience

—Your human personality experience is true for you while you are living it. However, it is constantly changing. At times, your personality experience can be aligned with truth, and at other times it can be aligned with human fear, confusion, and negativity.

E ven though we have spoken of the various aspects of your inner life as though they are *separate* streams of energy, in truth, they are all part of the whole of your personality experience as a human being. Thus, even though all of the complex aspects of your inner life that we have mentioned will each affect the way you create your human experience, when you are working to create a healthy inner life, you can make significant changes in all of your patterns by working with your personality experience as a *whole*. In other words, if you work intelligently with your whole experience, then it is not necessary to understand *everything* about all of the individual streams of your inner life, nor is it necessary to completely master every one of those streams before you move toward healing your personality and your body.

Just as with all of the separate streams of your inner patterns that we have looked at, in working with your personality experience as a whole, it is important to keep in mind that *your personality experience is not reality or truth*. It is simply your personal inner experience of life at the moment.

Your human personality experience is true for you while you are living it. However, *it is constantly changing*. At times, your personality experience can be aligned with truth, and at other times it can be aligned with human fear, confusion, and negativity. At times your personality experience can be feeding you in ways that promote a healthy life, while at other times it can be filled with self-created negativity that can challenge your health.

NEGATIVE HUMAN EXPERIENCE

As with the individual streams of your inner life, when your personality experience as a whole is *negative*, you can be certain that it is far from the truth about life. Your negative experiences grow out of human *fear*. (We use the word *fear* not only to mean *fright*, but to convey the many different human feelings that cause you to believe that something is *wrong*, or *bad*.) When your personality experience feels *positive*, you can say to yourself, "*Perhaps* this experience is aligned with truth. Perhaps it is not. That is for me to determine."

It is possible for your personality experience to clearly mirror the perfection of your soul, and of God itself. Ordinarily, this occurs when you are experiencing love, beauty, and harmony.

However, this does not mean that pain, sorrow, and despair set you apart from the perfection of eternal energies. As we have emphasized, negative experiences are *human creations*. They only exist in the inner personality experience of human beings living on earth. Such negativity does not exist in the experience of *eternal* beings. Thus, negative experiences are not a true reflection of the energies of souls, or the energies of God. Yet, even your temporary negative human experiences are, in a certain way that cannot be verbalized, contained *within* the eternal perfection of the energies of God while those experiences are unfolding inside your human personality.

Remember that when you are having negativity in your personality experience as a whole, it does not mean that there is badness in your life. It simply means that you are aligned with human fear. You can learn to identify the fear and heal it, which we will address in a moment. You can also learn to *change* your whole personality experience, just as you can change any of the individual patterns within that experience. To do this in your day to day work with yourself, you could say to yourself:

"My human personality experience is not truth. But, it is very *important* to me. It is not

a dream or imagination. It is a *personal reality* that I have created for myself in this moment, from all of the complexities that are involved in my personality. I remind myself that I can learn from this human experience. But, if the temporary reality of this experience does not please me, then let me change it and create another experience for myself."

As we have stressed in other areas, when working with your whole experience, it is important for you to always maintain the feeling that you have the freedom and power to *create* your experience as you desire it to be. As you work with your whole personality experience each day, remind yourself:

"Within my personality experience I have the power to *create* what I desire, to *transform* what does not please me, and to *expand* upon that which does please me."

You will also need to remember the freedom that you have to *respond* to your life in ways that please you, no matter how you may feel about what is happening in your life. Thus, it is important to remind yourself each day:

"No matter what takes place in my life, inwardly within my own private experiencing, or outwardly in terms of other people, events, places, and things, I can always change my *response* to my experience once the experience has occurred."

When negative experiences seem to rise up spontaneously in your life, appearing not to be chosen by you, you can still work with your response to those experiences. You can say to yourself:

"How do I choose to *respond* to this experience that seems to be out of my control? I can respond by choosing to fall into despair because of this experience, or I can respond by choosing to live the experience fully, and infuse it with strength, love, and understanding, and thereby transform it."

The way that you respond to the negative experiences in your life will determine the *quality* of your inner life. When you respond to negative experiences by falling into despair about them, believing that you will be damaged or destroyed by such experiences, then your inner life will be dark and painful. On the other hand, when you can respond to your negative experiences with all of your honesty, courage, strength, and understanding, then you will eventually heal the negativity, and you will bring forth the beauty of God into your life for all ones to share.

HEALING NEGATIVE EXPERIENCE

There are many different techniques that human beings have developed for focusing creativity, attention, desire, and will upon the healing of negative human experience. Those techniques would include such things as therapeutic conversations with ones of psychological training, meditation, hypnosis, introspection, visualization, and religious counselling. As with all things that human beings create, the *effectiveness* of such methods depends not upon the method itself, but upon *how the method is used*, and how it is integrated into the inner life of the human personality.

For example, imagine a male one who feels quite weak, and helpless, and unable to rise up and heal his negativity in any area. He decides to use a certain hypnosis process to make himself feel stronger, and he does it with the attitude: "I am one of weakness and helplessness. I am a lost cause, but I believe this hypnosis will help me be strong." Perhaps he would find a bit of strengthening of his confidence by using hypnosis. Perhaps there would be a certain amount of benefit to himself. Yet, because he is using the method with a sense of unworthiness, most of the positive change would be undermined by his feelings of weakness, helplessness, and despair.

On the other hand, if, in honesty and clarity, he would make his feelings of weakness, helplessness, and despair the subject of the hypnotic suggestions, aligned with the desire to heal the old patterns and draw forth the strength from within his being, then such a healing technique could be of great benefit to him. The difference is in his *attitude*. If his attitude toward himself is that he is really a weak person, and he simply uses a healing method to force upon himself a belief that he is strong, and he artificially repeats that belief without healing the fears and the negative attitudes that caused his feelings of weakness, then there will not be a great deal of improvement in his inner life. However, if he comes forth in his day to day life with an attitude of honesty, and a willingness to experience and heal his feelings, no matter how negative they might be, then most likely, the use of any human method of focusing the attention can be of benefit to him.

Accomplishing the necessary changes in attitudes and beliefs can heal negative personality patterns, whether any specific healing technique is used or not. Along with loving and honest work with the inner personality patterns, techniques and methods can help you accelerate the healing that *you create from within your own personality*.

In working with your personality experience as a whole, you would need to remind yourself that the healing *energy* lives within you, not within a method. You can remind yourself of this truth by saying to yourself:

"The most potent healing energy in the universe is the energy that has *created* the universe—the energy of God itself. That energy lives within me now. If I can work with myself in ways that help me to experience that energy of God as *love*, and if I can draw that energy into my day to day life, then it matters not what method I use to do it. It matters only that I do it. And, in so doing, *I become the healing one*. I become the one who brings the method, and the ways of working, together in harmony, strength, and love. I become the one who chooses how I will heal my negative patterns in order to unfold my personality experience in love and joy."

With this in mind, we will now look more closely at the inner reality that you are creating in your present life, and we will suggest a general approach to the healing of your negative personality experience.

Let us begin by comparing your inner reality to a large, hard ball with which you are playing. If you throw the ball about and play with it quite intelligently and proficiently, you will have much joy. However, if you are clumsy and impatient, the ball may occasionally hit you in the face, causing you pain. In the same way, the inner reality that you are creating within your human personality can either be lived intelligently, thereby bringing you great fulfillment and health, or, if managed clumsily, it can be the cause of pain and illness in your life.

To extend the analogy: You as a human being are in the rather strange position of being not only the one playing with the ball, but, you also *are* the ball. In a certain sense, while you are a human being, you *are* your inner experience. You are temporarily your feelings, thoughts, emotions, and all of the other energies and qualities of your personality life, and, you are continually creating your experience from *inside* those energies and qualities. Yet, you are, at the same time, the observer, or "experiencer" of your experience, witnessing it from *outside*. So, you are both of these at once: you are the *creator* of your inner experience, and you are the *responder* to that experience.

To heal your negative personality experience, you will need to intelligently live each of these roles. As the creator of your experience, you will want to find ways in your day to day life to *create* your thoughts, emotions, and inner patterns to be what you desire them to be. As the responder, you will need to learn to master your *response* to your inner creations so that you are able to rejoice in your inner experience, even when that experience does not please you.

As you work with yourself each day, you can use your ability to observe your inner life, and you can begin to notice the difference between these two aspects of your inner experience. You can learn to define and master your role as creator, while you become adept at responding to your experience in ways that please you.

If you find that you are unable to make an adjustment in one area, for example, in *creating* your inner experience, then perhaps in that moment you can make an adjustment in how you are *responding* to that experience. In such a case, you would first say to yourself:

"I am temporarily caught in the negative experience that I have created in my personality. I wish to heal that experience and *create* a new experience for myself."

You would then work in that moment to heal your inner negativity and turn your attention toward the truth, thereby creating a new experience for yourself.

However, if you come to feel that you are not successful in healing the negative experience and creating a new one in that moment, then you can turn your attention to the second aspect of your inner life—your *response* to the inner patterns that you have created. You would then say to yourself:

"It appears that I have not succeeded in changing my negative experience in this moment, so I now choose to change my feeling that it is *bad* that I have not succeeded. I can now create a *response* in which I can find some good in this situation that challenges me. In my new response, I can decide that my grappling with this continuing negativity within me will eventually bring about some kind of good in my life. I will learn from this work. I will grow stronger from it."

What is important here is that you are creating a *new* response to your inner experience that is more fulfilling than your old response. And, you can do this even though you were unable to change the experience of negativity itself.

When you are working in a general way with your negative personality experience, remind yourself that you have the freedom to focus upon both of these areas at the same time, or to work with them separately. When you are attempting to heal your inner life, you can choose the area of focus—*creator* of your experience, or *responder* to it—that you feel will help you make the adjustment that you desire in the moment.

HEALING FEAR AND GAINING TRUST

As we have emphasized, the cause of your negative personality experience is *fear*. We remind you that when we use the word fear, we are not speaking only of fright. We are referring to any sense of "badness" that you might experience within yourself, which creates the feeling that goodness is lost. It is the feeling that certain people, or things, or events, or experiences will bring some kind of badness into your life.

Since fear is the cause of negative personality experience, to maintain your full health, it will be important to learn how to heal the fears that you have created within your personality. You will also need to gain the trust that there is goodness in you, and in all of life.

As we have pointed out earlier, the beginning human forms that were created by the souls of you ones in ancient times were not infused with energies of fear, or feelings of badness. There was no negativity in the souls' creation of human personalities. The first negativity began to arise when human beings began to believe that there could be a loss of good in their lives. They created fears in many areas of human life. Rather than remaining attuned to the love that joined them to all other human beings, they began to create feelings of *badness* about experiences and situations that they believed could harm them.

In this present moment, you as a human being have within you the same tendency to create feelings of badness by imagining that people, situations, and experiences can harm you, or bring badness into your life. From your many times of living in human life, you have brought forth unconscious patterns that make you sensitive to what you feel can be harmful to you. Those old patterns are the roots of your fear. And, those old patterns combine with present experiences that feel bad to you. They combine with your present negative thoughts and emotions, prompting fear to arise within your personality.

Not only do you have the negative experiences that arise from certain *real* situations in your life, but those are exaggerated by negative things that you *imagine* in your fear. You can imagine situations in which you would be robbed, or beaten, or killed. You can imagine situations in which all of your money would be lost and you would walk in poverty. You can imagine situations in which ones would not love you, and you would live a life of loneliness. You can imagine situations in which your body would become diseased, and you would spend many years of pain before your death. You can imagine situations in which the earth would be polluted, and many ones would die, perhaps even yourself. There are a great many experiences that, to you, as a human being, can seem potentially damaging. You can imagine any of them and feel: "Perhaps these bad things *will* happen to me." From all of this, *you can come to feel that the earth is a very frightening place to live.*

The first step in understanding how to heal fear is to notice that *your capacity to be frightened is totally unlimited.* If you constantly create fear in yourself, then earth life for you will hold an unlimited number of things to be afraid of, and to worry about. You can assume that throughout your lifetime, *there will never be an absence of opportunities for you to frighten yourself.* However, it is very important to understand that no matter what you find to be frightening in the outside world, *the fear is being created inside of you.*

The capacity for creating fear lives within your personality. Your fear does not exist outside of you. Situations that you find frightening can exist outside of you. However, if you did not believe that those situations could damage you, there would be no fear inside of you, even though the situations would continue to exist in your outer world. Thus, the *process* of becoming frightened of the world takes place *within you.*

If you would think clearly about your entire life up to this present moment, you might find that you have been frightened about many things in your lifetime. Perhaps some of the things that you feared have happened to you physically. Perhaps you have lost money. Perhaps illness has diminished the full range of function of your body. Perhaps you have lost a loved one. Perhaps you have experienced pain in many different situations. All of those things that have happened to you, or that have frightened you, are now *past.* The key to your freedom in the *present* is to understand that even though you may have experienced pain in your mind, emotions, or body, *you* have not been damaged. You are not your thoughts. You are not your emotions. You are not your body. You are an *eternal* being who cannot be damaged by anything of earth.

Thus, when you are working to heal any fear inside of yourself, you will need to take a moment of silence with yourself and remind yourself of the truth that *you* cannot be damaged, no matter what happens to your mind, your emotions, or your body. To accomplish this, you can say to yourself:

> **"There may be many things in this earth life that have frightened me in the past. Perhaps there may be things that will frighten me in the future. The thing that frightens me may constantly change, but my fear is the same. It is the fear that badness will come to me in one form or another. It is always the same fear—that there will be badness in my life, instead of goodness, joy, and fulfillment. The *process* of fear is always the same in me, no matter what I am frightened of in any given moment. The fear is *my* process. I have *created* the fear, so, most certainly, I can *heal* it."**

We suggest that you write these words on paper and carry them with you. When you are inwardly working to heal your fear, draw these words forth and feed them to your mind.

Other ways of working to heal your fear have to do with your courage to *enter into* the experience of your fear until you can come to understand and believe that the fear cannot harm you. Here we are speaking of entering your *feelings* of fear about certain things or situations. We are *not* suggesting that you force yourself to physically enter into frightening situations, or associate physically with frightening things.

For example, if you have a fear of snakes that becomes quite disturbing to you, you do not need to say to yourself: "The only way to heal myself is to physically handle snakes." If you desire, you can say: "My fear is an emotion *within me*. My fear does not lie within the snake. Therefore, I believe that I can heal my fear quite well at a great distance from physical snakes. I will work with this fear inside me, just as I work with any other fears." Thus, you would spend time entering into your fearful feelings about snakes, not forcing yourself to go forth to be physically near snakes.

A METHOD FOR HEALING FEAR

When you desire to enter into your fear and work with it, we suggest that you do it in a gradual, persistent way that does not over-exaggerate the fear, or give it too much importance. To help you, we will describe a simple method that can be very effective in healing your fear.

Imagine that you arise in the morning and you notice a persistent, nagging feeling of negativity. You would then make the following attunement with yourself.

Step One. Enter into a gentle silence with yourself, relax your physical body, calm your mind, and still your emotions.

Step Two. Identify your *negative feelings*. Clarify what you are feeling. Ask yourself:

"What is the negativity that I am feeling right

now? What are my negative feelings about?"

Let us imagine that you identify this particular feeling as a sense of being left out of life. Perhaps you feel that you have not accomplished enough in your life. You are feeling a bit depressed that you are unimportant. You feel that your life has no meaning. Identify all of these feelings as clearly as you can, even though at times your understanding may be cloudy and confused.

Step Three. Identify the *fear* associated with your negative feelings. Ask yourself:

"What could possibly be the fear within these negative feelings that I am having?"

To answer this question for yourself, enter into the *negative feelings* as deeply as you can, experiencing them without holding back. Calmly see what it is like to feel the negativity as intensely as you can, while at the same time using your ability to *observe* the feelings and learn from them. Even as you are feeling these negative feelings, draw deeply upon your wisdom, knowledge, and intuition to bring forth all that you can understand about any fears that are involved with the feelings that are troubling you. Keep asking yourself:

"Why is this negative feeling so frightening? What is the bad that I believe will come into my life here?"

As you work with your negative feelings in this way, you may find several different fears. For this example, let us imagine that you identify the primary cause of the present negative feelings of being left out of life as a fear that your life is running out too quickly. You are fearing that you are moving toward death too rapidly. You feel that there is not enough time left for you to accomplish all of your purposes in life.

Once you have identified the fear as clearly as you can, you will enter into it and begin the healing.

Step Four. Begin to heal the fear by *experiencing* the fear. Say to yourself:

"Now is the time to begin to heal my fear. I will heal the fear by *experiencing* it, until I can understand that this fear cannot harm me. Let me enter into this fear now. This fear is not reality. It is only my *feelings*. My feelings cannot damage me."

In that moment, put aside everything in your thoughts and feelings except your fear—in this example, the fear of moving toward death without accomplishing your purposes in life. Begin to imagine vividly that your time on earth is indeed running out. Imagine that you will accomplish nothing before you die. Intentionally exaggerate the feeling of being useless and insignificant. As vividly as possible, imagine yourself going to a meaningless death without leaving anything of importance behind. Using your imagination, make your feelings of fear as strong as you can. Exaggerate them. Enter into them, and experience those fearful feelings as deeply as you can.

Continue to work inside of your fearful feelings for as long as you desire. When you decide that it is time to end this step, then you will release the feelings of fear.

Step Five. Release the fear and the negative feelings. Say to yourself:

"I have courageously entered into my fear and I have fully experienced it. I am satisfied that I have done enough work with it for this time. I now release the feelings of this fear. I now most definitely observe that *I have not been harmed by my experience of fearing. I am undiminished.*"

Use your imagination and creativity to create a deep experience of release. Imagine the fear and negativity falling away from you. Feel the release as deeply as you are able.

Step Six. After releasing your fear, you come to the final portion of your inner work with the fear. As with other areas of inner work that we have suggested, this important step involves using your imagination to turn your thoughts and emotions toward the *truth* of your being. During this step, you will also attempt to create feelings of love for yourself, for others, and for all of life.

The first part of this important step can be accomplished by saying and doing this within yourself:

"In this moment, I enter deeply into the *truth* of me, which is the eternal, perfect energies of my soul. I now feel the beauty of all life welling up within me. I feel the perfect magnificent force of God itself that lives within me. I draw the beauty and perfection of all of the truth of life into my feelings now. There is joy and fulfillment in my heart."

The second part of this step involves filling yourself with love. Begin with love for yourself, working with that for as long as it pleases you. Then, expand those feelings to include all people in your life. Finally, create within yourself feelings of love for all human beings, and for all of life. Say to yourself:

"I am filled with deep, unending love for myself. I feel this grow as a great womb of beautiful warmth that includes everyone that I know in my life. I feel it grow now to embrace all human beings. This wonderful love fills me now and joins me to all of life in perfect harmony and fulfillment."

Step Seven. The last step of your attunement is to gently return your awareness to yourself in the present moment. Do this *slowly*, taking as much time as you need.

It is important to remind yourself that healing your fear is a *process* of inner work. Once you become familiar with the process, you can *choose* to set it into motion within your inner life. As you learn more about this process of healing fear, you can use it wisely and lovingly whenever you desire.

USING THE PROCESS OF HEALING FEAR

You can set aside a period of ten or fifteen minutes each day to practice the process of healing fear that we have described. Do the work persistently, thoroughly, and joyfully.

We suggest that you first work with one of your *minor* fears. We also suggest that you carry out the process of healing fear with only one fear pattern at a time.

After you have worked for a while with this process, it will become familiar to you and it will be quite simple to carry out. Once you have trained yourself in the various steps of the process so that they become automatic, then, in addition to using the process in your special periods of inner work, you can also use it *briefly* many times each day with *minor* fears.

We do not suggest that you immediately use this process to enter into your most frightening negative patterns, unless you feel a deep sense of confidence in your love for yourself, and in your wisdom, clarity, and honesty about your personality. Unless you have such confident feelings about yourself, we do not believe it would benefit you to intensify and exaggerate your greatest fears without assistance from beloved ones, or from those with a thorough understanding of human fears, such as a psychological counselor or therapist.

We believe that as you work in the way that we

have suggested with your smaller fears, you will find that your confidence in healing fear will grow. When you feel that the time is right, you may wish to enter into some aspects of your larger fears in order to heal portions of them. If you feel that you are growing stronger, more confident, and more loving through this work, then you may wish to go deeper into the larger fears. Work slowly and patiently. There is no need to rush yourself in the healing process.

If you find that your inner work with your fear patterns begins to lead toward confusion, or toward more fear, then cease the work for a while. If you begin to feel deeply troubled in any way about yourself and your life, then it would be of benefit for you to seek the assistance of someone with a thorough understanding of the healing of mental and emotional challenges.

As you work with your fears, remind yourself that *you do not need to wait until all of your fears are healed before you love yourself and rejoice in your life.* Your fear patterns need not prevent you from celebrating life. *You can live joyfully, even while you are working to heal fear.* Fear cannot damage you. If you learn to feel that there is goodness and magnificence in your personality, then you can live a deeply fulfilling and healthy life, even if it is woven with some threads of fear from time to time.

YOUR TRUST IN LIFE

Another aspect of transforming your negative personality experience is your willingness to *trust*. In a simple way of speaking, we would say that trust, at least in the context of your human personality experience, is *the willingness to believe that there is goodness in life*, even when your inner experience might say that this is not true.

The area of trust is complex, and you will need to be intelligent as you work to gain trust in your life. You will need to understand that learning to trust that there is good in life does not mean that you will *ignore* what your personality believes is negative. In all of your days of earth life, you will need to acknowledge, live, and work with the negativity that you create within your own personality. As we have continually stressed, it is never of benefit to ignore your negativity, or to try to hide it away. If you wish to live a complete, joyful, and healthy life, you will always need to work with the negative patterns that you create. However, as you do this work, you are also free to teach yourself to trust that *no matter how negative you may feel inside yourself in a given moment, that does not change the truth that there is goodness within you, within all human beings, and within life in all realms.*

Thus, even as you are experiencing negativity in your personal experience of life, you can still trust in life itself. You can trust that there is goodness, even when your inner experience says there is "badness."

There will be times in your life when your experience will feed you negativity that you can recognize as old habit patterns of thinking and feeling that you are working to change. In such cases, you will usually accept the negative feelings as habit, and you will not be so concerned about them in the moment, since you know that you are gradually healing the habit. However, there will be other times when the negative feelings coming through your experience need your attention in the moment. In such moments, the issue of trust is not so important.

Let us clarify this. Imagine that you are standing at the middle of a long bridge in a wind storm. The bridge begins to tremble and shake. Then it begins to sway wildly. If you would work with your mind in that moment in a way that is not intelligent, *rigidly* attempting to follow our suggestion about trust, you might say to yourself: "I trust that there is goodness in this bridge, and that it will not harm me, in spite of the fact that my earth personality is telling me that this bridge is about to fall. My earth personality is telling me to flee to save my life. But, I choose to work on trust now and believe that the bridge is good." You continue to stand on the bridge, forcing yourself to believe that there is goodness in the bridge. The bridge continues to shake. Finally, it falls, and you die.

Looking at such a situation, you would need to say to yourself: "What have I gained by rigidly adhering to *teachings* that I have adopted about trust, while ignoring intelligent earth knowledge brought to me by my own personality in the moment?" This simple example is to show you that there is an intelligent *balance* needed as you work to gain trust that there is good in all of life. You will need to balance trust with your own experiences that say: "Here is a thing that is not good for me in my earth life.

Here is a thing that I need to avoid or change."

In some moments in your life, there will be situations in which other concerns will be more important to you than the issue of trust in life. There will be situations in which you will need to direct more of your attention toward your earth affairs than you will toward your inner work on trust. You will need to be intelligent, flexible, and creative as you balance these areas.

Having established this understanding of the need for intelligence and flexibility, we can now say to you: *The capacity to trust that there is only good in life is one of the most important abilities that you have brought into this earth life.* This capacity to trust that there is only good is one of the most important abilities to develop in your attempt to become consciously aware of the invisible, eternal energies of God that continually flow into your personality moment by moment. This capacity to trust is one of the most important aspects of your ability to love yourself and to love other human beings. This capacity lies at the heart of your ability to maintain intimate, fulfilling relationships with others. *The capacity to trust that there is only good is one of the most important aspects of creating health for yourself in this lifetime.*

For most human beings, the greatest obstacle to developing trust is the continuing unfoldment of *negative experiences* in your earth life. When you notice that there are painful human experiences that constantly arise, no matter how hard you try to create joy and love, then it becomes difficult for you to trust that there is good in your life. No matter how much you might desire good and beauty for all ones, you still see many human beings suffering and living in despair. No matter how much you might desire that this would be an earth of beauty and perfection, you can see that all about this earth there is hunger, disease, and painful death. Standing in the midst of those kinds of negative experiences, it is not only difficult to say, "I trust that there is only good in this life," but, it seems to be quite unintelligent to take such a position. Your human personality cries out to you and says: "There is no goodness here in the suffering and pain of human beings."

As we have mentioned, it is very important that you listen to your human personality. It is important that you acknowledge your feelings and experiences of negativity. If, out of fear of the pain of them, you begin to push away negative experiences in order to gain trust, you can create deep confusion for yourself. You can begin to live a fantasy, rather than the truth. The negative human experiences in the world are a portion of your present earth reality. You have had a hand in creating them, and you will need to take a hand in healing them.

At times, you will need to *live* your feelings of negativity that cause you to believe there is not goodness in certain situations and events, rather than trying to change those feelings. As you live your feelings of negativity, you will be motivated to *care* about human life. If you let yourself feel the negativity that others are living, you may be motivated to help those in earth that you believe need your help—acting and doing in ways that you choose.

You can also *observe* yourself grappling with all of the negativity that comes forth in your inner experience. As an observer of your experience, you have a great deal of power to do something about all of the negativity that you experience in each day—negativity that may have caused you to believe that there is not goodness in life. You have the power to change your *response* to the negativity, and to remind yourself of the *truth*. You can say to yourself:

> **"My *response* to my negative experiences lies totally within me, even though the negative situation might exist in the outside world. I am free to choose how I respond to all of the negativity that I am grappling with, and that I believe I am seeing about me in earth. I am free to choose the conclusions that I draw about these experiences."**

You are free to decide that all of the experiences of negativity that you are having *prove* that there is badness in earth. If you make such a choice, you will *respond* to your negative experiences with *further feelings of negativity*. You may even come to believe that there are forces of *badness* in human life that are causing all of the negativity. And, you know from your past experience that filling yourself with such feelings of badness will bring forth a life of darkness and pain.

When you are working as an observer of your experience, you can realize that you are also free to conclude that all of the negativity that you are experiencing, and that you see about you in earth, is a result of *human fear,* not of forces of badness. You are free to conclude that the presence of painful human experience caused by human fear does *not* eliminate the eternal goodness, harmony, and majesty that live within all human beings. You are free to conclude that all of the painful areas that you and others on earth are struggling to heal do not damage your eternal beings that are expressing through your human personalities. Thus, you can say to yourself:

"I choose to believe that all of the human-created fear does not diminish the goodness of life on earth and within the universe. I choose to believe that the *temporary* negative activities that grow out of human fear can never diminish the *eternal* goodness that lives within me and all other human beings. I choose to fill myself with the love that is eternal, that heals all human fear."

This kind of thinking and feeling *is* trust. This is the kind of thinking and feeling that you will need to create in order to *fully* heal negativity in your human life.

Yet, this trustful way of thinking and feeling does not often arise spontaneously within you in your daily earth experience, especially in this present complex and challenging period of human existence on earth. Therefore, you may often need to work to *create* trust within your personality experience.

We can assure you that, even when you are so caught up in negative personality experience that you cannot believe there is any goodness on earth, in that moment, your *capacity* to trust has not been diminished. That capacity still lives fully within you, and it is simply a matter of learning how to draw it forth, even when you are working with negative personality experience.

Creating trust in your inner experience involves healing your fears, loving yourself more deeply, and creating loving relationships with other human beings. Your trust will also be augmented by the work that you do toward experiencing the deeper eternal portions of your being. Finally, your trust will be enhanced by learning to look for the goodness in yourself and others, even when you are challenged by the negative personality patterns that confront you.

Trust *can* arise spontaneously within your experience, particularly when you allow yourself to love and be loved. Trust arises naturally within you when you allow yourself to create deep, intimate relationships with others in honesty and clarity. During such experiences, it is easy to feel: "Most certainly there is good here. It is quite clear and obvious to me because I *feel* it now."

As you work to gain trust that there is good in life, you will see that the process of building trust is quite similar to the process of loving yourself. It is also similar to the process of healing fear. Gradually, you will come to see that there is a certain deep way of attuning to love that can heal *everything* in your experience that you desire to heal.

PURPOSE AND MEANING IN LIFE

Another important aspect of healing your negative personality experience is your ability to feel a sense of purpose and meaning in your life. To begin to address this area, we will again make use of a simple vision.

Imagine that you are a small frog in a pond. Each day you come forth from the water to sit upon a lily pad that is floating in the pond. And, each day you rejoice in the warmth of the sunlight as you sit upon this pad. There is pure pleasure in this for you. Your life unfolds beautifully as a result of such pleasure. You are quite a satisfied frog.

Now, let us imagine that one morning you rise up and you begin to think that it is time to go sit on your lily pad. A portion of your frog mind that is quite curious, and that can create many questions and doubts, begins to ask: "But what is the *purpose* of sitting upon that lily pad? All that happens is that I feel warmth and a bit of joy."

After much questioning and examining, you become quite disturbed because you can find no purpose for sitting upon that lily pad, other than that it is pleasurable. You can find no meaning for it in the larger scheme of your frog universe. So, you decide *not* to sit on the lily pad, because it has no purpose or meaning. For many months, you do not go out of the water.

Eventually, from this choice, you die from lack of sunlight. You did not have the *conscious* intellectual understanding that there was a certain chemical re-

sponse in your body caused by sunlight that was necessary to keep you alive. Your conscious mind
thought that pleasure was the only reason why you
would sit on the lily pad, and since that was felt to be
unimportant, you decided to ignore it.

We build this simple image as a way of helping
you *feel* areas that can be quite complex when put
into words. We wish here for you to feel that many
things that you do in your life that seem to you to be
done only because they are pleasurable to you, actually have very deep and significant purposes and
meanings that are difficult for you to be consciously
aware of. Thus, in examining your life, and in working with your feelings of purpose and meaning, or
even a feeling of *lack* of purpose, you would need to
begin with an assumption that there are important
energies and interactions that take place *beneath*
your conscious awareness. In fact, given the present
human personality structure that focuses you primarily on your *conscious* life (as a way of gaining
more *intensity* in your inner experience of life), you
could understand that *a major portion* of the important energies and interactions in your present life
are taking place beneath your conscious awareness.

This is particularly true of your interactions with
other human beings. As we will describe more fully
in the next chapter, there is a vast network of unconscious energies that flow invisibly between you
and other human beings. Since this can be a difficult
area for your mind to grasp, we would ask that you
experiment for a moment with *imagining* the existence of such realities.

Imagine that you go forth into a marketplace, and you come into a small group of strangers without noticing them, or without speaking to them. Then, imagine that in that moment, you suddenly are given the eternal vision of your soul, and you are able to see *all* realities. With this expanded vision, you see quite clearly that you have just come into a grouping of human beings who walked physically with you on 'the earth in past times in which all of you were a portion of a great spiritual brotherhood. All of you were involved in bringing truth, understanding, and love into the physical earth life. And, there was a very deep personal love between all of you for an entire lifetime.

As you observe with your soul vision, you see the invisible energies of love and communication that go forth between yourself and these beloved ones. You see the *inner* beings of yourselves greeting and recognizing one another, even as your human personalities go about their affairs without noticing the truth. You are joyfully celebrating with them that you all could come so near again as physical human beings. With your soul vision, you can see that in one instant of earth time, you ones review together your intervening lifetimes. You instantly share many lifetimes in ways that teach all of you a deeper truth. Yet, at the conscious level, you are all strangers, and you pass by one another without being aware of the deeper truth.

These kinds of unconscious interactions *do* take place between you and the people around you each day. Yet, they can be quite difficult to understand from the ordinary earth point of view. However, it is quite simple for you to *imagine* such realities in your own way. By occasionally imagining the kinds of loving interactions that you could be having with others each day, you can begin to break down some of the rigidity of your human personality structure that prevents you from directly perceiving these hidden interactions.

Ordinarily, it would not benefit you in your daily earth life to have a clear awareness of these deep unconscious interactions between yourself and others. Such an awareness would be confusing for your present personality, and it would distract you from the *conscious* purposes and meanings that are so important to you in your present life. The reason that we speak in detail of this deeper area is so that when you find yourself caught up in feeling that there is no purpose or meaning in your life, you can say to yourself:

"This sense of a lack of meaning in my life is a *feeling* that I am creating inside myself. It is certainly not truth. It is simply another confused set of emotional and mental patterns that I have created in my personality. While I am working to heal these confused patterns, I now remind myself that even though I am not consciously aware of important purposes for my life in this moment, there are still all of the interactions of love and understanding that are flowing unconsciously between myself and others that involve important purposes, and that are very meaningful."

As with all of the other unconscious areas of your personality life that we have mentioned, a bit of knowledge of the hidden interactions between yourself and others can *inspire* you in the present, but, ordinarily, such knowledge of invisible realities cannot bring the personal fulfillment that you seek in your physical earth life. In other words, you cannot live fully as a physical human being on knowledge of invisible realities alone. In order to rejoice *consciously* in life, you need to experience joy and love *consciously*. Knowledge of the hidden aspects of reality is important primarily as a reminder to you of the larger truth of life, particularly when you have confused your conscious awareness by creating fear and misunderstanding in your personality experience. However, your real *human* joy in life will come as conscious experiences. Thus, it is important to create feelings of purpose and meaning in your *conscious* life.

In the area of purpose and meaning, as in all of the other areas that we have looked at with you, we suggest that you begin to work in *small* ways at first. It may be tempting to say to yourself constantly: "I must find that *large* purpose for which I have come into life. I must go forth to be successful in the eyes of all ones on earth, and accomplish great things." These kinds of desires come forth because each of you on earth has a great burning sense of purpose living in your heart. There is a force of desire for accomplishment that your own soul has planted in your personality matrix as a "prod" to keep you moving and searching as a human being; to spark in you a hunger for more meaning and more purpose in your earth life. This force is prompting you to *act*, and to fulfill through accomplishment. Thus, it is to be expected that you will feel: "There must be a thing of great importance for me to accomplish in this lifetime, or I would not have such deep feelings of yearning for accomplishment. I would not feel so unique and special. I would not have such a deep longing to align with a large purpose in this lifetime."

The intensity of this force of longing can cause you to feel that meaning in earth life depends on accomplishing one "large" purpose. This makes it difficult for you to understand and feel that purpose and meaning grow out of an accumulation of small moments in which you create a growing *appreciation* for the deeper significance of your simple daily life experiences. Thus, if, in the present moment, you have not yet developed this appreciation, and you are now unable to feel purpose and meaning in your life, you would most likely discover that even if you went forward to manifest great earth accomplishments, you would still carry with you your present sense of diminished meaning. Even large accomplishments will not fulfill you if you do not develop your ability to find purpose and meaning in the present small moments of your daily life. You will simply bring your present discontent into your accomplishment of great things in earth life, and you will feel discontent with your great accomplishments.

As with all aspects of your inner experience, there are different *cycles* in your experience of purpose and meaning that depend upon your thoughts, emotions, and earth activities. At times, when you are doing a thing that pleases you, it is easy to feel purpose and meaning. At other times, when you are bored or discouraged, it is difficult. What is important to remember is that your *capacity* to experience purpose and meaning, regardless of what takes place in your life, is another inner ability in your personality that you can consciously bring forth.

Just as with some other areas of fulfillment in your personality, the feeling of purpose and meaning does not always arise spontaneously in your earth experience. Most often, the feeling must be *created* by you.

As you would expect, your ability to create purpose and meaning is woven with all of the other complexities of your human personality. It is tied to your ability to trust, to your capacity to heal fear, to your ability to love, and to all of the other areas of inner mastery that you are working to develop. To intensify your feelings of purpose and meaning in your life also requires some inner work at certain times.

At any point in your life, you might feel: "For quite a while, I have felt that there is no purpose to my life. I have been confused about the meaning of life." If you have such feelings, then it is time to do some inner work with yourself. You can begin this work in the same way that you work with healing fear. You can say to yourself:

"This feeling of having no purpose or meaning to my life is *an inner experience* that I am *creating* inside myself. It is not true that I am

walking on earth without a purpose. This is a
***feeling* that I am unintentionally creating out**
of confusion and fear."

Then, the next step in your inner work would be
to decide what you desire to *do* about your feelings
of lack of purpose and meaning. You would ask
yourself:

"Do I need to enter into these feelings and
explore the fears and the confusions about
myself and my life that have caused me to feel
that there is no purpose and meaning? Or,
are my feelings telling me that I need to go
forth to act and accomplish more in the earth
arena, where perhaps I have been quite pas-
sive and uncreative for a while? Or, is this
feeling of lack of purpose due to the fact that
I am not experiencing enough love in my
life?"

You will first work to determine if your feelings
of lack of purpose and meaning are due to general
fear patterns in you that are making your entire life
seem dark and discouraging. If that is the case, then
you can work with the fear, and, as you heal it, the
sense of purpose and meaning will return to you.

If you decide that you have been too passive and
inactive in your life, then you will need to go forth
and do, and accomplish in areas that are important
to you. You will need to initiate fulfilling activities in
the physical world that will help you bring forth your
capacity to create purpose and meaning in your life.

Or, you might decide that you are not experiencing enough love in your life, and that is creating a sense of meaninglessness. By going forth to create loving relationships with others, you can re-spark your ability to create purpose and meaning.

There can be many factors in your personality experience that can cause you to feel a lack of purpose and meaning. Through patient inner work with yourself, you can come to understand those factors, and then you can go forth to change them in the ways that you believe will be helpful to you.

Often, feelings of lack of purpose and meaning come forth as a result of long-standing feelings of negativity in your emotional life in general. You will notice that during periods in which you feel quite stimulated and excited about your life, periods in which you are loving yourself and others, periods in which you are fulfilling your earth desires, it is not likely that you will feel a lack of purpose and meaning. By the time you begin to consciously experience a lack of purpose, you have built complex inner experiences that are marked by a lack of joy, and that are infused with confusion and turmoil from various areas of your life. Thus, even though you may work in the ways that we have suggested to increase your feelings of purpose and meaning, eventually, you will need to also address the underlying long-term negative mental and emotional patterns associated with different portions of your life that have culminated in the feeling of lack of purpose and meaning.

All of the ways that we have suggested for doing inner work with yourself will be beneficial in working to identify and heal such long-term negative patterns. In fact, if you would open your heart in all of the other ways that we have suggested, there would quite naturally spring forth within you this kind of feeling:

"There is a great purpose for me to be living this life, and it involves fulfilling myself and loving others. There are so many important meanings that infuse me, thrill me, and inspire me day after day."

Considering the area of purpose and meaning in *outer* earth activities, we would say that for each of you in earth there are certain kinds of work, creative and artistic activities, physical relationships, and earth projects that are particularly attractive to you. The reason that you feel a particular attraction to certain areas is tied to experiences, interests, passions, and fulfillments that you have had in your past lifetimes on earth. Those past influences can draw you to certain areas of earth activities through intuitive attraction. However, whether you accomplish successfully in those areas, and whether the activities come to have great purpose and meaning for you, will be determined by the *choices* that you make within your present personality.

In other words, it is not your past lives, or your "destiny" that will determine whether certain earth pursuits become your purpose in life. This will be *decided* by you, based on an intelligent and loving response to the *desires* that rise up within you day after day throughout your life.

As you work with the area of purpose and meaning in your life, remind yourself: You could go forth and do the most magnificent things in your outer earth activities, and if you did them in doubt, fear, and lack of love, then you would still feel a lack of purpose and meaning in your earth accomplishments. On the other hand, if you open all of your personality in love and trust, and if you work honestly to heal your fear and expand upon your capacities, then you can go forth and do even the most simple, menial task of earth, and you will experience deep fulfillment, enthusiasm, and excitement for life that will prompt within you feelings of accomplishing great purposes on earth.

Chapter 13

Your Inner Life
And The Outer World

*—Everything that you gain in the **outer** world, in terms of what you are able to physically attain for yourself, begins in your **inner** life.*

Your health is not only affected by all of the aspects of your inner experience that we have examined, but also by your relationship with other human beings, and with the outer world. Your life in the physical world will help determine the kinds of thoughts and feelings that you will feed into your body day after day, and that will play a large part in the creation of health or illness in your life. Therefore, a clear understanding of how your inner life interacts with the outer world will be an important part of what you need to know in order to manifest full health.

Your interaction with the physical world includes

not only the ordinary experiences of which you are aware, but also some extraordinary realities that lie beneath the surface of physical life. There are certain ways in which you and other human beings actually *create* physical reality, including the reality of your own physical body. If you can gain knowledge about your part in the creation of the physical reality of earth, then you will have a firm foundation for extending your understanding into creating your physical body in more healthful ways.

HOW YOU CREATE PHYSICAL REALITY

To begin to show you how you are involved in the actual creation of the physical reality of earth, we will look at the way that the eternal soul energies within your personality matrix interact with the physical persons and objects in your environment. We will also show you how your soul is involved with the eternal energies that constantly animate the physical universe. Then, we will help you understand how all of these forces relate to the reality of your present physical body.

As we look at some of these vast eternal areas, we would need to remind you that what we now bring forth in human *words* is a very pale substitute for the *realities* that we are attempting to bring to your conscious awareness. Thus, you can begin your understanding of these realities by saying to yourself: "Unconsciously, I do have knowledge of these eternal areas. Let me use the words of these teachings to spark my inner knowing so that I do not let my *mind* alone determine what I will take from these teachings. I will also attune my *feelings* and my *intuitive sensitivity* to these words."

To help you understand how you, as one human being, infused by eternal energies, interact with your physical environment, we will first focus upon the way your relationships with other human beings are built and maintained. As you are aware, your relationships with others can bring you a great deal of joy in life, as well as intense pain. All of your interactions with others in the physical world will have a strong impact upon the way you create your reality. As we will show you, your relationships with other human beings can even affect you in ways that you are not consciously aware of.

As you go forth into your human interactions in each day of your life, there are many different kinds of energies that constantly fly between your personality and the personalities of other human beings. At the most conscious level, these energies begin with your *physical perceptions*—what you gain from your five physical senses. You see other human beings, you hear them speak, and so forth. At the next deeper level, you *think* about those persons, and you have *feelings* about them. Beneath your thoughts and feelings, at the next deeper level, there are energy interactions that are *unconscious*. You are not aware of these complex, hidden energies that are continually flowing between yourself and others.

Looking at these unconscious levels, we can say, in a manner of speaking, that there are various "kinds" of unconscious energies at this hidden level. First, there are the unconscious energies that maintain very elaborate, unseen interactions between your personality matrix and the personality matrix of other human beings *in your immediate environment.* If you could be aware of these energies with your conscious mind, you would discover that they contain memories of past lifetimes on earth that you have shared with some of the people presently around you, even, in some cases, with strangers that you pass on the street.

A portion of these unconscious energies flowing between yourself and others in your immediate environment will *teach* others about areas of earth life that you have learned that they have not yet learned. In a similar way, they will teach you through their energies what they have learned.

There is also contained in these unconscious energies, a memory of the eternal energies that *created* your human personalities. This is a certain awareness of your soul, and of the souls of the people around you.

All of these unconscious energies would be considered a *personal* level of communication, since they involve an exchange of energies with the human beings that are in your immediate environment.

The next level of unconscious energies that we will show you is related more to your eternal soul. Here, we must take you a bit deeper into the structure of a larger reality where the energies are much more complex. We will need to use some simple descriptions to portray these complex energies for you in words.

We could say, in a simplified way of speaking, at

this deeper level, *all human beings upon the face of the earth are constantly communicating with one another.* This is accomplished through the use of "refined" eternal energies that are used in the same way in which all *souls* use them to communicate with one another, outside of time and space.

At this deep level of energy communication, your human personality and your soul forces essentially merge and become the same. This is the level of energy that connects your personality matrix and your soul.

If you could stand at this deep level of unconscious energy communication between all human beings, and if you were able to perceive with your present *human* conscious awareness, you would become aware that you are completely joined to all other human beings on the face of the earth by a complex web of interweaving energies. At the same time, you would be fully aware of yourself as an eternal *soul*, engaged in the process of *animating your own human awareness.* In a way difficult to describe, you would be aware that *you are creating yourself.* You would experience you-as-a-soul creating you-as-a-human-being. If you could stand in this extraordinary point of view with your present awareness, you would also be experiencing what you as a human being would consider to be *the most profound experience of all of life—an experience filled with total and complete awareness of the magnificent and perfect nature of all human personal reality, all physical reality, and all eternal reality, with all of it woven together into the indescribable energy structure that*

makes up the physical universe, and all of it perme-
ated with the divine energies of love and harmony that
are God.

It is from *inside* the complex interaction of these
various profound energies that your physical reality
is continually created, moment by moment. Within
this interaction of extraordinary energies, the souls
of you ones stand in *total mastery* over all of the
physical earth energies, including what you would
speak of as the subatomic particles, the atoms, and
the molecules of physical matter.

Also, within these interactions of energies, there
goes out the energies of unconscious knowledge and
wisdom that infuse human personalities. It is here
that you have total *unconscious* knowledge of all of
the reasons and purposes for earth life. It is here
that you understand the profound importance of
human relationships carried out in love. It is here
that human beings communicate with all of the souls
in order to say what you desire to be the new unfolding physical realities.

For example, it would be here, within the interaction of these profound energies, that the energies
originate that eventually produce an earthquake in a
certain physical place on earth, or a volcano in another place, or any form of natural event that can
bring an impact upon human beings. Within this extraordinary world of energies, the *unconscious* portions of human beings give "permission" for the
souls to influence the molecules of matter that make
up the physical earth, and to set up those forces that
will bring about the physical changes of earth. It is

here that the souls who overwatch the nature forces of earth are interwoven with the souls who overwatch the human beings. Together, all of the beings, human and eternal, who are concerned with the unfoldment of life on earth, make the choices and the manipulations of energy that maintain and animate the physical reality.

As we attempt to describe these realities in human words, there is a certain distortion that is unavoidable. We remind you that what we are describing as interactions of *energies* could be more precisely understood as an interaction of *awarenesses* of souls. The realities involved here are roughly equivalent to what you experience as thoughts and emotions, except that the soul awarenesses involved in these interactions are eternally vast, unlimited, and profoundly magnificent.

These interactions that determine the nature of physical reality cannot be understood in the context of earth *time*. In one eternal instant, choices can be made that could determine the structure of the physical earth for millions of years, influencing the earth matter—the air, the rocks, the trees, the underlying crust of the earth—in such a way that in a certain time period of the future there could occur either an earthquake, or a volcano, or perhaps a severe storm or flood. Thus, some soul choices could take millions of years of earth time to manifest in physical reality. On the other hand, there could be "permission" given by the unconscious portions of presently living human beings to quite quickly bring about an immediate change in physical reality.

Thus, the souls and the human personalities *choose* the major events of the physical earth. The souls choose consciously, while the personalities choose unconsciously.

Those choices manifest as the *physical evolution* of the earth and the physical universe. Thus, the choices made by the souls and the human personalities will align perfectly with the observable natural unfoldment of earth in its evolution. In other words, the souls would not choose to create an earthquake in an area of earth where there is not already a physical splitting of the deeper layers of the earth. They would not choose to create a volcano where there is not already the physical earth conditions to bring about the eruption. Thus, all of the souls who overwatch human beings will interact with the souls who overwatch nature in order to "find" the perfect location for the event that will affect earth, and they integrate their influences with natural earth forces as they are unfolding from an observable human point of view.

To understand this clearly, you would need to recall that your souls are acting and choosing out of an unlimited wisdom and a complete love. Any choices made about the structure of the physical reality are made for the good of all human beings living upon the face of earth.

In some cases, this can be difficult for human beings to understand. For example, if you look at a great flood on earth, and you see it destroy homes and take human lives, it is difficult to feel: "Here is goodness and love."

In dealing with such earth events that appear to be negative, you will need to work in your own way to see through the illusions of negativity. You will need to respond to, and work with, your feelings of sadness and emotional negativity that naturally arise from painful earth experiences. If you are stirred in your heart by compassion for those involved in such events, then you may wish to rise up and go to them and help them physically. However, when you have done all that you can do with your feelings and with the events themselves, you will need to decide how you will *respond* to those negative earth events.

As we have previously discussed, if you respond to negative events by saying that there is badness in those events, then you will deepen your human confusion and pain. If you respond to negative earth events by saying: "I feel sadness; I would have preferred that this event did not happen to my fellow human beings, but, I must assume that in some way there is a purpose here, and eventually, somehow, there will come growth and goodness from these events," then you will eventually discover a deeper truth about such physical realities. This is a particularly difficult area for human beings, and there is not a simple way to resolve the confusion here. You will need to work patiently in your own way to come to an understanding that satisfies you.

On the other hand, when you consider joyful earth events, such as sunshine and comforting warmth, rain that brings forth the food, the beauty and magnificence of the earth's physical environment, it is not difficult for you to feel that there is good. It is easy to understand *beauty* as the manifestation of God. Therefore, it is only in the areas that human beings speak of as negative that you will ordinarily have difficulty believing that God, your soul, and you have created that event as an important experience in the unfoldment of life on earth.

YOUR INTERACTION WITH OUTER REALITY

Your physical body stands as a transition point between, on one side, your *inner* life of thought, emotion, desire, and all of your *subjective* reality, and, on the other side, the *outer* world of other people, places, things, and events, which make up the *objective* earth reality. In working to create health in your life, you will need to understand the way in which your inner life is brought into contact with the outer world.

Let us begin in this area with a look at how you as a human being *create* the circumstances and events that take place in your outer life on earth. First, we would remind you that everything that exists and occurs in your experience of the outer world grows out of the great complexity of interaction between these factors: (1) your human choices and actions as one individual; (2) the choices and actions of other human beings; (3) the interaction of human choices and actions with the physical environment of nature, and the physical world created by human beings, such as buildings, automobiles, and other physical objects; (4) the shared social attitudes and viewpoints of human societies; and, (5) the soul energies that sustain earth life. This is what creates your everyday ordinary reality as a human being living a physical life on earth.

To help you understand how you have participated in the creation of the outer world, we will begin at the most personal level—your inner life. In earlier portions of these teachings, we have attempted to help you understand some of the complexities of your inner life. Now, we will remind you of how your inner life affects your experience of the outer world.

First, the *quality* of your inner life, whether it *feels* good or bad to you, will determine how you feel about the outside world. When you feel depressed, the outer world will often seem to be a threatening and frightening place. Other people might look unkind or menacing. On the other hand, when you are happy, for example, when you are in love, the outer world can look quite beautiful to you.

How you see the outer world will influence your willingness to allow yourself to *desire* things in the world. If you see the world as a harsh and demanding place, in which there is scarcity, then, you will tend to be hesitant to allow yourself to desire abundance, because you inwardly believe you cannot achieve it in such a restrictive world. If you see the world as a happy, joyful place, you will feel freer to desire for yourself the goodness that you see in the world.

Your inner attitudes toward the outer world will also determine how much confidence you have to use your will in order to *act* upon your desires. Feeling strong within yourself will give you the confidence to go forth to act and accomplish what you desire. Feeling weak and helpless inside will make it difficult for you to act.

The way that you work with your desire area within yourself will then determine what you *do* day after day, in terms of actions and accomplishments in the outer world. If you smother your desires, you will become frustrated and do very little, or, what you do will seem uninspiring and not fulfilling. If you work passionately with your desires, you will accomplish a great deal, and what you do will usually be more satisfying and rewarding.

Then, what you do will determine how *successful* you are, from the point of view of fulfilling your own desires. If you do nothing, you will have very little success in fulfilling your desires. If you act strongly and vigorously on your desires, you can expect to fulfill many of them.

The success you have in desire fulfillment will then determine what *exists* in your outer life in the physical world—whether you will have many friends or no friends at all, whether you will have wealth or poverty, whether you will live in an environment of beauty that you *choose* to live in, or a challenging environment that seems to be *forced* upon you out of necessity.

Everything that you gain in the *outer* world, in terms of what you are able to physically attain for yourself, begins in your *inner* life.

In the same sense, everything that other human beings bring physically into your outer life begins in *their* inner life. Their inner experiences result in their choice of actions in the world, which interact with what you set into motion from *your* inner life. Thus, in day to day earth life, your reality is made up of your inner patterns, which prompt your outer actions, which come into interaction with the actions of other human beings, who are acting in accordance with the inner life that they have created for themselves. All of this interaction is impregnated with *choices* that you all make, both as human personalities, and, as eternal souls. Thus, the outer events in your day to day life grow out of a great deal of inner complexity, most of it not seen by you.

To clarify some of this complexity, imagine a male human being who is not consciously known to you, but who lives in your present city. This man, in his *inner* life, has come to be extremely frightened of other human beings, for many reasons. Because of his fear, in the inner life of this man there has grown a particular *hatred* for human beings who fall into the grouping that you belong to. He hates the sex, the race, the age, and the personality type that you are.

In the inner life of this man, there has come to be such distortion that he now desires to *kill* those kinds of human beings that you are. So, he goes forth and obtains a revolver, and then he wanders the streets looking for someone to kill. His search, growing out of the turmoil in his *inner* life, brings him to a market place.

Let us say that you, in your inner life, have noticed *hunger*. Thus, you go forth to manipulate your environment in order to fulfill your *desire*. You go to the market in order to trade the money that you have earned for food.

Your *conscious* purpose in going to the market is to fulfill your desire to eat. You certainly do not go forth in that day consciously desiring to be killed. Yet, your inner life has led you to take actions in your environment that have brought you to the same place at the same time as the man who has come, in response to *his* inner life, to kill someone.

When the disturbed man sees you in the market, his hatred for your type of person flares up. He draws his revolver and he shoots you. The result is your physical death.

Now, in this kind of outer event, from your point of view, it would be very difficult for you to believe that you have *chosen* your outer experience. In thinking about such a situation, you would most likely feel that you have been crushed by your environment, by the choices, the willing, and the acting of another human being.

Such events in your outer reality, that appear to be *imposed* upon you by forces outside of your control, are so challenging that, for most ones, it will require a diligent inner work over a long period of time before you truly feel that you understand them. To help you move toward such an understanding, we will explore our example a bit further.

To begin to understand how you created your own death at the hands of this disturbed man in our example, you would need to return to what we earlier described as that place in your deep unconscious energies that is a communication point between your present personality, other human beings, your own soul, and all of the souls who have projected human personalities into earth. Within this communication point, you as a human being are now *unconsciously* participating in the lives of all human beings presently walking on the face of earth.

In our example, you are participating in the life of the disturbed male one who shall eventually shoot you and kill you. You are attuned to the *soul* of this male one. Your soul and his soul *consciously* understand, just as your personality and his personality *un*-consciously understand, that there are many deep connections from the past between you and this male one. Your souls desire to use the present experience of you and the male one to accomplish important purposes in the lives of each of you.

For this example, let us say that the souls of you ones are aware that in another lifetime of past earth, you as a human being, living physically with the one who is now the disturbed male one, made choices that caused you to act in ways that were extremely painful for the male one. At the same time, from your own soul's point of view, you look at your *present* human life and you see that you have accomplished most of the important purposes of this lifetime. Although it may not feel that way to your *conscious* earth personality, your soul can say: "I am finished with earth for this lifetime. I desire to withdraw my personality projections from the physical body. I shall now create a death possibility for the body."

Your soul would then consider the past connections between yourself and the present disturbed male one. Together with the soul of himself, your soul would see in his present personality the fear, the disturbed emotions, and the mental imbalance. The two souls would determine that the imbalance in his present personality is so great that perhaps the only way that his fears can be healed in his present lifetime is through the influence of an extremely dramatic earth event. Such an event could be his subjective human experience of going forth to let his hatred grow so strong that he comes to believe that the only way to gain power over life is to kill another human being. The souls would hope that his human response to his deed would eventually be a sense of the futility of such actions, a sense of remorse, a painfulness that would prompt him to search his human heart, that would sensitize him to feel the inner life of his victim, and the family of the victim.

With such a viewpoint, the souls would allow for the *possibility* of the man shooting you. They would not *cause* him to do it, and, it would be possible that he could release his fears in some other way, *before* the pressures of his mental and emotional disturbances resulted in his choice of murder.

This decision of the souls, combined with the choice of your soul to bring about death for your present personality, would result in the establishment of energies within your personality that would combine with your ordinary impulses of hunger and the desire to buy food. All of those energies would combine in an extremely complex way to prompt you to go to that particular market place, where you might possibly be killed. Thus, in effect, you as a soul have *offered* your present human personality and physical body as a *possible* victim for the murderer that you will meet at the market.

The souls of you ones actually give "permission" for this murder to take place, if it becomes the *choice* of the human personality of the disturbed male one. Your souls make this decision from the highest wisdom of the universes in which they are attempting to create influences for the male one to have freedom to do as he pleases on earth. Yet, they are attempting, above all, to create influences that will prompt him to open his heart and heal the greatly exaggerated fear and disturbed mental and emotional patterns that he has created in his lifetime. Your soul is combining the possibility of your death with the attempt to shock the personality of the male one into a new understanding.

Although this is a very crude way of expressing complex realities that lie beyond present human language, at least it will give you a sense of the *love* that exists in your soul for that human being who will soon become your murderer. It will help you feel the love that exists in *his* soul, even for his disturbed personality.

This example will also give you a beginning understanding of how the souls of all of you, along with the unconscious portions of your personalities, work at deep levels to create the outer events of your life, even the events that seem to happen to you accidentally. It will help you sense some of the "hidden" causes of the outer events in your life.

YOUR ACTIONS IN THE OUTER WORLD

An aspect of your outer reality that is much simpler to understand, even though it may at times seem difficult to actually master, would be those areas of your life in which you consciously *act* to create what you desire in the physical world, whether it would be health, prosperity, love, or whatever it might be. These are the areas that ordinarily will receive most of your attention day after day—the areas in which you consciously go forth to physically manipulate the earth objects and environment in order to satisfy your desires.

If you desire health, you will try to eat well, exercise, rest, and so forth. If you desire a home, you will go forth into earth to act in ways that will earn money, then you will find the home, purchase it, and move into it. If you desire a mating one, you will go forth and act to begin relationships with others. This is the area of your life in which you use your will to act upon your desire in order to create the outer events that will please and fulfill you.

As you would imagine, the *inner* reality that you create in your personality patterns will be the primary determinant of whether your *actions* on the outer environment will be fulfilling for you, or whether they will be frustrating and painful. All that we have spoken of earlier, in terms of your ability to love yourself and others, and your willingness to heal the fear within your inner life, will affect your actions in the world as you seek fulfillment in your outer environment. As with other areas of your inner life, as a general principal, in order to cover all of the complexities, you could say to yourself:

"The more I can love, and the more I can heal fear inside myself, the more I will fulfill myself through my actions in the outer world of other human beings, things, places, and events."

What you create in the outer environment is a reflection of what you are creating in your inner world. The success you have in acting to fulfill your desires will depend on your inner feelings of confidence in your own capacities to create and act. Your degree of confidence is tied to your capacity to love yourself. This is related to how much you can trust that there is goodness in the world, or how much you fear that there is not goodness, which can cause you to fight with your outer environment.

The qualities of your inner life will also affect your capacity to communicate with, and to love other human beings. This will relate to your cleverness, ingenuity, and creativity as a human being, which will affect the successfulness of your actions in the world.

In this area of the relationship between your inner qualities and your outer actions, there are not so many hidden mysteries. You can look about you at other human beings and easily observe the kinds of inner human qualities that result in successful action in the outer world. These are the day to day inner patterns of creativity, persistence, strength, sensitivity, and all of the observable personality qualities that human beings develop in order to fulfill themselves by acting in the outer world. By developing all of these qualities, and by combining them with love for yourself and others, you will move toward successful accomplishment in the physical world.

YOUR PLACE IN THE PHYSICAL WORLD

As you can readily observe, you are living in the midst of many other human beings who are all working to fulfill themselves as individual personalities. You are a part of many large groupings of human beings in families, cities, nations, and within the entire earth community. Understanding your place in all of this is very important to you as a human being attempting to create health, and desiring to fulfill your personal desires within the context of the present human society.

To begin the understanding, you could say to yourself: "Of course my most important concern will usually be *my desires for health* and *my fulfillments* as a human being. It is the fulfillment of desire that is one of my primary purposes as a living human being. If I ignore my own desires, or hide them out of fear that they are wrong or bad, then it will be very difficult for me to love myself and to love my life."

Thus, you begin by acknowledging the importance of your own *personal fulfillment* in relationship to other human beings. If you acknowledge the importance of your own desires, then you will develop more respect for the desires of those about you, and you will be able to intelligently seek your own fulfillment within the context of your social environment.

There may be times when you find your own *at-*

titudes blocking your ability to participate in the outer world. For example, if you would have a feeling of *detachment* from your society, and from the world in general, and you would feel, "I am not a part of the larger unfolding of this earth, and the people of earth are not important in my life," then you may be overbalanced toward *preoccupation with self*. If, on the other hand, you would have an attitude that would say, "I am so unimportant as an individual; all that matters is other people, and the earth, and the large universal issues of earth life," then you could be blocking your participation in the world by a lack of appreciation of your own individual worthiness.

As a general way of understanding your place in a world filled with other human beings, you could say to yourself:

"First, quite naturally, I will be concerned with my own personal fulfillment. But, I also wish to weave this with a deep, loving caring for other human beings, particularly the ones personally involved in my life. Also, in a broader altruistic sense, I desire to care for all human beings, to wish good for them, to do whatever is possible in my life to give to them, and to help them."

This is a kind of generalized ideal that can help stir within you the appropriate sense of *belonging* to the human race.

As with some of the other inner streams that we have looked at, it is necessary for most people to consciously *work* toward such ideals, because the sense of belonging to all of humanity does not always arise spontaneously within human beings. Although you have an *unconscious* knowing that you are joined together by energies of love, often, your *conscious* feeling will be one of *separation*. This is because the human personality is usually engaged in such an intense search for personal fulfillment that you have little time or energy for exploring the deeper connections. Thus, it is often necessary to "teach" your personality to become sensitive to the underlying connections of love that join you to others. The sense of the great loving community of human beings living all about the earth might need to be *cultivated*, just as you cultivate your awareness of eternal realities.

An increased awareness of the unity of all human beings can be brought into your conscious life by a persistent practice of willfully focusing your attention. This can be done by setting aside all of the distractions of your physical earth life in order to focus upon the deeper reality that you desire to perceive. To accomplish this, you would need to take a period of time each day to attune in silence and use your imagination to create thoughts and feelings of the energies of companionship and love that join you to others. You would *create* the experience of being one family, whether you spontaneously feel it or not. During your attunements, you would need to guide yourself with a great *idealism*, so that no matter what you have come to believe about other people, even if you believe that they are your enemy and you must condemn them, you can gently lead yourself to understand that in truth *they are a portion of you*. During your attunements, you would guide yourself by using your thoughts and your feelings to create this truth. You could say the truth to yourself in this way:

"*All* human beings, including myself, are infused with the eternal energies of God that are *love*. All human beings are joined together by this love, and this love joins me to all human beings."

You are also joined to the human beings around you by past experiences on earth. All of you alive now in physical bodies have walked so many times on the face of earth that you have come to know quite a large number of other human beings. For most ones alive in this period, there are many other human beings now living physically in the world who have walked with them in physical form in past earth lifetimes. Therefore, not only are there the eternal energies of love that have always joined all generations of human beings in deep unconscious ways, but there is another layer of uniting energies that is made up of unconscious memories of *personal* experiences that you have shared with human beings who have lived on earth with you in the past, and who are now alive in the present.

This layer of energy that comes from the past personal relationships that you ones have established with one another through so many human lifetimes has been *growing*, generation by generation. The more times you come into earth as a human personality, the more energy there is available to you from the accumulation of personal relationships. At this particular time on earth, there is a very strong energy of past associations between human beings, and the primary quality of this energy is *cooperation* and *love*.

Of course there have been many challenges between human beings in the past, and you ones have often created negative experiences in your past relationships. However, the negative energies from those past relationships are extremely small when compared to all of the love, cooperation, beauty, and harmony that have been created by billions upon billions of human families throughout endless generations of humanity that have passed through earth.

Therefore, in this present period of human life, there are great energies of love and cooperation between human beings that extend about the earth. And, there is a growing *awareness* of these unifying energies in the minds and hearts of many human beings.

However, if you look about earth and you notice that there is war, racial conflict, social strife, turmoil, and struggle between human beings, you may be tempted to conclude that there must be forces of disintegration loose in the physical world. You may conclude that there are forces of negativity causing human beings to strike out against one another. In spite of the turbulent interactions that seem negative from the earth point of view, the great energies of love that we have spoken of are still growing and expanding. If you look closely enough, you can find evidence of this love in the personal relationships between people in all societies. You can find, in the hearts of vast numbers of individuals, a growing concern for other human beings.

In this time, there is a change taking place in the earth society as a whole. More and more, through your communication systems, through your teachings, your learnings, and your personal growing and loving, you ones are becoming more able to live the magnificence of love that truly joins the human community.

In future years, you can expect to see this resulting in tangible agreements between groups of human beings and nations that gradually will dissolve the kinds of fears that have led to war. You will see a love that will bring much deeper cooperation between human beings of different nations that will result in experiences of unity and love throughout earth. Eventually, you will come to love and trust one another in ways that will most certainly transform the face of earth.

As you live your life each day, if you keep in mind all that we have said about the way in which your inner life determines your interaction with the outer world, you will be able to feel that you are an important part of the magnificent transformation of the human race. Participating in this transformation will help you feel that there is a deeper purpose to your life. With renewed purpose and meaning, you will find it easier to experience yourself as a loving companion to other human beings. All of this can inspire you to a wonderful fullness in your inner life, which of course will help you stimulate forces of rejuvenation and health within you.

Your personal contribution to the magnificence of human evolution comes from the choices that you make in your day to day life. Choosing in fear and negativity will perpetuate the barriers that exist between human beings. Loving yourself and others, and using your creativity to help others and serve them, will accelerate the coming of a future filled with health, harmony, cooperation, and love for all human beings.

Chapter 14

Healing Your
Physical Body

—The healing process that reverses the disease process involves an action that is often difficult for human beings to accomplish. It requires the courageous acceptance of the negativity that initially set the disease process into motion.

A s we have stressed in earlier chapters, your thoughts, feelings, and other inner patterns, when not properly managed, can disrupt your health. Thus, you can understand that your inner life of thoughts, feelings, and so forth will also play a large part in the *healing* of your physical body.

Many people will unintentionally limit their healing abilities by creating distorted beliefs about health. For some, physical health is often felt to be a valued prize that is being denied them by life. When illness comes, there is a feeling of great disappointment and resentment against life because the prize is being withheld. Others, when they are ill, will feel that bad fortune has come their way and ruined their life. Also, there are those who have begun to learn something about the human causes of illness, and when they become ill, there is often a sense of *failure* — they feel that they have failed in doing the human things necessary to manifest health.

As we now examine the area of healing your physical body, it will be important for you to try to create a feeling that health is what was *intended* for human beings. It is not something that you must earn. It is your right. And the more you stir up this kind of feeling within yourself, the more likely you are to harness your inner forces in ways that will eventually enable you to create and maintain health for yourself in this lifetime.

ATTITUDES TOWARD HEALING

Before we look at ways to heal the physical body, we must explore more fully how your success with healing will be closely tied to the *attitudes* that you hold toward healing. Some attitudes will help you heal, while others will block you.

There are many different attitudes that you can create in your inner life concerning what health is, what denies health, and what can restore it. In this area, instead of searching for one perfect attitude to hold, it is most effective to guide yourself by asking, "What is the *effect* of my present attitudes upon myself and my health?"

Through a simple trial and error process in your

day to day life, you can test various attitudes about health, and you can learn about the impact that they have on your life. For example, most human beings can see that when you are ill, attitudes of resentment and bitterness about the illness will *not* heal you. They will not even bring you comfort. In fact, with careful observation, you will discover that such attitudes will *intensify* your illness and suffering.

In general, we could say that *attitudes that allow you to feel that you have power and control over your health will help you in your healing*. To create such attitudes, you need to realize that you somehow have been involved in the *creation* of your illness. Without an attitude that at least moves in this general direction, it will be difficult for you to believe that you have the power to heal your body. You will tend to attribute the *cause* of your health challenge to forces beyond you. This will lead you to believe that the *healing* must also come from forces beyond you. This will make it difficult for you to rise up from ill health and heal your own body.

Another attitude that can cause blockage when you are ill is the attitude that goodness and health are far away from you. When you are ill, you might feel that there is not goodness in your life because you feel caught up in the bad feelings of illness. At such moments, it seems that health has vanished—it is distant from you.

To feel the complexities of this kind of situation, imagine that you are looking into a long dark tunnel. You can see a light at the far end of the tunnel. However, between your eye and the light, there appears to be a large area of darkness. The illusion is that there is darkness in the tunnel. But, in truth, there is light passing *through* the tunnel. If there were only darkness in the tunnel, you would not see the light at the other end. So, the dark tunnel is the illusion *through which* you perceive the light. In human life, you perceive the truth by seeing *through* the illusion.

So it is with your human personality when your health is challenged. At times, when you are in the dark tunnel of illness, it can seem that the light of health is far away from you. The illusion is that goodness is gone. There is no joy. There is no God. However, all of the energies of life—the energies of God—are pouring forth into you, *through* your dark experience of the illness. Those energies of God exist *inside* you, not at a distance from you.

When you are ill, your challenge is to *feel* those eternal energies of goodness and love through the temporary dark, negative feelings associated with the illness. You will need to say to yourself, "This feeling of *badness* about my illness is an illusion, even though the pain and suffering are quite real." You will need to work with the illusion of badness until you learn how to pass through it. Eventually, you will need to *believe* that the energies of your soul, and of God, still live in your personality and in your body, even when your body is ill. Such a belief can release an extraordinary healing power within your personality.

You will also need to adopt the attitude that healing is not an unusual thing. In a sense, each of you continually heals yourself many times each day, without noticing it. If, in this moment, you are not presently struggling with an illness, you could say, "I am quite successful at healing myself. I have healed everything that has ever challenged me in this lifetime." You are also in this moment carrying many tendencies toward illness within your body, and you are constantly, day after day, healing those areas. They are *not* manifesting as illness. *There is a constant healing process that goes on within your body that you are not aware of.*

You will also need to have an attitude of respect for your human *desires* to have health. It is never beneficial to say, "Since our souls and God sustain and monitor life, then I will allow them to make the choices about whether I will manifest health or illness in this lifetime. If God wants me to be ill, then I will be ill. I should not have my own desires for healing and health." Such an attitude, of course, would not serve you. Even though the energies of your soul and of God do constantly feed you and sustain you, *they do not choose for you* in your human life.

Thus, it is more beneficial to say:

"I *desire* full health in this lifetime, I deserve it, and I will draw upon the energies of God to *create* it."

Then, you would do all that you can, inwardly and outwardly, to try to manifest health, knowing that if *you* do not act, then the energies of your soul and of God may be interfered with in your body, and your illness might not be healed.

It is very important to adopt this kind of attitude toward your health. In fact, in a way, we could say that it is even your *responsibility* as a human being to take charge of your health in this strong, potent way—to decide what needs to be healed, and to find ways to heal it.

Another attitude to consider is the way that you think about the *energies* that are involved in your healing. To help you clarify this area, we will briefly review the important interactions of those energies.

As we have pointed out, in each human being, there is a strong and potent flow of eternal energies that constantly pour into your personality matrix, and those *eternal* energies mingle with your *human* energies. This creates the complex interaction of the many kinds of energy that we have described earlier. At the deepest level of this interaction, you are receiving the eternal energies from your own soul, from guiding souls to you, and from God. At the surface level, there are the energies of your own human thoughts and feelings. And, in between, there are many different kinds of energies with which you are not presently familiar.

To work effectively in the healing area, you do not need a perfect understanding of all of these complex energies. A simple vision of them can be very effective in guiding your work with these healing energies. To help create this vision, imagine that all of the eternal energies within you are symbolized as the *supply of water* that feeds a large fountain. The water comes into the base of the fountain full and strong, unimpeded in its flow. However, before the water has a chance to spray forth strongly from the top of the fountain, someone places a large rock upon the spewing portion of the fountain. The result is that, although the *supply* of water coming into the fountain is strong, only a weak spray of water issues out of the fountain.

Now, if you were not familiar with the workings of fountains, you might become confused and say, "My fountain is broken. I will never get enough water from it. All is lost." However, if you have knowledge of fountains, if you are seeing clearly without distortion, you would say, "There is a rock on my fountain. I wish to have more water from my fountain. I must remove the rock."

This is a simple way to guide yourself when you feel, "I do not have enough healing energy. I am not able to heal myself. All is lost." At such a moment, you would need to say to yourself, "It is not because the eternal forces that supply my fountain of energy have suddenly diminished and dried up. It is because I have unintentionally blocked the flow of energy." You would need to encourage yourself to see that you have placed the "rock" of unhealed negative feelings and thoughts upon the fountain of healing energies. Because of that, the energies that you are perceiving seem small. If you will remove the rock, by healing the negativity, then you will feel that the flow of healing energies is very strong and potent.

To successfully heal your physical body, you must also develop an attitude of *expectation* that you will heal. You will need to gain a strong confidence that within your present personality there is a great ability to heal your body, and you expect to successfully use that ability. To accomplish this attitude of expectation, most ones will need to grapple with, and release, present beliefs that they are limited in their capacity to heal.

You will also need to create a sense of *appreciation* for the many healing abilities that already live within you. Often, your limiting attitudes about your abilities make it difficult for you to appreciate how strong those abilities really are. To help feel this, imagine that you have been imprisoned for twenty years. Suddenly, the door of your cell is thrown open. You rush out into the beautiful sunlight, and you see the trees and the sky for the first time in many years. In that moment, you are not likely to say, "I am so inadequate, and imperfect. I desire this and that, and I do not have it. My life is terrible." Instead of focusing upon your own negative thoughts and feelings, you would be caught up in a great *appreciation* of the extraordinary beauty of life that you see around you. You would pass through your own negativity to appreciate the truth about life. This is what you need to do in terms of your own negative attitudes about your healing abilities. When you are feeling that you have no healing abilities, say to yourself:

> **"These limiting feelings are the old patterns of belief that I have created. I now release myself from that prison of negative belief, and with a new freedom of creativity, I now open myself to feel, and appreciate, the powerful**

healing abilities that live within me."

In your healing work, you would also benefit by creating feelings of appreciation and gratitude about all of life. You can strive to feel that each day you are throwing aside the door of *all* imprisoning thoughts, feelings, and beliefs that you have built within yourself. You have the capacity to look about you and rejoice in the miracle of your life. Whether your life totally pleases you or not, it is still an extraordinary occurrence. The fact that you can stand as an eternal being, temporarily experiencing life inside a human physical body, is a miracle. And the capacity to feel that, and rejoice in it each day, is very important to your healing work.

As you work to create such rejoicing, gently remind yourself to begin with your body, and rejoice in the miraculous nature of it. Rejoice in the people about you, and the love that you can have with them. Celebrate the sky, the trees, the beauty of nature. The willingness to open yourself in gratitude to all of this beauty can accelerate the many healing capacities within you. Take time in each day to make this opening, and you will feel the prison doors of limiting inner patterns being thrown wide. You will go forth to rejoice in the creation of joy and health.

THE NEED FOR COMFORT

When your body is ill, you will have a need for *human comfort*. When you are caught up in the challenges of illness, it is difficult to immediately be efficient and effective in your healing work. First, you need to be comforted by other human beings so that you can begin to feel that you are safe, that you are not moving toward annihilation. You need more warmth than usual, more joy, more reassurance, more laughter and play.

You do *not* need more pressure to be perfect in your daily activities, or in your relationships, or in your healing. You need the sense that there is a great deal of time to accomplish anything that you desire. And, you need to feel that if it does take some time to heal your body, it will not be destructive to live for a while unhealed, although it might be frustrating and painful. You must convince yourself that it will be less painful to pass through the period of illness if you can take a more relaxed attitude toward it.

Without this sense of relaxation, you might tend to put pressure upon yourself to heal quickly. Of course, the more you pressure yourself, the harder it is to heal, and, when you fail to heal quickly, you can become more frightened, and then you put more pressure upon yourself.

If you feel such pressure, you can work with it as you would any negative thoughts or feelings. You would enter into and experience your negative feelings about not healing. By living through such feelings, lovingly and patiently, you will heal them. That healing, along with the comforting you will receive from others, will be of great service to you in your healing work with your physical body.

Another reason that you will need comfort is that, often, your willingness to love your physical body is diminished when you are struggling with ill health. When you are ill, you need to bring forth greater love for your body. Yet, when you are ill, it is easy to feel that your body is a burden. You can feel critical toward your own body because it is challenging you. By drawing near to other people and asking them to comfort you, you can begin to release such negative feelings, and, drawing upon the love that they give you, you can begin to work toward loving your body again.

LOOKING AT EXPECTATIONS

Your expectations about health will play a large part in blocking or releasing your ability to heal your body. Most people expect their bodies to be healthy, and they become disappointed when they are challenged by ill health.

To help you feel the way your expectations can affect you, imagine that you have come to unwrap a box that has been given to you as a present by a wealthy friend. As you begin to open the present, you have an expectation that it is a very valuable jewel. However, after the box is opened, you discover that the present is a wonderful sweater.

Now, the most beautiful sweater in the world cannot thrill you as much as a valuable jewel. So, you will feel a great disappointment. You will experience a sense of incompleteness and lack. Your negative experience will be caused by *the disappointment of your expectations*, not by the sweater. If you had been expecting the present to be a pencil, then you would have been very happy when you discovered that it was a beautiful sweater.

Most human beings will expect and desire health. They want a perfectly functioning body that will bring them great joy. Thus, any manifestation in their body that is less than perfect will be disappointing.

Therefore, when you are ill, and you are ready to begin your healing work, you may have to heal some disappointment that arises from expecting perfect health and receiving instead the illness that you have. You would work with such feelings of disappointment by entering into them, experiencing them, and healing them from within, just as you would with any other negative inner experience.

YOUR RESPONSE TO ILLNESS

There may be times when you feel that you have done all that you know how to do to create health, and yet you continue to have an illness or malfunctioning of your body. When those times arise, remind yourself that it does *not* mean that you lack the capacity to maintain health in your body. You would need to say to yourself: "This means that there are *fears* in my personality that I am not aware of—unconscious patterns of fear, or other unconscious negative energies that I have created in such a way that illness is now a part of my present reality. If I am unable to *heal* the illness in this moment, then the question now becomes, how shall I *respond* to the illness?"

As we have mentioned, if you respond to illness with a sense of anger, and a feeling of resentment because life has visited illness upon you, such a response can complicate the illness. On the other hand, if you respond with a sense of honesty and say, "I do not rejoice in this illness, it is painful, it feels bad to me, I do not desire it," then, you can enter into those feelings and you can heal them, just like you would heal any other negative feelings.

After you work to heal your negative feelings about the illness, then you would try to move toward a more hopeful *response* to the illness. You could say to yourself:

"To the best of my ability, I will attempt to respond to this illness with understanding, patience, and love. I will attempt to rise up in courage and strength. I will attempt to find a goodness that can eventually grow out of my experience with this illness."

This is the kind of response that is the most beneficial when the complexities of illness become so great that you cannot understand them. However, since the response to illness is an area of such uniqueness within each individual, filled with so many complexities of inner patterns of thought and feeling, you will need to work with your own personality patterns to find the most beneficial way for you to personally respond to illness and loss of health within your body.

CREATIVITY AND HEALTH

Before we turn to the actual process of healing, we need to look at an area that is not usually associated with health and healing. That area is your human *creativity*. Your creativity comes from a strong stream of inner energies that can affect your health in dramatic ways.

As you attempt to work with your creative energies during this present period of human existence, there is a certain pervasive influence of which you will need to be aware. At this time in earth, there is a kind of *pressure* upon all human beings that has an impact upon your inner life and your health. We would call this pressure, "the accumulated burden" of humanity. We are not speaking of a badness here. We are speaking of a widespread sense of *toil* and *burden*. It can also be felt as a sense of *strife* and *strain*.

This pressure is unintentionally exaggerated by the ways in which you ones teach *human history* to your children. From the early stages of childhood, you begin to agitate your children by communicating to them a history filled with burden, strife, disharmony, and war. Because you are retelling real events that have occurred in human history, you believe that you are telling your children the truth about life. However, your "truth" creates a certain kind of dark energy cocoon, or sphere, within which you and your children must function. This dark energy is not a "bad" energy. It is simply "heavy." It is this sphere of dark energy that causes the pressure of burden and strain upon humanity.

For your purposes, let us call this dark sphere of burdensome energy, *oldness*—meaning the old accumulated attitudes, beliefs, and descriptions of past human events. This sphere of oldness refers to the entire tradition of human history that emphasizes *struggle*, *conflict*, and *war*.

What this human history overlooks, for the most part, is that *billions of unknown human beings in the past have created an extraordinary variety of positive human experiences*. Since those simple, everyday positive experiences have not dramatically affected societies and nations, they have not been written about in your human histories. Yet, the creative energy generated by so many past human beings, who have loved and rejoiced in life, has a great impact upon you in the present. In fact, it has a stronger impact upon your *true* being than does your human tradition of recording history in a negative way. However, human beings are quite fond of *intensity*, and often, the human negativity is much more intense for you than the joy, the love, and the harmony. Thus, you tend to become fascinated with the intense and dramatic events in your history, many of which are negative.

Although the truth is that all of the past *positive* human creations have a much more powerful impact upon the human race and present human life than negative historical events, to your *conscious* selves this dark sphere of *oldness*, that we have described, has a more dramatic impact. You pay more attention to it. You worry about it, and you struggle with it. While you do so, you ignore a larger truth about life.

To illustrate this, let us imagine that you have come to a wonderful party. At this party, there are dozens of people that you love and rejoice in. However, there is one person there that you hate. And, you become so busy feeling disturbed by the hated one being at this party that the entire party seems to you to be a failure. Even though there were so many ways you could have rejoiced in that party, your negative response led you to *create* a miserable experience for yourself.

Now, the "party" of earth life that you are presently living through—your entire present life—has to do with many things that are quite extraordinary. There are literally millions of wonderful things in your life that are associated with your personality, other people, places, and things. There are legions of wonderful guests at your party. You are free to create joyful experiences with all of these things. However, most of you do not. Most of you tend to notice the guest that you do not like—the challenges in your life. You tend to respond to the negative pressure from the sphere of oldness which influences you to focus upon the drama of negative experiences in your life. This creates a vague sense of heaviness and dread that constantly weighs upon you, stirring up a kind of negative emotional pressure that tends to drag you down.

Depending upon your personality and bodily makeup, this pressure of heaviness can have varying affects upon your health. For some of you, the pressure simply causes fatigue. For others, it can accelerate illness and disease.

Even though we are speaking of this collective negativity as a *pressure*, it is not a force that overrides your choice. If you *choose* to create negativity in your present life, then you can align with the pressure of oldness, you can take it into you, and then it can affect you. However, if you make choices in love, honesty, and creativity, then the sphere of oldness will not be a significant factor in your inner life.

Therefore, in understanding creativity and health, you would need to realize that when you are able to bring a feeling of *newness* into each day, particularly if it is aligned with love and a sense of the magnificence of life, then you will not be weighed down by this dark, oppressive force that can hamper your healing work. If you constantly strive for creative, new ways to respond to life, then your inner stream of creativity, instead of being unintentionally used to exaggerate a sense of heaviness and dread, becomes expressed as a potent energy of aliveness, brightness, brilliance, and unlimited potential. Experiencing this energy will help you establish a sound base for your healing work.

As you focus on newness in each day, you have first the *inner* aspects, which include creative new attitudes, feelings, thoughts, and so forth. Then, you have the *outer* world of creative new activities that you can do day by day. These can be activities in which you try to create new experiences with other human beings in the ordinary family relationships, in the friendships, or even relationships with strangers as you respond to them and interact with them each day. These can be creative activities in which you strive for newness in your work, or in your activities within your society. These can be, if you choose, artistic activities. All of these outer activities, based in a search for newness, are very potent ways to stimulate your personality toward lightness, openness, and feelings of greater possibility and potential. Such feelings then feed back into your personality the expanded experiences of greater potency that create a stimulating and healthful impact upon your physical body.

Your creativity is one of the powerful energies woven into your personality matrix by your soul. Like the other soul energies within you, the energy of creativity exists deep within your personality matrix as an *unlimited* capacity. In truth, every human being has an unlimited creative capacity, yet, as you look about, you may notice that human beings manifest that capacity to differing degrees—some a great deal, and some very little. Most humans tend to feel that they are not so creative. Thus, for many, the first step in utilizing your own creativity to the fullest degree in creating health, and in healing, is to convince yourself that you have unlimited creative capacities.

Convincing yourself that you have unlimited creativity can be done by inner work carried out during periods of silent attunement with yourself. This kind of work will be especially important when you are challenged in the areas of health.

To carry out this inner work, you would sit with yourself in a period of silence, relaxing your body as much as possible, and filling yourself with feelings of love. You would remind yourself that the purpose of this work is to help you free yourself from old habits of thinking and feeling so that you can enter into a p 45

Long term:

Lungs — Those who squeeze the joy out of their lives

Throat — Swallow the truth + fear to speak yr truth out loud

Shoulders — Feeling of carry tremendous burdens in life

Legs + feet — Fear of sadness in the future? Stay to walk forward

Digestion — Too much pain in life to take in, cannot disgust-life so its to painful

Kidney — Fear that painful emotions cannot pace through you without taking?

Loss of energy (chronic fatigue) — Smothering desires. Desires fuel the engine of personality.

deeper experience of your true nature. Then, you would say to yourself:

"I now release all feelings of limitation of my creative abilities. I am filled with the eternal energies of God that have created all realities. Those unlimited creative energies are flowing through me now. They spark my own personal creativity that is also unlimited. I can now turn my unlimited creativity in any direction in my earth life."

In addition to this kind of inner work, bringing forth your creativity into the tangible affairs of your outer life will require *practicing* creativity in your day to day activities. You will need to give yourself many opportunities to actually create in a physical way so that your unlimited creative capacities are brought from your inner life into a tangible expression in the outer world.

You can devise a simple plan that will encourage you to practice your creativity each day. In working to create your plan, you can consider creativity to be: the process of bringing forth *newness* and *uniqueness* in life. The plan itself can be quite simple. You will choose at least one specific creative arena that you will work with every day, and you will determine a period of time that you will devote to that activity. Your chosen creative activity should be directed toward a tangible earth arena that interests you, whether it is artistic, or whether it involves your work, or relationships, or other areas. The amount of time spent on the activity each day could be as little as ten minutes. You will decide the time on the basis of your desires. How much do you desire to accomplish? What is important here is that you *do* the creative activity *every day*, and that you do it for at least the amount of time you specify.

After you have clarified your plan for yourself, write the plan on paper. This will help you remain clear about what you desire to accomplish. Each day, read your plan in the morning, then act creatively in your chosen area, working to bring forth *newness* and *uniqueness* by drawing upon your unlimited creativity. Use your imagination to think of new creative ideas, as well as creative new ways to *act* upon old ideas. If you are working in a health area, you can bring forth creative new visions of yourself manifesting the fullness of health in many ways in your life.

If you choose to direct your practice of creativity to *artistic* areas, you can create particularly satisfying experiences for yourself. That is because human artistic expression brings forth deep energies that are more closely woven to eternal realities than would be energies generated by the human activities that are of a more practical nature. This is not to say that artistic creativity is *better* than practical creativity. It is that artistic expression is an arena in which you can more easily explore some of the *mysteries* of your personality and of life, free from the kinds of restraints that you might feel when you are engaged in practical activities. This deepened experience can be set into motion even if you give only a small period of attention to artistic creativity in an area that pleases you, whether it is simply singing a song to yourself each day, drawing, painting, writing, sculpting, dancing, or whatever pleases you.

If you decide that your creative practice will be directed toward artistic creation, for example *drawing*, then, begin your period of creative practice by saying: "Whether I believe I am an artist or not, I will now sit with myself and I will draw a picture. Through my creativity, I will bring forth a new thing that has not existed before." Then, you would draw for the period of time that you have chosen, every day. You would draw for *yourself* and your own creativity, not to please others. The *result* of your drawing would not be so important. It would be the daily creative practice that would be beneficial to you.

Perhaps you may decide to turn your creativity toward a relationship. Then, you would begin your practice each day by saying: "In this time, I shall focus upon this relationship, and I shall find a new truth about the relationship, through my own creativity. I shall imagine a beautiful new aspect of this relationship. I shall create it inwardly now, and then I will go forth to put it into practice." You would spend your work period creating many new ways to understand and carry out the relationship.

No matter what you choose for a focus for your creative activity, your willingness to set aside the time each day to turn your attention toward your creativity will eventually spark the release of more of your unconscious creative capacity into your conscious life. You will also notice that as a result of working diligently during this small practice period each day, your creativity will eventually begin to spring forth spontaneously in many other areas of your life. Gradually, you will learn powerful new ways to focus your creativity into the healing of your physical body.

THE PROCESS OF HEALING

Now we will look closely at the actual *process* of healing the physical body. This will establish the foundation for a *method* of healing that we will suggest.

If a human being were able to carry out certain inner personality adjustments in a perfect way, and if all areas of the person's life were harmonized in a certain way that we will later describe, then a *healing process* would be accelerated in the physical body. That healing process would reverse what could be called the "disease process," which is the impact of human negative energies that cause the malfunction of the cellular structures within the physical body.

To help you understand the process of healing, we will need to look again at the cause of illness. Then, we will examine the healing process that reverses that cause.

As we now look at the cause of human illness, we will need to review some of the areas previously spoken of, then we will expand upon them. First, we would remind you that although we can make some relatively accurate generalizations for all human beings, you will need to remember that these areas cannot be specifically applied to every single human being who creates illness within their body. Even though cellular responses in the human body appear to your scientific eyes to be similar, the process of disease has slightly different causative patterns when it appears in different parts of the human body. However, building now upon our earlier discussions, in a general way of speaking, we could say that the cause of illness is: *The process of sending constant emergency signals to the cells of the physical body by creating steady and persistent feelings that there is danger to the human personality.* This is our first generalization.

Here, we must emphasize what we have discussed earlier. The feelings of danger to the personality are created through various negative thoughts and emotions—fears of many kinds—that cause a person to feel, "I am under threat; there is badness here; I am about to be damaged."

However, as we have stressed, the negative feelings and thoughts in themselves are generally not enough to cause the abnormal cellular process of illness in the physical body. The disease process is actually caused by *the inability of the human personality to bring negative inner patterns to conscious awareness, to live through them fully, and to resolve them and heal them over a period of time.* When human pain and suffering are not adequately vented, then the disease process is most likely to be initiated.

Now, these are only beginning generalizations, and it is not wise to approach these generalizations with a simplistic viewpoint. If you would say, "All those who do not heal their fears for a number of years will create disease in their body," you would soon discover that this is not true for all human beings. The generalization is not always true because there are so many individual factors to consider. As we have pointed out, there are some souls who have chosen to manifest physical bodies that will maintain health for a lifetime, no matter how much the personality wallows in unhealed fear. Other souls have created human bodies that will bring forth a great over-sensitivity to negative patterns, and even if the human beings work honestly and diligently to heal negativity, they might still manifest illness within their physical body.

Yet, it is generally accurate to say that the cause of illness lives within the human personality. It is a matter of negative thought and emotional patterns that are not healed thoroughly enough. This can also be complicated by a failure to feed, exercise, and rest the body in intelligent ways. Other complications include physical irritants in the environment—such as various human-created chemicals that interact with the physical body. However, unless they are extremely strong chemical irritants, they alone will not usually cause illness in most human beings. In other words, at this point in time, your physical environment by itself would not cause a great deal of disease, except in those who are particularly over-sensitive to disease because of their soul's choices.

As we have described earlier, when you swallow your negative personality experiences over periods of time without bringing them to the surface and working with them, you create negative human energies that become barriers between the perfect energies of your soul and your physical body. This can eventually disrupt the process of healthy cellular reproduction in your physical body. It can interfere with the full potency of the blood. The perfect eternal energies that ordinarily feed the blood are temporarily distorted and disrupted in ways that make it difficult for the blood to perform all of its intended functions—functions that you call *the immune system*. At times, the negative energies that come from your confused inner patterns can also interfere with the functioning of your heart. Eventually, under the pressure of the negative human energies, the nerves of the body do not respond perfectly, and the glandular responses can be affected.

All of these kinds of bodily changes are very slight at first. However, they eventually begin to feed into the electrical and chemical responses of your brain. As this occurs, the disrupted brain functioning begins to create certain energies that reinforce the negative kinds of influences that you have set into motion by your unhealed inner negative experiences. The brain, in its electrical and chemical communications, begins to send back to the body a certain kind of "negative pressure" which can flow into all of the bodily systems. This kind of negative brain influence can cause an even greater depletion and weakening of the blood, heart, nerves, glandular systems, and so forth, which then causes those areas to respond in an even more negative way. This incitement of negativity throughout the body then in turn feeds even stronger negative energies back into the brain. Then, the brain feeds more negativity back into the body, and the circular process continues to accelerate.

In this way, a quite destructive cycle is set up within the physical body. That cycle eventually becomes the physical manifestation of *the process of disease*. It is that process that produces illness and malfunction within the body. It is that process that needs to be reversed in order to bring about healing of the body.

Now we will turn from the process of disease to the process of healing. The healing process that reverses the disease process involves an action that is often difficult for human beings to accomplish. It requires *the courageous acceptance of the negativity that initially set the disease process into motion*.

As part of the "animal" nature of the human physical body, it is a "natural" impulse to run from negativity. As human beings, you will not be inclined to eagerly embrace negative thoughts and feelings. When illness manifests in your body, you strongly desire to eliminate it, to escape from it. Yet, the ordinary human impulse to rush away from negativity actually undermines the healing process.

The healing process is set into motion when you are willing to enter into your own negative thoughts and feelings in a way that acknowledges the understandable human tendency to run from negativity and eliminate it, and, when you can accept the negative experiences and move beyond them. For example, you might need to say, "I wish to *eliminate* this pattern of fear from my mind and heart," or, "I desire to *escape* this disease in my body." Then, you would say, "These impulses to eliminate and escape are understandable. But, I now see that they are based in my fear of negativity. I accept that as natural to my *human* nature. Yet, I realize that such impulses will not heal me. I cannot heal negative patterns by fearing them and hating them. I can only heal them by accepting them, and then, *by transforming them from within*."

The true healing of all human negativity begins with the willingness to embrace the negativity. This does not mean that you must like it, or enjoy it. It means that you must be willing to courageously *accept* the negativity as a part of your human life. In a certain way, you need to be willing to believe that you have *agreed* to accept the negativity as a condition of living in human form.

Let us expand upon this with a simple vision. Imagine that you have decided to go fishing. You find a worm and put it on your hook. Then, the worm would ask you, "How can I get off of this hook?" You would say to the worm, "I do not want you off of the hook. I want you to stay on it. I desire to use you to fish."

Now, in a certain playful way of speaking, your human personality is the worm on the hook. Your soul has *chosen* to create your present personality, and has voluntarily placed it into a human body, which is the hook upon which you often squirm. Your physical body has been born into a world where there is a great deal of human negativity. Your body is also subject to certain laws of disintegration and deterioration, which can cause you physical pain and suffering.

In the face of this, your first challenge in healing is to begin with the courage to *accept* what you-as-a-soul have chosen for yourself as a human personality. You need to say, "I am a worm that has been put on a hook. At least, I will be a dignified, courageous worm. I will not frantically try to wiggle off the hook."

When you begin in this way, what you will eventually discover is that you are actually a *magical* worm. If you stay on the hook, you will be eaten by the fish. However, once you are eaten, you will discover that you will be transformed. *You will become the fish.*

Once you accept your own negativity, whether it is mental, emotional, or physical, *you become a larger being. You are no longer manipulated by your animal fear of negativity.* You become the being who eats the negativity, who has unlimited capacity to swallow it, and transform it by digesting it, living through it, realizing you cannot be damaged by it. Often, the clearest feeling of the power of the forces of God inside human beings comes from courageously overcoming what seemed to be a negativity that they feared would destroy them. This brings about extraordinary feelings of accomplishment and mastery of earth life.

Thus, to begin the healing process, you will need to learn to embrace your negativity. You do not need to pretend that you like it. Simply say, "It is time to be the worm on the hook. I will do it fully and courageously, even though it is painful and frightening." The sooner you embrace the negativity, the sooner you will discover that you have *created* it. And, the sooner you will begin to transform yourself by living through the negativity.

After you have worked to embrace your negativity, you would work with this understanding: *The most potent way to stimulate the healing process within your personality and your body is to create the feeling, "I am safe. I will not be destroyed by life."* In other words, you stimulate the healing process when you can feel:

> **"No matter what challenges may arise in my physical body, they will not destroy *me*. They might destroy my body. And that body will end in death anyway. But, I am not that body. I am an eternal being. I am safe. I cannot be destroyed."**

These kinds of feelings lead to a confidence in life, and in the eternal rejuvenating energies of life that constantly feed you.

This does not mean that in your healing work you must strive to *always* have these perfect feelings, or to never have any negative feelings about illness in your body. You will simply work patiently for the attitude of safety, goodness, and love whenever you can. As often as you can, you will try to stir up a sense of trust and faith in the energies of God that sustain you, love you, and keep you safe in your eternal existence.

At other times, as we have noted earlier, the

healing process involves changing certain negative attitudes that are associated with illness. For example, in some cases, there might be a challenge of *self-preoccupation* and *pridefulness* involved with an illness. Many people, when they are healthy, become so self-involved in their own day to day concerns that they become caught up in self-preoccupation, and they forget to pay attention to their sensitivity to others. They also become caught up in their own pride, losing themselves in their personal accomplishments. Often, an illness will tend to break the individual's self-preoccupation and pride, causing a softening, and a stirring up of needs in the person that will prompt them to begin to ask other people for help. Many times, this kind of softening, and the beginning of the healing of rigid emotional patterns involved in the self-preoccupation and pridefulness, will stimulate the healing process.

One aspect of the healing process that is extremely difficult for most human beings to understand is that healing can often involve the *death* of the physical body. In other words, the healing process for the *personality*, as it strives for deep learning about life, might possibly involve the continuation of illness for the *body*. For example, imagine a male one with a cancerous growth in his body, and whose soul has chosen that he will leave earth through death by cancer. It would be unlikely that he would be able to stimulate the healing process in such a way that he would eliminate the cancerous growth in his body. Most likely, the cancerous growth would bring about the death of his body. In his case, the healing process might be shifted to negative thoughts and emotions that would be stimulated by his fears of death. He might find himself healing that negativity in inner ways that, in the long run, are much more important than frantically trying to save his physical body for a few more years of earth life.

However, even when a soul would choose death through illness for the physical body, there is always the possibility of, let us call it, *infinite creativity*. Infinite creativity can come about when a human being consciously chooses to align the personality fully and completely with love, when there is a miraculous kind of trust in life, and when there is created an extraordinary awareness that the forces of God live in the human personality.

For example, imagine a soul that chooses a death for the physical body to be caused by the disease of cancer. If the human personality living within that body would so master the challenges and fears that have been set before it that are associated with cancerous tendencies—mastering physically, mentally, and emotionally during the human lifetime—and the personality would show an extraordinary kind of love, patience, and courage, along with the conscious alignment with spiritual realities, then, it is possible for the personality to spark such an intensity of human goodness that the soul can make a choice to change the direction that would have led to death by cancer. In such an instance, there could be a physical healing of the body, even though the cancer might have been considered incurable by human beings.

We wish you to feel the infinite freedom that you

have as a human personality within a physical body. And, we remind you that *you are also that eternal soul making the larger choices for your present human lifetime*, which include the choice of death for your physical body. As a soul, you have all of the energies of God at your command to use in those choices. So, it is beneficial for you to believe in quite miraculous potentials for human beings, for they are always there, and they can always be stimulated if the human desire is great enough.

We will extend our understanding of the healing process by turning now to certain *preparations* that would be important to make as you get ready to begin the actual healing of your physical body.

PREPARING TO HEAL

After you understand the importance of your attitudes, the disease process, and the healing process, it will become clear to you that an effective way to prepare to heal your physical body is to: (1) work consistently to heal your negative thoughts, feelings, attitudes, beliefs, and so forth; (2) work to stir up feelings of security, magnificence, love, and goodness within your personality; (3) set your intention to align your thoughts and feelings with energies of your soul and of God; and (4) begin to create a confidence in your ability to actually change the way that the blood, the nerves, the glands, the brain, and all cells function within your physical body.

These preparations are the ones that are the most likely to release your potential for manipulating the matter of your physical body in a way that can bring about the reversal of the disease process, the elimination of symptoms, and the healing of the physical body. These preparations can eventually lead you to a healing that can return all of the systems of your physical body to perfect functioning.

Let us now take a closer look at the process of aligning yourself with the energies of your soul and of God. An important aspect of inwardly aligning with eternal energies is to try to think in terms of a kind of "precious substance" that lives within the personality of all human beings. For lack of better human words, we would need to call this substance *the divine spark of perfection*. We are attempting to put words to an energy that could be likened to the spark of life in a human body—that energy that creates life when the male and female come together to procreate. Without that spark of life, there would only be sexual union. With the spark of life, from the merging of the male seed and the female egg, there comes about another living human being.

We are attempting to make this precious substance, or spark, *physical* for you so that it will be easier to understand. The actual divine energy itself is *not* physical. Therefore, *it does not depend upon the coming together of opposites*—male and female in the case of human bodies. The very structure of this divine energy contains within itself *a perfect wholeness that is undivided*.

It is this perfect, whole divine energy that constantly feeds all human personalities, and, through your personality matrix, this energy feeds your physical body. However, as we have stressed, your human personality stands *between* this divine energy and your physical body. Your human personality is either the clean magnifying glass that enhances the divine energy, or the dirty one that blocks the energy.

To build upon what has been described earlier, we would say that when the personality becomes distorted by human negativity, the divine energy, in a way, (at least in terms of its *physical* manifestation inside a human body) is "translated" from its perfect *whole* state, into a temporary configuration that is *split*. Some of that divine energy continues to feed the cells of the body in a growthful way. However, other "portions" of the divine energy are weakened (in their *physical* manifestation), and, in a manner of speaking, they are "drained off." They do not reach the cells. They simply change form and leave the physical body.

The result of this is that the divine spark, the nurturing and rejuvenating energies that were *intended* for the cells of the physical body, are weakened in their work on the physical level. As a consequence, some of the cells of the body will not receive enough of the energy they need to carry out their normal, *healthy* functioning.

Thus, the divine spark of life, while it is feeding the human body, temporarily becomes "dependent" upon the human personality. The personality is allowed to determine how strong the divine energies will be when they finally reach the cells, and the various structures of the physical body.

Therefore, in your preparation for healing, not only will you need to rejoice in, respect, idealize, and venerate the divine spark of life that sustains all physical bodies, but you will need to realize that you, as a human personality, have the power to block that extraordinary energy in a way that can diminish the health of your body. You also have the power to *augment* the intensity of that divine energy as it comes into your physical body. *It is the augmentation of the divine energy that will bring about the healing of your physical body.*

Thus, in a way, the healing of your body depends upon your ability *to invite more of the divine energy through the threshold of matter, into the cells of your body*. Your preparation to do this consists of *imagining how this works*. That is why it is beneficial for us to attempt to thoroughly paint a picture of this process so that you can take the picture into your mind and use it to guide yourself in your healing work.

The next step in aligning with the divine energies is to set aside a period of silence in each day during which you *practice* attuning your human personality to those eternal energies that we have described. Such attunement will make you better prepared to succeed in healing.

Let us imagine that you have spent many years preoccupied with the pleasures of physical life on earth, and you have had little interest in eternal realities. Then, you are stricken with a serious illness, and you try to work with the kind of healing method that we will suggest. You may have some success in inviting more of the energies of God through the threshold of matter to help heal your body, but you could also expect some degree of unfamiliarity with working with the eternal energies, simply because you have not previously practiced using them.

Experiencing eternal realities is not something that you can learn in the ordinary human way of mental study and intellectual mastery. It is an area that requires *direct experience* in an inner way. A day to day attunement in silence is the most effective way to gain that experience. Daily practice in attunement to eternal realities, at least for a small period of time each day, can teach you how to *feel* your eternal nature, and how to consciously align yourself with the energies of God. This will not only help you to have greater success in your healing work, but it can also bring deeper purpose, meaning, joy, and love into your day to day personality life.

Also, each human being, in their own way, is attempting to bring forth, from unconscious levels, knowledge about life, and about healing, that they have accumulated from many times of walking on earth. Taking a period of attunement in each day can accelerate the bringing of that knowledge to your conscious awareness. Once you have brought that knowledge into your mind and your heart, in a sense, the way you function as a healer will be raised to a new level. Your capacity to heal will be accelerated.

At your *normal* level of functioning as a human being, only a portion of your knowledge and healing capacity is being brought to the surface. As you persist in a day to day attunement, a change will occur in your personality. There will be the stimulation of more confidence, strength, and love. This will change the personality structure so that the "tough hide" of self-preoccupation and confusion that covers most human personalities will be gradually thinned. The personality patterns that interfere with drawing eternal energies into tangible reality will be adjusted, and your personality will become freer and more flexible, and much more of the eternal energies will be able to flow through you.

All of this is to speak of the *conscious* level. There is also an area that, generally, you will not need to be so concerned with, but by simply reminding yourself of its existence, you can encourage yourself. That is the area of healing that takes place at an unconscious level, and that takes a while to manifest on the surface. For example, if you are working to heal an inner negative pattern, let us say a pattern of *jealousy*, and you work diligently for one month and notice no change in your feelings, you could comfort yourself by saying:

"I may not have tangible evidence of the healing that I have made, but I now remind myself that beneath my conscious awareness, I have made some important changes in my inner patterns. And, later, these will blossom forth as beautiful new thoughts, feelings, and positive changes within me."

You may often need to remind yourself that a great deal of good is taking place inside you that is not available to your conscious awareness.

As you prepare for your healing work, you will also need to take into consideration *the present condition* of your physical body. If you presently have an illness that is of an emergency nature, that is threatening your life, you will not be so interested in long term improvement in your thoughts and feelings. First, you will need to try to improve the present condition of your physical body, through medical treatment, or whatever means are available to you. However, as you attempt to improve your physical condition, you can also try to work with the healing of your negative thoughts and feelings as best you can. Such work might encourage you to have faith in your capacity to heal your body.

Another way to prepare for your healing is to remind yourself that you will need to be *patient* in your healing work. You will need to understand that even after you have begun to make the needed changes in your various inner patterns, the body itself will take some time to respond to those inner changes. That is because the physical aspects of you are less flexible and more dense than are your personality energies. Thus, your physical body is slow to follow the changes that you make in your thoughts and emotions. Therefore, it will usually take longer to heal illness in the body than it will to heal the underlying personality patterns that might have caused the illness. The body will be slow to catch up with significant changes that you make in your inner personality energies. Thus, the process of healing the physical body usually involves a gradual, day by day change, rather than a sudden and dramatic elimination of symptoms.

As you prepare for your healing work, you will also need to realize that *opening emotionally* is, in a sense, a prerequisite for healing. In working to invite the divine energies more fully through the threshold of matter to become stronger energies of healing in your body, you need to be aware that your *intuition* can enhance those energies. However, your intuition is intimately woven with your emotions. Thus, when you tighten or close emotionally, you also constrict your intuitive capacity, which hampers the inflowing of the divine energies into the cells of your body.

We are not suggesting that you cannot heal when you are tight and squeezed emotionally, but, the outpouring of the energies of God that are at your command, and that you can bring through the threshold of matter, will be squeezed down into the narrow emotional opening that you have allowed. Thus, there will be less potency to the energies that are allowed through, and there will temporarily be less forcefulness to your ability to heal your body.

A METHOD FOR HEALING

In light of all that we have examined together so far, we can now suggest a general method for healing your physical body. Of course, this is not a *magical* procedure that immediately makes you a perfect healer. The many complex energies involved in healing are simply too resistant to human manipulation to be *instantly* mastered. Therefore, learning to heal your body with this method will require persistence and patience over a period of time. However, while you work steadily and persistently toward mastery of your healing abilities, the work can be quite thrilling, and extremely satisfying in itself.

The following method can be effective with what we would call the two general "categories" of physical conditions to be healed. The first category would include those conditions that you might say are "tolerable." In other words, even though such conditions do not please you, even though you would wish to heal them and make perfection in your body, if you do not succeed, you will not be seriously debilitated in your life.

The second category would include those conditions that create a deeper and broader disruption to your health. These are the areas of serious impairment, disease, and malfunction, including diseases that threaten the life of your physical body.

Step One. The first step in your healing would be: *To bring your attention fully upon the situation and circumstances of that which is challenging your body.* In order to heal your body, you would need to deeply engage the *experience* of your physical challenge. This is the step in which you *accept* the negativity of your condition.

Let us say that you have a troubling pain in your knee. The first impulse would be to try to carry out a healing that would eliminate the pain. However, in order to fully heal your knee, it will first be necessary to be willing to *fully experience the pain in your knee.*

Thus, you will set aside a period of time in which you will enter into a silence with yourself, and, during this period of silence, you will *not* try to heal your knee. *You will try to feel the pain in your knee as intensely as you can.* You will also encourage any negative feelings or fears that you might have about your knee. You will try to bring such feelings to the surface, and while you are experiencing the pain in your knee, you will also completely fill your thoughts and feelings with all of the negative patterns that might be associated with your physical pain.

You will decide how long a period of time you wish to work in this way—it might be five minutes, or it might be more. At the beginning of the period, you can say to yourself:

"At a later time, I will work to heal the challenge to my body. For now, I wish to deeply experience what it is like to be in this painful situation. I notice my physical sensations, my feelings, and my thoughts. I let them all penetrate me now. I do not resist this experience."

This is the actual process of accepting your negativity. This step is necessary in order to begin to dissolve any *fear* that you may have generated about your physical challenge. It will also begin to open the door to a greater awareness of fears that may be involved in manifesting the health challenge in the first place.

As you explore your symptoms, your feelings about them, and your thoughts about them, in the way we are suggesting, you will become familiar with them, and they will not seem to be enemies, nor invaders. They are temporarily *you*, feeling less than perfect. They are you, having discomfort and pain.

At this point, if you have a tendency to fear that your condition might become more serious, you might take a few minutes to imagine that you have a serious, life-threatening illness. Engage your imagination and stir your fears as deeply as you can. Even imagine a horrible death. Whatever is frightening to you, for a few minutes, bring it to the surface. This will help diffuse underlying fears of further serious illness.

Step Two. After you have worked with the first step for as long as you feel is necessary, it is time to begin the healing. Say to yourself:

> **"I now choose to heal my body, because it
> *pleases* me to walk forth in a perfect body, not
> because I am frightened of pain. I now *choose*
> not to suffer any longer. I wish to eliminate
> the physical challenge to my body."**

Your healing will always begin with *thoughts* and *feelings*, not with the body. So, you would say to yourself:

> **"I now release into myself, and I bring to my
> conscious awareness, all negative thoughts
> and feelings that are associated with the ill-
> ness in my body, and that may somehow be
> the *cause* of my present challenge."**

Then, take five or ten minutes to patiently explore those patterns, to intensify them, and deeply experience them so that you can recognize how they are connected with your physical challenge.

If nothing comes forth during this time, then assume that by your willingness to invite your negative patterns to the surface, you have made some *uncon-scious* openings that will be of service to you at a future time. In the future, you will have some insights arise that will help you understand which of your negative thoughts and feelings caused your present health challenge.

Step Three. You will now begin a process that is essentially a *disengagement* from your ordinary personality patterns. You can accomplish this by imagining that you are floating away from your physical body, and you are leaving your ordinary personality patterns behind. You can imagine that you are aligning with your own soul, with guiding souls, or with God. In that moment of disengagement, you are shifting your attention from your "animal" nature, which is rooted in your physical body, to your *eternal* being, which is rooted in your soul.

Your thoughts and feelings are closer to your eternal nature than to your animal nature. Therefore, if you direct your thoughts and feelings toward *imaginations* of yourself disengaging from your body, floating away from it, separating from it, *you can stir in your thoughts and feelings their capacity to imitate, or mirror, eternal energies.*

Your thoughts and feelings are a kind of flexible bridge that you can move about at will. You are free at any moment to link your thoughts and feelings to your animal nature, or to align them with your eternal being. In this moment of healing, you would *consciously* direct your thoughts and feelings toward your eternal nature by creating a strong imagining of disengaging from your physical body. Do this to the best of your ability. It may take time until you feel that you are becoming proficient at this step of the inner work.

Step Four. After your thoughts and feelings start to become "lighter," or more flexible and fluid, you are prepared to turn your thoughts and feelings toward the *truth*. At first, you can say the truth, or think it, or imagine it. Gradually, as you work persistently in this way, you will learn to actually *feel* the truth inside of you as a deep experience.

Each person will have their own way to accomplish this step. The essence of what you are attempting to do is to convince your human personality that: (1) there is an extraordinary, eternal perfection that is your true nature; (2) perfection lives within you in that moment, buried deep inside your human personality; and (3) your eternal perfection is not diminished by the present challenge to your physical body that you are now healing.

From a lovingly detached point of view, you would work inwardly to create the following *thinking*, *feeling*, and *knowing*:

"I am a magnificent eternal being. In this moment, I am filled with a perfection that cannot be diminished by this present challenge to the health of my physical body."

It is one thing to understand and think about the words that we are now using to describe this step. It is an entirely different matter to actually *experience* the *realities* that we are speaking about. You will do all that you can to guide yourself to a direct experience of these realities. It may take some time to accomplish this, but the reward will more than justify the time that you spend. And, remind yourself that, within your personality, there already exist the abilities to accomplish this kind of experience. You simply need to take the time to bring those abilities to your conscious awareness and *use* them.

Step Five. From deep within yourself, draw forth feelings of *strength* and *potency*. Then, say to yourself, and *feel*:

"As I make this adjustment in my thoughts and feelings, I have now taken a position of *power* over all aspects of my human personality. All of the old, limited habits of thinking and feeling are now put aside, and I stand with a clearer awareness of my soul. I stand with a great desire to *augment* the perfection of the energies of God that feed my body. Using my will, my desire, and my authority, I now take command over my human life. I command that more of the perfect energies of God shall now cross the threshold of physical matter and pour forth into the cells of my physical body."

As you say this, you would attempt to inwardly *live* the reality of it as fully as you can.

We are using human words to try to describe energies and realities that can be difficult for human beings to perceive. We are creating word images in an attempt to stir certain feelings and insights within you that can guide you to an *experience* of these realities. Thus, in human words, we would describe your accomplishment of this step in the following manner: You are standing above your physical body, close to your eternal soul nature. However, you still stand within your personality matrix. From that position, you are assuming authority over the physical world, and over your physical body. *You are becoming the master of your body, by virtue of the power of the energies of God that live within you.* The healing energies stream from God itself. *The decision as to where those energies will be focused in your physical world will be made by you.*

Step Six. Here, the words of earth are inadequate to express the next movement properly. Therefore, use your inner sensitivity to attempt to expand your *feeling* of the words that we must now use.

In this position of power and authority that you have assumed, *begin to visit your divine self upon your own human body with a desire to achieve perfection in your physical form.*

When you are in this position of assuming power, you do not wish to notice any contradictions to your belief in God, and in your own capacities to direct the energies of God. Simply begin to carry out this divine visitation in your imagination, in your own particular way. Experiment with yourself until you feel you have discovered the most potent way to create this experience for yourself.

Since there are no human words or images to accurately portray the divine energies that you are working with, when you visit your divine self upon your physical body, you will need to use ideas, images, or feelings to "symbolize" the divine energies. Some may choose to visit their body as *a force of light*, reinvesting themselves back into the body, particularly into afflicted areas of the body. Some may visit themselves as deep, pure feelings of love. Some may feel that they are visiting their body as the Christ force. Some may simply imagine, as best they can, that they are merging themselves with the actual energies of God, and that they are visiting those energies of God upon their physical body. Use whatever will deeply stir your experience of this merging of the eternal and the human.

Step Seven. Now we come to the very heart of your healing work—*the actual penetration, through imagination, intuition, feeling, and thought, into your own physical body.* You will make this penetration from the lofty position of command that you have obtained.

Ordinarily, when you are ill, and you enter your body with imagination, it is with a sense of *dread*—a feeling that the challenge to your body is bad. The purpose of all that we have suggested so far is to give you a new way to enter your body. You will now enter your body from the point of view of an eternal soul. From that point of view, it is quite clear to you that *the challenge to the health of your body is not bad*. You would say to yourself:

"No matter how serious this health challenge might seem to my personality, I see now that it is not *bad*. It simply has stirred negativity within my personality and my body, but I see clearly now that all negativity is temporary. It is of earth. And I am eternal. The negativity cannot damage me."

From this position, most of you have the capacity to learn, eventually, how to heal your physical body. You would say to yourself:

"Wielding the energies of God itself, I now penetrate into my physical body, and I visit powerful, perfect, divine energies upon the afflicted portion of my body."

Using whatever way you choose to experience this visitation, you begin to infuse your body with divine healing energies. For example, if you are using the image of light, you will see the light of God itself entering your body and infusing itself into every cell of the body. You will see and feel that light to be particularly strong in the part of your body that you are healing.

Step Eight. At this point, you will begin to use your imagination and feelings to try to deepen your connection with the eternal energies. You will do this according to your temperament and your beliefs. Some have developed the capacity to call upon *a living master* that they have assimilated into their own personality. Others will be able to call upon eternal souls who are guiding-ones to themselves.

Others upon the force of the Christ itself. Others upon certain understandings concerning past times of earth, in which they were associated with extraordinary beings. Whatever will spark a deepened connection to the eternal realms, you can use it. The more *belief* you can generate during this step, the more intensely will you invite the energies of God into your body.

At this point, try to feel deeply the power of your spiritual connection *intensifying* the energies of healing that you are visiting upon your body. Imagine a deepening of the healing that is taking place, because you are now being augmented by the deepened spiritual connection that you have made.

Now, if the challenge to your physical body is of the serious, life threatening type, you would need to add something else to this step of the healing process. Comforted by the love of your deepened spiritual connection, you would need to create *a willingness to give up your physical body for this lifetime.*

This is a very delicate area, because, for some, it may stir the human fear of death. Thus, you would begin by saying this to yourself:

"I desire the largest truth that I can understand in this moment. If that truth is that my personal challenge is now to rejoice in my death, then I wish to know that. If it is that my challenge is to exercise my human *choice* in my life and *heal* this illness, then I wish to know that."

The only way to decide which of these choices is

the one that you need to make is to use your imagination *to enter into the choice of death* in order to *test*
that choice with your feelings to see if it is the one
you believe you should make. You would use your
imagination to practice feeling that choice from inside the experience of it.

From the expanded state of awareness that you
have attained from carrying out the previous steps,
you would imagine that your task is to give up your
physical body and go to your death, as gently and as
lovingly as possible. First, enter into a deep feeling
of love, as much as you are able. Then, begin to
imagine going quietly to your death. Imagine that
your greatest learning will come from simply accepting death.

After doing this as deeply as possible, you should
begin to have a clear feeling about whether this is
really the path for you to follow, or whether this is
the wrong decision for you. If you feel a sense of
burden, heaviness, and wastefulness about this
choice, or if you clearly feel that this is *not* your path,
then say to yourself, "I have decided that it is not my
time to accept death. That is not the true path for
me at this point in my life." It might take a number
of days of working with this step to come to any
clarity about this area, or, you might know immediately what is the truth about this choice.

If you decide that your true path is to heal your
physical body, then you would take up the healing
work with strength, courage, stamina, and passion.
You would try to heal, *not because you are frightened
of death, but because you love life*. With this kind of

attitude, you would dedicate yourself to the healing, totally and completely.

As you work with this step of the healing method, you would try to create a sense of *destiny*. In other words, while you were testing the choice of death, you were trying to decide whether you would *choose* to focus upon living or dying. However, now that you have become convinced that your true choice is to heal, then you would try to stir up the feeling that it is your *destiny* to heal your body. You would know that your soul is aligned with that healing; that all of the energies of life will help you change the disruptive cellular responses in your body; that those energies will help you dissolve and eliminate all challenges that have caused the illness in your body.

Step Nine. After you have worked with your healing for as long as you desire, then slowly and gently return yourself to complete, full awareness of yourself in the present moment. Take as much time as you need. Do not rush yourself.

The method that we have suggested here is quite a direct and potent way to heal your physical body. The effectiveness of the method will grow as you use it in trust of your own magnificence, your own healing capacities, and the energies of God within you.

As you work to heal your body, it is important to remember that the energies of God, and of your soul, will continue to pour forth into you, whether you heal your physical body or not. You are always cared for, you are always sustained, you are always safe, whether your physical body is healthy or ill.

While you live in human form, you must decide what you *desire* to manifest in the physical world, and how you will turn the energies of God toward such manifestation. If you wish, you can *choose* to be healthy.

Yet, your soul understands that if you go into illness, and even if you die a miserable death from it, there is no badness in such experiences. Your soul knows that you are not diminished, or damaged, or harmed. You are still eternal. Your soul can rejoice in *any* experience that you have, whether you find it pleasurable or painful.

However, for you as a human being, it is important to live a life of beauty and personal fulfillment. The desire for health in your earth life is yours to fulfill. Step forth boldly into your life and fulfill your desire in any way that pleases you, knowing that you are always drawing upon the eternal energies that continually flow into your human personality.

Chapter 15

Creating A
Healthy Life

—When you go forth to be kind to other human beings, to help them, and to serve them, you stir up areas of feeling inside you that can be activated in no other way. Those feelings feed into your personality in a way that can not only bring joy and fulfillment for you, but they can also stimulate the health of your physical body.

J ust as in your work to heal illness, when you come forth to create health for yourself in your day to day life, your success will be directly linked to the way you create your inner reality. As we have attempted to show you throughout these teachings, the health of your body *depends* upon the health of your inner life. Therefore, your *creation* of health in each day will begin with the kind of harmonious inner life of thought and feeling that we have described in earlier chapters.

However, in order to create full health, you will also need to pay attention to your outer world. You will need to make intelligent choices about the physical aspects of your life, such as what you eat, how you exercise your body, how you relate to other human beings, and other interactions with the physical world that you will have daily.

Your work in creating a healthy life will be done in four important areas that involve a constant interaction between your inner life and the outer world. You will need to wisely manage these four areas day by day throughout your lifetime. The areas are: (1) working to maintain an awareness of your eternal nature; (2) working patiently and lovingly to heal your personality fears and negative patterns as they arise each day; (3) healthy living in your physical world, which includes diet, exercise, rest, play, social activity, and giving to others; and, (4) *creating love in your life day by day*.

We have already examined ways to maintain an awareness of your eternal nature, and we have suggested ways of healing personality fear and negativity. We will now look at the second two areas, which are healthy living in daily life, and the creation of love.

CREATING HEALTH WITH DIET

First of all, we will look with you at the relationship between food and health. Concerning the foods that are put into the human body, you must assume that there are certain parameters within which you have total freedom, and, if you go outside of those parameters, you will have challenge. In other words, you are free to put *any* food into your body, and it will sustain the life of your body by the way in which the nutrients are extracted from the food and fed into the various cells of your body. However, even though your physical body can survive on any food, some foods serve your body better than others. Within what we would call the "normal human eating range," there are certain foods that are more effective in creating health.

Outside of the normal eating range would be found such things as poisonous plants, rocks, and other things that are not food material for human beings. At the edges of the normal range, there are some things that you *could* eat, but you would not consider them ordinary parts of your diet. For example, certain flowers, blades of grass, and so forth.

Within the normal range of foods that you could eat, the only difference between those various foods is their *effectiveness and efficiency of functioning*, in terms of the health of your body. For example, if each day you put a great deal of fat into your body, the body is fed and sustained, but not at its most perfectly efficient level, and not in ways that you would consider conducive to optimum health. Eating a great deal of fat can energize the body and allow it to live on the physical earth, but other foods would be more effective in creating full health within your body.

For clarity, let us create a *spectrum* of substances that you could put into your body. Imagine that this spectrum is represented by a horizontal line that runs from the left to the right. At the far left end are the *inedible* substances, simply because they are indigestible—rocks, metals, and so forth. That is a small part of our spectrum on the left side that represents *heaviness*. On the far right end of the line are things that you could eat, but they would damage the body, such as poisonous plants. They are also a small portion of the spectrum, and they represent the quality of *intensity*.

The largest part of the spectrum is a very large part on the center of the line, which represents things that are *acceptable* to the body as food. Everything in this large middle area will keep the physical body alive.

In this large middle area that represents foods that are acceptable to the body, at the very center of that area, are the foods that are *most* efficient and effective in maintaining human bodies at their most beautiful and healthful level. Here you would find the fruits, vegetables, and small amounts of proteins that are light, such as the fish and the fowl. These are foods that most of you now realize will benefit your body.

On the left side of this middle area that represents acceptable foods, you would have the *heavy* foods, such as fats and heavy proteins. These foods will sustain the body, but they create a heaviness that acts against the lightness of experience that is intended for physical bodies.

On the right side of the acceptable area would be foods of strong *intensity*, such as the sharp, spicy foods. These foods tend to be too intense, or over-stimulating, and they act against the mild and soothing experience that is intended for bodies.

If you eat foods *only* on the left side in the heavy foods, or *only* on the right side in the intense foods, your body will survive, but you may have some physical responses that do not serve you well, that will make it difficult for you to create full health. On the other hand, if you eat foods *only* in the middle of the acceptable area—which are the fruits, vegetables, and light proteins—your body will respond with optimum strength, vigor, and health. This is assuming that you do not distort the area of eating with negative attitudes, which we will examine next.

In making your choices of what to eat, it is a matter of the *quality* of the experience that you desire. If you like the experience of heaviness in taste, and you are willing to live with a fat body, then, you will eat fats. They will sustain your body, but they will not give it the optimum influence for creating health.

If you wish as perfectly functioning a body as possible, you will eat foods in the middle range. They will do all for your health that food can possibly do, in accordance with the personality patterns and soul impulses that you are working with.

If you wish intensity of taste, then you will eat the foods that are stimulating. The intense foods are exciting to many human beings, but they have certain limiting effects upon the health of the body, primarily resulting from overstimulation of the nerve and glandular systems.

The foods in the middle of the acceptable range

have a kind of *amplifying* effect upon certain beneficial forces within the body. In other words, when the
body is digesting the fruits, vegetables, and light proteins, the rhythms of the digestive system, the way in
which the body utilizes the foods, and the way the
body throws off waste, are all stimulated in a manner
that is most harmonious and beneficial to healthy
cellular reproduction within the body. The cells are
most gently encouraged to feel "safe," or whole, or
perfect. There is less tendency for the cells to feel
that there is a threat that needs to be resisted.

In looking to the area of eating the flesh of animals, including the fish and the fowl, as well as the
cows, and so forth, it is important for you to understand that the intelligent exercise of human *choice* is
more important than trying to rigidly follow certain
narrow dictates that you consider to be perfect rules
to live by. What is important here are your own personal attitudes toward eating meat. If you would feel,
from a moral point of view, "It is horrible to eat the
animals," and if you try to do so, there would be
mental and emotional resistances set up in your body
so that the flesh of the animals would not make the
most effective feeding of your body. This would
come about because of your *attitude*, not because of
the nature of the meat itself.

On the other hand, if you would believe, "The
eating of meat is quite wonderful, very delicious, and
good for my body," then your body would be more
receptive to all forms of the meat. You would receive nutritional benefit from eating the meat.

However, in a general way of speaking, there are

some real differences in the meats, and the way the human body responds to them. Some of them are harder for the body to break down and digest, and some have more fat in them than others. Thus, there are some similar responses that most bodies will have to the range of meats, assuming that you like the meat, and you eat it with a positive attitude.

As a general guideline, we could say that the eating of the fish is preferable for the body, for many reasons having to do with metabolizing the fish, and the ease of extracting nutrients. The next preferable meat would be the fowl. Then, there would come the meats that you would consider to be the red meats. The red meats will of course have nutritional value, however, if there is an over-indulgence in them, there can be a less than perfect feeding of the body, due to the heaviness of such meats, and a certain kind of "wildness," in terms of a mismatching of the substance of the red meat to the intended function of the human stomach.

This mismatching of the red meats is slight, because human bodies have made certain adjustments over time. In other words, in the beginning of human existence, the human stomach was not formed in a way that it could perfectly digest the red meat. However, because of human desire and will, which led human beings to eat the red meat, over the ages, the stomach has adapted to work with greater efficiency in such digestion, as long as such meat is not over-indulged in. Therefore, there would not be any "badness" about eating red meat, even though in some physical bodies, it may create slowness of functioning, and some challenges to the health. The red meat is simply not as effective and efficient as fish and fowl would be in the creation of full health within the physical body.

We remind you that physical bodies do vary. For some, a small amount of red meat can be a challenge. For others, a larger amount would not particularly challenge the body. Therefore, you will need to learn the response of your particular body to the eating of such meat.

Some human beings believe that the greatest health comes from eating only the fruits, vegetables, cheeses, and so forth. They will avoid meat altogether, engaging in what you call, vegetarianism. If your belief is strong that this is a beneficial path for you, then you will need to test it for yourself. However, we would caution you that without at least occasionally taking the fish or fowl into your body, there is a possibility of depriving your body of some important nutrients. Yet, if your belief in the goodness of a vegetarian diet is strong enough, then your body may not be hampered by avoiding meat. Again, you must learn through experience whether such a choice is beneficial for your particular body.

Now, let us examine the *spiritual forces* involved in the feeding of the physical body. First of all, we would say that the souls intended for the physical human bodies, as you now know them, to be fed by physical food, just as the animal bodies are fed by physical food. The human body was created to digest some substances and to reject others. It was created in a way that makes rocks inedible, some substances poisonous, and some foods able to provide optimum health for the physical body.

In the beginning of human life, the area of human eating was controlled by the eternal souls, as they experimented with ways for bodies to function effectively in a physical world. At that point in time, human beings had a conscious awareness of their souls, and what those souls desired to accomplish with the human personality. Thus, under the clear direction of the souls, the early human beings would choose to eat in a perfect way.

Then, as the human perception of the souls gradually slipped into the unconscious areas of human awareness, the area of eating was "turned over" to human beings, and they were given the freedom to do as they pleased. Therefore, eating is now a matter of human *choice*, and you decide what foods to take into your body.

You would understand that the normal food range that we have described earlier is essentially the range intended by the souls. The souls created human bodies to thrive on the diet of the middle of the spectrum—the fruits, vegetables, and lighter proteins. However, in your cleverness and creativity, and in your search for pleasure in the taste of food, you ones have created some unusual things to eat that push the edges of the food range a bit further than the souls might have chosen. Yet, you are given the freedom and the power to do that, if it pleases you.

The souls established certain laws, or principles for the unfoldment of physical matter, including the physical matter of a human body. They intended for the structure of the human body to evolve in a way that would be in alignment with the laws of physical matter. In other words, it has been so established that if a human being eats a poisonous substance, the physical matter of the body will respond according to physical laws, and the poison will damage the body, or cause it to die. If a body is not fed at all, then it will deteriorate and die of starvation. The human body is of earth, and it will respond to the laws of the physical universe.

To the souls, the feeding of physical bodies is not as important as it is to you as a human being. The souls understand that the physical body is an important and useful vehicle, but that it is quite temporary. They understand that they have given you the capacity to rejoice in your life, whether you are fat or thin, hungry or satiated, eating of light foods or heavy foods. Your soul will not fall into despair if you become fat, or unhealthy. Eating well is valuable *for your own personal human experience of life*, in which health produces more happiness, more clarity, more inner joy and fulfillment. However, you can still accomplish your important purposes in life, whether you eat perfectly or not. Yet, it is more difficult for most human beings to accomplish at the highest level when they are unable to create health in their lives.

In addition to what you eat, in creating health for yourself, you will also need to look at your *attitudes* toward diet. As you can understand, your various attitudes—your many thoughts and feelings—toward food will be an important factor in determining how those foods affect your body.

The first area to understand here is the way your emotions and thoughts affect the food intake, assimilation, and elimination. In a general way of speaking, even though there are exceptions, we could say that if you approach food, and the eating of it, with a great deal of negative thinking and feeling about food, then there is less efficiency in the assimilation of that food. For example, if you are constantly frightened that you will become too fat, then when you eat, this fear can interfere with the way your body works with the food.

Also, your attitudes about life in general will affect your eating. If you eat when you are depressed, the food may not digest properly, and it might not be fully utilized by your body. If you have constant fear, doubt, and worry throughout your life, then there will be disturbances set up in the digestive processes of your body, which can eventually bring about challenges to your health.

Therefore, when you are trying to create health through diet, you will need to be aware that un-healed negative attitudes toward food, and toward life, over a period of time, can interfere with the way your body uses whatever food you put into it. On the other hand, as a useful generalization, we could say that the more calmness, happiness, joy, and understanding you have in your attitude toward food and eating, and toward life, then the more you leave the body free to function perfectly in the way that it takes in the food, assimilates it, and eliminates the waste.

As a general guideline to yourself, you can say, "If I am extremely agitated, upset, frightened, or depressed, I may wish to choose to eat later when I am calmer. Or, when I am mentally or emotionally challenged, I may choose to eat a small amount of food."

You will also need to be aware that very *strict* beliefs about what you eat, and why you eat, can also interfere with your creation of health. For example, if you say, "I must *only* feed my body certain foods, or I am afraid my body will deteriorate and become ill," then, eating becomes a guarded, defensive activity. The tension and fear caused by such an attitude begin to disrupt some of the capacity of the assimilation system in your body. In such a case, even if you are eating the perfect foods, because of the fear associated with your eating of them, your body will not receive the optimum benefit from those foods. For you, it might be more beneficial to eat foods that are a bit less than perfect, but to eat them in relaxation and joy.

In general, when you approach your food, it is always wise to try to make a bit of relaxation before eating. It is beneficial to clear your mind, to calm yourself, to create some feelings of pleasure and joy. This will encourage the best assimilation of the food. However, you would not wish to be overly strict about this, or to be worried if you do not feel perfectly relaxed when you eat.

Your attitudes about *yourself* will also affect the way your body responds to food. If you feel unworthy and inadequate, it will be difficult for you to maintain a completely healthy diet. You will tend to feel, usually unconsciously, "This body does not deserve the best from life." You might unintentionally disrupt your eating patterns, feeling that you could never be perfect, so you cannot have perfect food. You might tend to desire foods on the extreme ranges of the scale—foods that are too fat, or that are over-intense. In an extreme case, if you develop severe habits of self-depreciation, you could so interfere with your digestion and assimilation processes that you could undernourish your body.

Generally speaking, those who are loving with themselves, and feel that they deserve goodness in life, will tend to be drawn to foods that are healthy. They will not usually develop such strong desires to eat foods in the extreme ranges, either too fat, or too intense. This is not to say that if you like foods at the extreme ranges then you do not love yourself. This is simply a generalization that applies to some people.

There are many different attitudes that you could have that can affect your eating in various ways. Thus, this entire area will need some careful study by you. You will need to work patiently and gently, observing your various attitudes, understanding them, and discovering how they interact with the food that you eat, and with your body's assimilation and elimination processes.

EXERCISE AND HEALTH

If there would be a physical body that would lie dormant, without any activity for a long period of time, as with one who is ill, you understand that the process of "atrophy" would occur in that body. There would not be enough physical stimulation to prod the body to continue its healthful growth and rejuvenation. You can see that if *no* exercise can cause the body to atrophy, then *very little* exercise will only partially balance the tendency to atrophy. The body will atrophy somewhat. This should indicate to your mind that if you wish your physical body to maintain its *full* strength and health throughout your lifetime, there is a need for a certain amount of exercise.

Now, in this, again, you must consider the individual, unique personality and body of each human being. You can observe that some human bodies stay quite strong and healthy with very little exercise. Some will tend to be unhealthy even with a great deal of exercise, because the attitudes, thoughts, and feelings will interfere with the way the exercise affects the body.

As a general way to guide yourself in this area, you could say, "Throughout this lifetime, if I do not *use* my body, in terms of some kind of physical activity, then I might gradually lose my flexibility, my stamina, and my physical strength." It should be clear that the less you use your body, the more rapidly your strength and flexibility will decline. This is particularly true of older bodies.

However, this does not necessarily mean that the more you exercise, the healthier you will be. To expand upon this, let us make an imaginary scale to represent exercise.

The scale consists of a horizontal line running from the left to the right. We will look at the various increments on the scale, beginning on the far left side, and moving to the right.

On the left end of the scale is, *no exercise at all.* Let us call this the "abnormal" range. Associated with this range is usually heaviness and atrophy.

Next to that, moving to the right, is, *a small amount of exercise.* For most present human beings, we could call this the "normal" range.

To the right of that, in the very center of the scale, is, *a perfect amount of exercise.* Of course, this is the area of optimum health for each individual.

Then, to the right of that, is, *a bit too much exercise.* This might, or might not be detrimental to the health of the individual, depending on the unique life circumstances, and the personality and soul patterns.

To the right of that, at the far right end of the scale, is, *too much exercise.* This can also be considered an "abnormal" range. This is exercise that is detrimental or damaging to the physical body because it is too intense, or excessive, or too violent, as are some of the more violent human sports.

However, as you can understand, in each of these categories, you could not say that the type of exercise, or the amount, would be the same for each human being. For example, you could not say that the perfect exercise for all human beings is to walk one mile, although the activity of walking is quite beneficial for most human beings. Yet, for some, the perfect exercise would be something more vigorous. For others, walking might be too strenuous, and they might need to do some simple stretching of the body.

As you work in the area of exercise, you will learn, given your own moment in time—whether you are youthful, of moderate age, or old age—what is the most appropriate and effective exercise for yourself. It will take some experimentation to find your own perfect balance. However, we do emphasize that physical movement is quite important in creating health for your body. To remind yourself of this, you could say to yourself each day:

"My body is, in essence, an *animal* structure, and animal structures are based in *physical* reality. When my body does not fully partake of physical reality, to the point of being robust and active in the physical world, then the animal nature is not being fully utilized, and accelerated. To create the optimum health for myself, I will give attention to the area of physical movement and exercise."

This will be of particular importance for those human beings who tend to be overly intellectual. They will often retreat into intellectual activities and ignore the need of the animal body for its share of stimulation and participation in earth life.

Looking now at the spiritual realities and the way that they are involved with exercise and your creation of health, we would remind you that as the souls created human bodies, and the personalities to live inside those bodies, the souls intended for human beings to fully explore the entire range of physical experience on earth. They intended for human beings to move about with their bodies and explore the physical world; to use their bodies to act against physical forces, to lift them, to move them, in order to develop physical strength, flexibility, and agility.

The souls planted impulses in the personalities to inspire them to use the body in physical pursuits that bring stimulation to the cellular functionings of the body, particularly the brain functioning. Thus, the souls set forces into motion that would prompt you to engage in physical exercise as a way of stimulating the physiological mechanisms of your body, and, as a way of providing a broader arena inside that body for the mind and the emotions to experience a fuller range.

The souls created the human brain to work with the physical body, and all of its processes, in certain ways that *depend* upon vigor and physical stimulation from the body. Without that stimulation, the function of the brain can actually be inhibited or distorted.

Also, the brain was evolved in a certain way that encourages the personality to engage in physical activity. This is accomplished by certain chemical and electrical responses in the brain that occur during exercise, and that excite glandular activity and accelerate the circulation of the blood. This results in a sense of greater well being inside the personality, and creates a feeling of passion for life.

REST AND SLEEP

We will now consider the area of rest and sleep in relation to creating health in your life. This will be a matter of intelligent, day to day work to determine the most effective balance of rest and sleep against your physical, emotional, and mental activity.

To clarify this area in a simple way, you could think in terms of a bank account, in which the prerequisite to spending is depositing. When you have spent more money than you have actually deposited, it is quite a negative event in your financial life. In the same way, as you can clearly see, in your physical world, when you expend a great deal of energy, and you have not built up reserves with the proper rest and sleep, you can create a negative situation in the area of health.

As you work to create health, imagine rest and sleep (along with your food) as the deposits of energy that you make in your body. Then, the outgoing energies that you expend through thinking, feeling, and physically acting and doing, need to be intelligently balanced against those deposits. Most human beings are familiar with this balancing, and usually accomplish it quite well. It simply involves the daily assessment of the amount of rest that you need, in light of the amount of food you eat, the kind of food you eat, and the extent to which you exert yourself in the world.

To illustrate the balance of deposit and withdrawal, let us say that there is a perfectly healthy male human being who does extremely vigorous physical work, such as chopping the trees. And he would place a great deal of alcohol, and the foods that are too intense, into his body. Then, he would need to be aware that these substances are a kind of *smaller* deposit in the bank account of energy. He would need to know that a great deal of physical work, in combination with a less than ideal input of food and drink into the body, would require more rest than usual for his body.

On the other hand, let us say that he would eat quite perfectly of the fruits, vegetables, and light proteins. Then, with the same amount of physical work, he would need less rest than his body required when the input of food and drink was not ideal.

Let us now imagine a later time when the same male one is eating perfectly and resting the proper amount, and he is rejected by his mating one. There is a great deal of despair in his heart. This emotional turmoil takes much energy from his physical system because of a certain kind of emotional pressure that causes disturbances in the nerves, the cells, the brain functioning, and so forth. In such a moment, he would need to be aware that, because of his despair, he would need more rest than before the despair came along.

Certain intense *mental* activity within you can also cause a drain upon your energy reserves. However, at times, this is not realized by some human beings. For example, if there is a female one who would sit and make complex mathematical calculations day after day, she may feel, "Since I am not exercising, since I am not using physical stamina and energy, then I do not require extra rest." She would need to realize that her mind is also a drain upon her energy. She would need to understand that when the mind is exercised steadily for more than the usual kinds of human activities, this is a significant withdrawal from the bank account of energy. Therefore, in working with your own daily balance of energy deposits through rest and sleep, and your withdrawals, in terms of activity, keep in mind that a great deal of energy is required for vigorous mental work.

Now, let us look at the *kind* of rest that is available to you. These areas are often misunderstood by many ones.

Let us say that there is a female one who consistently, before entering her sleep period each night, takes a moment or two to put aside the worries, the doubts, the complexities, and even some of the excitement of her physical day. She also does some relaxation of her physical body, and some releasing of the physical tensions within her body. Then, she would make a sleep period of eight hours. This would make a very strong and large deposit into her bank account of energies, and it would promote a certain kind of rejuvenation and stimulation of her physical body.

Then, let us imagine the same female one, who, over a period of time, forgets to make these relaxations and releasings before sleep. Let us say that she begins to spend a great deal of time worrying about her financial difficulties just prior to sleep. As a result, she carries worry and fear into her sleep period. Because of this, her sleep period is of a different quality than when she was relaxing before sleep. The same female body and personality, with the same eight hours of sleep as before, would not be depositing as much rejuvenation energy into the physical-psychological system of body and personality. Therefore, in order to *perfectly* balance her energy account, she would need a bit more rest than she did when she was releasing and relaxing prior to sleep.

Those who consistently disturb themselves before sleeping will interfere somewhat with the rejuvenation effect and the re-stimulation of energy that occurs during the sleep period. We are not saying that if you are occasionally troubled or worried before sleep that you are severely limiting your energies. Yet, if, over a period of time, you consistently carry tensions, worries, doubts, turmoils, and fears into the sleep period, and you wish to create full health for yourself, then you will need to either make some adjustments in your mental and emotional patterns before sleep, or you might consider a small napping period during the day in order to increase your amount of rest.

Now, again, we are speaking in terms of the creation of *optimum* health—drawing as much health from your rest periods as possible. Yet, we are not suggesting that if you have less than the optimum balance of energy output and rest that you are harming yourself. Many ones can remain healthy with less than the perfect energies from their rest and sleep. You can use our suggestions as a guideline, and you can decide how much health you wish to create for yourself. If you feel, "I am too busy with important matters to have perfect rest patterns, and I am willing to accept a slight diminishment of energies," then you are free to make that choice. However, if you consistently, over a long period of time, ignore the proper kind of rest and sleeping patterns, then you will find that you are doing a disservice to yourself and to your health.

Remind yourself that the sleeping period is important for a number of reasons. Not only does it bring rest and rejuvenation to your physical body, and deposit new energies into your energy account, but it is also important for maintaining vital energies that are critical to the psychological balance of your personality. During your sleep, when you enter into the "blank" period of sleep—when you are not dreaming, and you temporarily have no conscious awareness—you move forth into a certain deep relationship with your own soul, and with eternal energies beyond earth. Those energies actually *teach* your personality in ways that you are not conscious of. You bring those teachings back to yourself, either consciously as dreams that affect your personality (and at times the dreams can be a confused version of the teachings), or, as *unconscious* energies of wisdom and rejuvenation that will amplify the eternal forces that are constantly pouring forth into your personality during every moment of your life.

As we have stressed, while you are awake, you are constantly being fed by the energies of your own soul, of guiding souls, and of God. While you are asleep, in the dreamless sleep period, you are receiving *accelerated* energies from those sources. If you go for long periods of time without the adequate kind of sleep, without undistorted sleeping periods, then those kinds of amplified eternal energies that your personality and body are used to receiving in healthy sleeping periods will be diminished. This can begin to trouble you greatly, and can lead to the depletion of your physical energy. If distorted sleep patterns are carried for a long period of time, they can eventually disturb your thoughts and emotions, and they can begin to stir up tendencies toward illness in your physical body. Therefore, in working to create health in your life, it is important to give loving, patient, and intelligent attention to your rest and sleep patterns.

HUMOR AND PLAY

In every human personality there is an interesting kind of inner "mechanism." In truth, it is a set of energies woven into all personalities, and those energies create an impulse that is similar to your impulse to eat, to drink, to rest, to have sexual fulfillment, to express creativity, or to love. Because of this particular set of energies, the human personality has an inborn tendency to seek what you would call play, laughter, and lightness, as a counterbalance to the heaviness of the burdens of human life that most of you carry.

Now, just as all of the other impulses and energies inside you, such as your thinking, feeling, desiring, and so forth, need to be harmonized in order to create a healthy life, so too does the impulse of desire for lightness, playfulness, and laughter need to be woven into your life. If you deprive yourself greatly of play and humor over a long period of time, then the impulse, the energy that is prodding you

364 HEALING THE HEART, HEALING THE BODY

toward that kind of fulfillment, is, in a way, distorted. There is the creation of certain *frustration* energies. Because the impulse toward play and laughter is being ignored, tumultuous kinds of energies are created inside the personality. It would be the same as if you ignored your impulse to be loved for a long period of time. It would stir up frustration and turmoil.

When your impulse toward play and humor is blocked and the tumultuous energies are created, then your capacity to create optimum health is temporarily diminished. If the distorted energies caused by this frustrated impulse are carried for a long period of time, the result can be the same as swallowing negative thoughts and feelings. You can begin to stimulate the disease process in your physical body. Therefore, in order to create the optimum health for yourself, day by day, you will need to give some attention to your natural impulse for play and laughter in your life.

As with all other areas in your inner life, you are the only one who could say what is the perfect balance in your daily life between work and play. How much play and laughter do you need in order to satisfy that inner impulse? Again, this is relative to all of the other factors in your life. In other words, if you are having a period of great challenge and struggle in your life for any reason, you would say, "Now, I need even more of the play and the laughter to help offset this." On the other hand, if you are having a joyful period, you are succeeding and fulfilling in many areas, then you would sense that the need for play and humor is not as great as in a more difficult period of your life.

However, you will always need *some* play and laughter throughout your life, so you will wish to give attention to this area. You will need to be alert to your own patterns and rhythms. Each evening you might say, "How many times did I laugh in this day?" If you would answer that you did not laugh at all, then you have a great need in the following day to balance your life with laughter. You would also say in the evening, "Did I take a few moments in this day to play, and to feel that sense of lightness that comes from recreation?" If you would answer *no*, then you have some balancing to do. On the other hand, and this would be less common for human beings, if you would say, "All that I have done today is laugh and play," then you would say, "tomorrow I might do a bit of work." The tendency of most adult human beings is to not laugh and play enough. Therefore, you might be alert to see if you are one of those who deprives yourself of this important experience in your daily life.

Play and laughter are not only joyful and satisfying, but they are actually a catalyst to the health-giving energies that live inside you. They stimulate those energies in a way that is beneficial for your heart, your brain, the blood in your body, and the various physical systems involved in creating health.

SOCIAL ACTIVITY AND LOVE FROM OTHERS

In the way that the human personalities were created by eternal souls in the beginning of human life, there has been planted in the human personality a strong impulse to link with other human beings, to love them, and to be loved by them. Among the many impulses planted in you by your soul, one of the strongest and most important is this impulse to link with others. This great impulse is intended to draw you into social relationships with other human beings.

You can understand that if this is one of the strongest impulses within you, then the *frustration* of that impulse can be one of the strongest disruptions to your personality, and to your health. Therefore, as you work to create health, it will be very important for you to satisfy this impulse toward human social activity.

This can be a difficult area for some human beings. Some of you, because of your fears associated with painful relationships, have learned to hold back, or partially smother your natural tendency toward social interaction. For some, it has been painful experiences with your father and mother, or other family members. For many, the pain has been associated with romantic relationships and marriage. Others have patterns of fear in relationships that come forth from painful experiences in past lifetimes on earth. Because of your fears, some of you have unconsciously convinced yourselves, "I do not need other people. Other people are not trustworthy. They are not lovable." Such thoughts and feelings smother your natural impulse toward social interaction.

Some of you who have avoided a great deal of social interaction have learned to focus your attention upon *yourselves* so fully that you now feel that you are simply being *independent.* You have convinced yourselves that it is good to be alone. Even though there is a certain benefit in learning how to love yourself and being independent, you need to see if there are fears of pain that are woven with your emphasis on independence. You need to notice if you are receiving enough love in your life from other human beings. If you are not, then you are cheating yourself out of some very important fulfillments that can come from loving social interactions with others. Not only are you robbing yourself of important fulfillments and joyful completions in this lifetime, but, if you constantly deprive yourself of this love from others, and the joy of social interactions, that can eventually become another factor that can interfere with your health and strength.

Again, speaking in terms of the *optimum* creation of health, you could sum up this area by saying to yourself:

"As part of my healthy living and creation of health, I need to make certain that I have some satisfying social interactions with other human beings. I need to make certain that I am loved by others. Even if I feel strong and independent, and spend most of my time alone, I will look and see if I need to make some changes and extend myself to try and satisfy the important impulse toward love from others that has been placed into my personality by my own soul. If I ignore social interaction and love from others altogether, I can establish blockages that will make it dif-

**ficult to create the fullness of health that I
desire in this lifetime."**

Focussing upon these kinds of thoughts and feelings can help you gain a balance between independence and self reliance, and, a loving interaction
with the human beings around you.

GIVING TO OTHERS

We will now look at the area of *giving* to other human beings. This area is one that needs to be carefully balanced against what you are *receiving* from
others. The way that you maintain the balance between giving and receiving will be another important
factor in your creation of health.

To clarify this, we would ask that you imagine
that you are a small squirrel in a tree. You rush out
on to a limb to pick a nut to eat. If you are an intelligent and experienced squirrel, you know that if you
go too far out onto the limb, you will come to the
weak part of it, it will bend or break, and you might
tumble down to the ground. If you do not go out on
the limb far enough, then you will not reach the nut,
and you will not eat. You learn from experience
what is the perfect balance point for you to feed
yourself, and to protect yourself from pain.

To establish your own balance in giving to others,
you will need to look at how much time you spend
preoccupied with yourself in order to feed yourself
joy and fulfillment, and how much time you are *over*-
preoccupied with yourself. If you go too far toward
self-preoccupation, you can begin to create painful

experiences for yourself. However, a certain amount of self-preoccupation is important in order for you to feed yourself, to nurture yourself, to fulfill your desires, and to accomplish what you need to accomplish in this lifetime. If you go beyond the balance point for you, then self-preoccupation becomes less beneficial. When you go *too* far beyond that point, your self-preoccupation can begin to cause you pain. When you begin to over-preoccupy with yourself, not only do you begin to lose interest in others, which prevents you from giving and receiving love, but you also tend to become distorted in your thinking and feeling, because you do not allow enough of the thoughts and feelings of others to be taken in by you to stimulate growthful new ways of thinking and feeling.

If human beings give *all* of their attention to themselves, they can become confused, and their personalities can become distorted by selfish tendencies and self-serving attitudes. They can become very narrow in their perceptions of the world. To avoid this, you would need to say to yourself, "Giving to others is a kind of balancing activity that in one way keeps me from becoming distorted, and, in another way, stimulates new kinds of feelings of love and fulfillment that I could not create for myself."

When you are concerned with other human beings, and you take your time to give to them, then you open certain feelings of *altruism* and *idealism* that are extremely important to your personality and to your health. These are feelings that you cannot open toward yourself. You can be kind and loving toward yourself, but that simply is a part of your own private self-involvement. When you go forth to be kind and loving to other human beings, to help them, and to serve them, you stir up areas of feeling inside you that can be activated in no other way. Those feelings feed into your personality in a way that can not only bring joy and fulfillment to you, but they can also stimulate the health of your physical body.

The area of giving to others is so important in human life that, in the long run, from the point of view of your own soul and what it is attempting to accomplish with your human personality, it may even be more important to serve others than to serve yourself. Now, we make this statement quite cautiously, for we would never suggest that you ignore yourself and your own needs. If you are not concerned with fulfilling yourself, then who shall be? However, most of you are usually quite adept at seeking your own fulfillment, and preoccupying with yourself. For most of you, if there is any adjustment needed, it is toward paying more attention to others, being more loving of them, and giving to them in deeper ways. If you do more in those areas, not only will you give more into earth life, but you will also stimulate yourself in a way that will create more health for you.

To complete our look at ways that you can create a healthy life, we will now need to turn our attention back to your *inner* experience and look at some abilities that you have within you. We will look at ways that you can use your inner abilities to create visualizations and affirmations of the health that you desire. These abilities can help you augment your work in the physical world.

VISUALIZING AND AFFIRMING HEALTH

You can augment and intensify your energies of health by creating imaginary *visions* of what you desire. Here we are not speaking only of mental pictures and visual *images*, but also of verbal *thoughts*, and deep *feelings* about what you desire. You can use your images, thoughts, and feelings together to visualize and *affirm* full health for yourself.

Creating inner visualizations and affirmations of the healthy life that you desire can trigger non-physical energies within your personality matrix that can flow forth and shower themselves upon the earth reality, softening rigid patterns, and stirring up creative energies in your environment. These strong non-physical forces also unconsciously communicate with other human beings, helping align them with your desires for a healthy life. Thus, visualization and affirmation can be important and effective in creating a joyful and healthy life.

However, such work *alone* will not create full health for you. For most human beings, there is not yet the complete development of the intensity of inner abilities that would allow you ones to literally manipulate physical reality with inner energies alone. Thus, in order to manifest the health that you desire, the inner energies released through your visualizations and affirmations will need to be combined with your *acting* in the outer world, which includes proper eating habits, exercise, rest, your relationships with others, and so forth.

To do the actual inner work of visualization and affirmation, it is most effective to set aside a special attunement period during which you can release the distractions of your ordinary earth life. This is not to say that your visualization work must be *limited* to such periods. You can also extend your visualizing and your affirming into *active* areas of your daily life. However, the most intense work with your creative capacities and your inner energies of manifestation will usually be done during deep periods of attunement.

We would suggest that you work in the following manner to draw upon your capacity to visualize, and to affirm the fulfillment of your desire for creating health.

First, decide the period of attunement time that you will set aside for your visualization, determining when the period shall be, and how much time you will spend. Then, each day, come to your attunement period with a sense of creativity, playfulness, joy, and love.

Step One. Begin your attunement period with a relaxation of your physical body. Spend a gentle moment lovingly disengaging from your ordinary thoughts, letting them slip away as best you can. Then, calm your emotions.

Step Two. Begin to create feelings of love within your own heart. This will prepare you for the visualization.

Step Three. Begin your actual visualization by calling to your attention your desire for a strong and healthy body.

Then, begin imagining your physical body, creating as strong a visual image, or thought, or feeling of your body as you can. Try to create inside yourself a clear vision (or thought, or feeling) of the perfectly strong and healthy body that you desire to have. The principle here is to inwardly *create* the perfection that you desire. If you have a well developed ability to create visual images, then in this deep attunement you will try to *see* your body as strong and healthy. Or, if you are more adept at using *words* in your mind, then you may wish to mentally *describe* the perfect body to yourself in words, verbally guiding yourself through a description of your strong and healthy body.

Step Four. After you have done this inner work for as long as you desire, then *slowly* and gently bring yourself back to your ordinary awareness. Do not rush yourself in this step.

The most important aspect of using visualizations and affirmations in the creation of health will be the *feeling* that you will generate while you engage in your inner work. No matter how you choose to visualize your ideal of health, as you work with it, also attempt to spark feelings of joy and enthusiasm about it. The more you can *feel* the reality of what you are inwardly building, the more intense will be the inner energies generated, and the more confidence you will stir in yourself. This will eventually enhance the effectiveness of your manifestation. So, as you are doing your visualization, to the best of your ability, attempt to feel your visions as reality, just as a small child will clearly and dramatically imagine and day-dream in ways that seem quite real.

You may find ways to elaborate upon the basic attunement that we have suggested for visualizing and affirming. You may wish to *write* about your visualizations and your affirmations. You might decide to draw them or paint them. You may wish to sing about them. Your creativity used in these ways, combined with your feeling and your will, can be a very potent force in the manifestation of health that you are attempting to bring about.

CREATING LOVE

Now we come to one of the most important aspects of your work in creating a healthy life. That is your ability to *create love*. Creating love can be considered the crowning achievement of all of your work. If you can infuse everything that you do in your inner and outer work with a powerful feeling of love, then you will establish a strong momentum that will help you create the full health that you desire in this lifetime.

In thinking about all of your different inner experiences and energies that we have examined so far in these teachings—your thoughts, beliefs, feelings, attitudes, desires, and so forth—you can understand that in any moment of your earth life, no matter which of the complex threads of your inner life you are experiencing, if you can add to that moment a feeling of *love*, for yourself, and for all other human beings, then you will bring the energies of your soul and of God more fully into your body, your mind, and your emotions.

Thus, the real secret to creating health is to create love within yourself each day of your life. If you can use your creativity daily to bring forth all of the energies of love that live within you, then you can manifest a strength and forcefulness in your body, your mind, and your emotions. Being able to create love within yourself, *whenever you desire to do so*, is the base upon which you can create a healthy life.

As with the other areas of your inner experience that we have examined, to learn to create love within yourself whenever you desire means that you must learn to bring the *truth* of your being into your conscious awareness, no matter what your thoughts or feelings might be doing in the moment. Once more, we remind you that the truth of your being is this: You are *temporarily* a human being who has been created by an eternal soul that has infused you with the energies of God itself, and you have within you *now*, and you have *always* had within you, a capacity to *create* love. *This divine capacity to create love cannot be diminished by anything that you experience in this lifetime, or in any other lifetime.* You have an ability to create the *experience* of love inside of you in any moment, and that experience will bring the *energies* of love into your conscious life. There is nothing that can prevent you from using your ability to create love, except *your own personality choices*.

Whether you *use* your ability to create love, or whether you *ignore* it, depends upon the many complexities in your personality that we have discussed. However, no matter how complex your personality patterns might be, the first step in learning to create love in any moment—just as with all of your other inner abilities—is *believing* that you have the ability to do it. *Establishing a belief in your ability to create love in any moment is the first step toward actually creating that love.*

One way to work to establish this belief is to continually feed appropriate thoughts of truth into your mind. We would suggest that you *write* the truth to yourself in this way:

"I have within me the capacity to create love in any moment of my life, regardless of what my mind and my feelings might be doing. *Nothing can prevent me from using my ability to create love, except my own lack of belief in that ability, and my unwillingness to use it."*

After you have written this on paper, carry it with you and read it often. When you read it, also attempt to *feel* it. This will help you to tangibly place this truth into your conscious mind. You can do this whenever you please, even in moments when you cannot believe it is true.

The next step in creating experiences of love involves practicing relieving yourself of emotional and mental burdens whenever you choose. We have examined this area earlier when we spoke of disengaging from the intensity of your immediate experience. However, since this area can be confusing, we will look at it again in the context of creating love.

First, as we have stressed, you must remind yourself often that it will *not* benefit you to try to relieve yourself from your negative experiences because you are frightened of the pain of them. If you attempt to bring forth your capacity to create love, motivated by a fear of your own painful experiences, you will eventually create *more* fear.

However, if you are working honestly and lovingly each day with your negative patterns of thought and emotion, as we have suggested earlier, then it can benefit you to use your ability to step back from the complexity of your inner reality and turn your attention to creating love in that moment. By temporarily putting aside your ordinary thoughts and emotions, you can enter into a feeling of the eternal portion of yourself in order to use the experience of your eternal self to bring forth your capacity to create love in that very moment.

Here is a simple procedure for accomplishing this kind of work. Although the procedure is simple, success with it will require patience and persistence over a period of time.

First, we would remind you again of the *two modes* of inner experience that we spoke of earlier. The first mode is the *experiencer* mode—living intensely *inside* your inner experience, and being caught up in your experience. In that mode, you are the *creator* of your experience.

Mode two is the *observer* mode—stepping back from the intensity of your experience to observe what you are experiencing. In this mode, you are the *responder* to your experience. As we have described earlier, you step back from your experience by creating a *loving detachment* from your subjectivity of the moment, *not by numbing your feelings*. This detachment is a *temporary* mode. It would not benefit you to attempt to cultivate this mode continually throughout the day, for it would simply result in a loss of *intensity* of your subjective experience. However, it will be necessary to use this second mode in a limited way in order to fully exercise your capacity to create love in any moment.

When you are experiencing love in your ordinary earth affairs, then you can rejoice in it, and you can increase the intensity of the experience by allowing yourself to remain in the first mode of being caught up in the experience. In that moment, love is arising from your earth circumstances. You can simply rejoice in the love, and encourage more of it.

However, when you are having experiences in which you feel that there is no love, in that moment, if you remain in mode one and stay immersed in your experience, there will continue to be no feelings of love. This is a moment in which feelings of love do not arise from the *situation*, or from the *circumstances*. This is a moment in which feelings of love are *not* a byproduct of your *earth* experience in mode one. In such a moment, the love is an aspect of your *eternal* reality. Therefore, to feel love in that moment, you will usually need to attune to an eternal love.

To attune to this eternal love, you will need to

step back from your temporary experience of mode one and gain the loving detachment necessary to feel what lies *beneath* your earth experience. This requires shifting to mode two and becoming an *observer* of your own experience.

Again, we must remind you that it will *not* benefit you to draw back from your experience of mode one out of fear of painful thoughts or feelings. However, if you have worked honestly to understand your emotions and thoughts that are involved with any negative experience you might be having, and you have done all that you believe you need to do in terms of dealing with any *issues* or *persons* involved in the experience, and you have attempted, to the best of your ability, to understand and heal any fears that might be associated with the moment, *then* you may decide that it is time to step back from the intensity of your experience so that you can create within yourself the sense of witnessing and observing your experience, as a preparation for attuning to love.

When you decide that you wish to create love in a certain moment, you would begin by gently disengaging yourself from the earth experience of that moment. Then, you would begin to remind yourself of the truth with your own thoughts. You could say to yourself:

"I am an eternal soul. In this moment, I release the human thoughts and feelings that I have created. And, as I release this experience of earth life, I turn my feelings toward the eternal truth that lives within me. This truth

within me is an energy of love, beauty, perfection, and all good. In this moment, I am allowing my awareness of this loving energy to grow. I am allowing my feelings to be totally saturated with the love of this eternal energy of good. I am allowing my thoughts to think about the beauty and majesty of this energy of love. I am impregnating my experience of the moment with this love that is eternal. In this moment, I am *creating* this love inside my personality."

Now, this is the necessary work as described in *words*. However, the actual inner work itself will need to be done by you as a real change and shift of your thoughts and feelings. You will need to shift from thoughts and feelings that are wrapped up in your earth life of the moment, to thoughts and feelings of the eternal truth.

Learning to work in this way, shifting from the experience of being caught up in your human thoughts and feelings, to the experience of the eternal force of love, requires practice and persistence. Yet, it is very important work, for this is the base upon which you can build your capacity to create love in any moment of your life. After you have learned to make this inner shift in your thoughts and feelings of the moment, then, whenever you desire, you can enter that deeper awareness of your eternal nature, and, from within that deepened experience, you can create feelings of warmth, harmony, and love within yourself.

If you work persistently each day to learn how to

shift your awareness to the eternal energy of love that lives within you, eventually you will come to the point in your life at which you can open your heart and pour forth love into your own experience, no matter what your inner reality of the moment might be. If you attain that capacity and develop it, gradually you will learn that you can also use this ability to come forth to help others create love in their lives. Thus, developing your capacity to consciously create love for yourself in any moment can also have a beneficial impact upon all areas of your life, and upon the lives of those around you.

Keep in mind that you need not have *perfectly* healed all of your fears in order to create love within yourself. You do not need to perfectly understand all of your challenge patterns in order to create love for yourself, for others, and for life. You need only be willing to turn your attention to the truth, which is the eternal force of love within you.

To bring together the truth of yourself with the health you desire to create, we suggest that you say to yourself each morning:

> **"I desire a body of strength and health in which I can rejoice throughout this lifetime. I am worthy of the gift of perfect health. It has been given to me by my soul, and I now accept it. Throughout this day, I will create love within myself, and in so doing, I know that I am bringing forth the perfect influence to create health in my body."**

These kinds of thoughts and feelings will help you use your ability to create love as another aspect of manifesting health in your thoughts, your emotions, and your body.

LOVING YOURSELF

In your earth life, many times the creation of health will depend primarily upon *your ability to love your own personality*. As you begin to closely examine your attitudes and feelings toward your own personality, if you are alert and learn to notice your various inner cycles, you may find a correspondence between periods of ill health in your life, and deep feelings of lack of love for your personality. Conversely, you may find that during periods when you are feeling a great deal of respect and love for your personality, there will usually be greater strength and health in your body.

The day to day attitude that you hold toward your own personality will usually fluctuate. It can range from great love for yourself, to feelings of inadequacy, and perhaps even hatred for your personality at times. These fluctuations are primarily *emotional* in nature, but they are fed by your thought processes. Yet, even though your *feelings* of love for yourself may rise and fall, as we have pointed out, within the fluctuations of your inner emotional cycles, there is a steady stream of love *energy* within you that is never diminished. Thus, in your own inner experience, you need not have the perfect feelings about your personality in order to love yourself. You do not need to feel deep, thrilling emotions of love for your personality in order to love yourself. You can be having a terrible time emotionally, feeling discouraged and depressed, and still you can rise up within those feelings and say to yourself:

> **"These are negative *feelings* inside me. They are only temporary emotions. They are not truth. The truth is that there is a perfection of love *energy* living within me. The truth is that I respect that love, and I rejoice in it. The truth is that I love my personality, and I rejoice in great gratitude for the opportunity to live within my present personal reality. It is a magnificent gift to be able to live this present personality that is me."**

If you judge your love for your personality on the basis of your emotions alone, you can deeply confuse yourself. At times, you may have rather lengthy periods of negative feelings about yourself. If you come to believe that those negative feelings are the truth about you, then you can eventually come to believe that there is badness in you, and you will find it difficult to consciously love yourself.

Thus, when you feel, "There is badness in me, I am not a good person, I am unworthy," or when you have any of the negative feelings that arise when you temporarily are not consciously loving yourself, you will need to remind yourself that such feelings come and go. You will work with them as you would work with any emotional pattern that you desire to change, using your intelligence, your sensitivity, and your love. You would also use your capacity to be lovingly aware of yourself, stepping back from the entanglements of your negative personality patterns, and seeing yourself with a broader, wiser, and more loving vision. You can do all of this to stimulate love for your personality, even when you are feeling quite negative.

We are not saying that it is *easy* to do this when you are having a negative experience. Often, you will feel that it is quite difficult to rise up in a time of sadness, pain, and despair to work with your mind and emotions to convince yourself that you are worthy and loved. Yet, no matter what you are feeling, there is nothing that can prevent you from at least *saying* to yourself:

"Even if my emotions feel negative, I am still a magnificent being. There is still great love for my own personality. I do love myself."

If you are willing to *say* this, even in moments when you cannot *believe* it, then you have begun the change. Then, it is a matter of working persistently until you can *feel* it. We can promise you that the love flows within you at all times as a powerful *energy*, but it is satisfying to your personality when you can feel it as a human *emotion*.

We can also assure you that you *can* change your negative feelings about yourself, no matter how strong they may be. You have brought the wisdom, strength, intelligence, and love into your personality that will enable you to make these kinds of changes, if you desire them. It is a matter of persistence, doing it again and again, along with a willingness to rise up and practice turning toward the truth each time that the negativity arises—remembering that the truth is that you are filled with an energy of love in all moments of your life.

PRACTICING LOVING YOURSELF

In your work to create health, just as you will be practicing each day to heal your negative thoughts and emotions, you can also practice loving yourself. The practice of loving yourself always begins with the *observation* of your inner experience. First, you will need to notice how you are feeling about yourself. This is particularly important when you are caught up in confusing or challenging inner experiences, or when you are swept away by worry, doubt, or fear, and you are not aware that you are being swept away. When you do not notice that you are filling yourself with negativity, then you are not able to exercise your freedom to cease doing it.

Thus, the first step in your daily practice of loving yourself will be the simple task of *observing* your inner experience to notice when you are *not* loving yourself. As you practice this observation, you may notice periods in which you feel inadequate, unsuccessful, or unworthy. As you notice such feelings, remind yourself that you are in the first mode of your subjective life—you are the *creator* of your experience, and you are caught up in it. In that moment, say to yourself:

"As the *creator* of my own inner experience, I now notice that I am creating negative

thoughts and feelings about myself. By taking a moment to make this observation of what I am inwardly creating, I am quite naturally switching myself to the second mode of experiencing my inner life. I am becoming the *observer* and *responder* to my own experience. I now have the power to use my imagination, creativity, and will to change my *response* to the negativity that I am creating. Or, if I choose, I can use my will to go back to the first mode of my experiencing, to become the creator, and create *new* thoughts and emotions about myself. I can even create the inner experience of love for myself, now, in this moment."

If you find that you are not successful in changing your negative thoughts and feelings about yourself in that moment, then you can remind yourself: "It is not badness that I am not loving myself in this moment. Let me find a way to *respond* to this experience of not loving myself that is more satisfying to me." You simply decide to respond with a feeling that the negative feelings about yourself are not bad. Eventually, you can find yourself in the rather unique position of being able to love yourself at the same time that you are feeling quite negative about yourself.

Now, let us turn for a moment to some specific ways in which you can work as the *creator* of your inner reality. Imagine that you are awakening in the morning from a deep sleep during which you had frightening dreams. Perhaps you saw yourself totally abandoned by loved ones, isolated and alone, feeling great sadness and pain. You are now feeling quite insignificant and unworthy. You feel: "I am such an unimportant person. There is no one who loves me. I am so lonely." In that moment, you are caught up in negative thoughts and feelings about yourself. If you would step back in that moment and do your loving observation of yourself, you would see that *you* are creating the negative feelings about yourself, even though you are doing it in response to the dream. Most certainly, in that moment, you are not loving your personality. Once you become aware of this you can say: "I wish to work in this moment to love myself."

In this example of feeling lonely because of the dream, the first step in working to love yourself, just as with your work of healing negative inner experience, is to *enter into* the feelings of loneliness that you are creating, so that you may work with them directly. First, you would *feel* them as deeply as you can for a moment. Then, you would begin to examine the feelings from inside of them. You could say to yourself: "Are these feelings of loneliness old habits that I am healing? Perhaps they have simply been sparked by my dream, and they do not need my attention now? If so, then let me *release* the feelings of loneliness that I have created in response to my dream. Let me now create feelings of love to replace the loneliness."

If this inner work is successful, then you have accomplished what you desired by *re-creating* the feelings of loneliness and changing them to feelings of

love. If you were not able to do that, then you can
begin to intensify your inner work to address the
fears that lie beneath the emotions. You could say to
your own mind and heart:

> "These feelings of loneliness are my own emo-
> tions. They have been triggered by fears in
> me. Now I remind myself that emotions can-
> not harm me. Fears cannot harm me. Emo-
> tions and fears can be changed. I have created
> them, and I can change them. I enter now into
> my deep feelings of loneliness, and I open my
> mind and my heart so that I can clearly per-
> ceive the fears that lie within the loneliness. I
> can begin to imagine what frightens me. I can
> begin to experience those fears now. The
> deeper I can feel them, the more I can under-
> stand them. By entering into my fears, I show
> myself that no matter how large the fears be-
> come, they cannot harm me."

When you enter into your fears in this way, you
are working just as you would in healing any negative
emotional pattern, as we have discussed in earlier
chapters. First, you observe the fear pattern lovingly,
then you attempt to understand what could have
caused the pattern, and then you work to change the
pattern in the moment. As you work with the fear,
you can say to yourself:

> "I am healing this fear because I desire to
> come to a greater love for myself in this mo-
> ment. I desire to love my personality now. I
> desire to dissolve this fear that causes me to

feel unlovable and unworthy. And I do it from within the fear, knowing that it cannot harm me."

You will find many other ways to think and feel as you work directly inside of your emotions and thoughts, as you exercise your freedom as *creator* of your inner experience. Yet, even as you experiment with your own unique ways of working with your inner patterns, the focus of your work will always be your desire to *love* yourself, not to criticize or condemn yourself. Work toward a loving attitude by continually returning to this thought:

"I am dissolving and re-creating these negative patterns within my experience so that I may love myself more in this moment. I am creating the trust that will enable me to love myself."

Each time that you work in this way with your negative patterns, do it for as long a period of time as you believe to be necessary. You need not feel that you must *completely* heal yourself before you go to the next step of the attunement. When you feel that you have at least *begun* to dissolve the negativity from inside of it, when you feel that your thoughts and emotions of negativity toward yourself are at least diminishing, then you can begin to turn your focus toward the truth. You can use the power of your mind to suggest the truth to yourself. For example, you could say:

"In this moment, I am releasing all belief that

there is badness within my being. I am turning my feelings toward that stream of eternal love that expresses within my personality. I am feeling it now. I am rejoicing in it, and I am creating a great love for the personality that is me."

By using your mind to *say* the truth to yourself in this way, you begin to trigger unconscious patterns within your personality that are aligned with that continuing stream of love energy that exists beneath your conscious awareness. By consciously making this affirmative statement of truth, you send a signal to your personality to release the *illusions* of negativity that you have built, and to turn your attention toward the truth. This eventually will enable you to peel back the layers of resistance set up by the negativity, thereby allowing the energies of truth to rise up into your conscious awareness as thoughts and feelings of love for yourself.

As you work persistently with yourself in this way, you can create your own inspiring thoughts that will help you love yourself more. You will notice that the more you use such affirmative statements of truth, the quicker your feelings will respond to the statements. Eventually, you will learn that *you can initiate very deep feelings of love for yourself simply by saying the truth in your mind.*

The more you practice loving yourself in this way, the more you will find a new flexibility and freedom in your feelings that perhaps you have not noticed before. Your feelings are much like rubber. They can be stretched, pulled, and twisted. Often they are pulled and twisted by fear. Once you have begun to practice guiding your thoughts toward your own magnificence, allowing your feelings to follow, you will begin to notice that you can change your feelings at will. You can learn to create feelings of love for your own personality whenever it pleases you.

Feeling love for yourself is an *ability* over which you can take mastery. As with all other areas of your inner life, there will be volatility and variation in your capacity to exercise your mastery. There may be times when you feel that forces beyond your control are causing negativity in your personality that makes you feel unlovable and unworthy. This can happen often in relationships with other people. If a person would criticize you, or curse you, or reject you, then quite naturally you will feel a certain sense of unworthiness. These are simply the fluctuations of the inner complexities of your human experience. You can work with them in the many ways that we have suggested to you in these teachings. However, none of the complexities of your life can *force* you to feel badness about yourself. You can still *choose* to love yourself, no matter what you are experiencing. *Your ability to love yourself cannot be diminished by your negative thoughts and feelings. This ability cannot be diminished by challenging earth circumstances and situations. Your ability to love yourself cannot be diminished by anything.* Only your false *belief* that you are not lovable can temporarily *hide* your ability to love yourself from your conscious awareness.

It is very effective to practice loving yourself in situations in which you feel that it is difficult to create that love for your personality. It will be particularly important to practice during periods when you believe that you do not deserve love, that you are unworthy of love. By using the second mode of your inner experiencing, which is the *observer* and *responder* role, even in the middle of a negative experience, you can step back from the negative thoughts and feelings of that moment, and you can say to yourself:

> **"Here is a brilliant opportunity to practice loving myself, for I am feeling quite negative and unworthy in this moment. If I can generate love for myself during this particular negative period, then I have certainly advanced and strengthened my capacity to love myself. And it will be even simpler to love myself when I return to calm and stability in my emotions."**

This kind of inner work on loving yourself will build a foundation of loving feelings that you can draw upon whenever you feel the need.

LOVING ACTIONS TOWARD YOURSELF

In order to intensify your abilities to love yourself, you will need to make your love tangible by rooting it in *actions* that you take in the physical world. Loving yourself here will involve taking beautiful, loving actions toward yourself each day. Those loving actions will stimulate your mind, emotions, and physical body.

A simple but very effective way to work with yourself in this area is to promise yourself that for a certain period of time, perhaps for one month of time, you will give yourself a small gift *every day*. This would be a tangible, physical gift. During this time period, every morning as you arise from your sleep, take a moment to plan the gift that you will give to yourself in that day. Do this just as enthusiastically and joyfully as you would plan to give a gift to a beloved one. Take the same care and the same interest that you would show if you were planning a special gift for your beloved one. Thus, each morning, you would say to yourself: "What will be my gift to me today to celebrate how much I love my own personality?"

It is important to do this *consistently*, every day. If you feel that you will forget to do it in the morning, you could write a message on paper, reminding yourself to plan your daily gift to yourself. Then, you could place the message near your bed, or upon your mirror.

The gift that you give yourself each day can be a small gift, or, it can be as large as you desire it to be. Perhaps you will say: "In this day I will take myself to a fine restaurant, and I will celebrate myself with a feast." Perhaps on another day you would say: "Today, I shall give myself the gift of an article of new clothing, or a flower, or a book." On another day you may decide to give yourself the gift of a walk in nature, or a visit to a museum, or time spent with a friend or loved one. Each day you would choose a physical item, or a physical experience that pleases you, and you would do it *only for the pleasure of it*. You would not do this for growth, or education, but for pure pleasure. The day to day willingness to actually give yourself a gift, or do loving things for yourself, will graphically demonstrate to your personality that you are indeed worthy of having time and energy spent on yourself, simply for the joy and pleasure of it.

As you work each day in your inner and outer life to increase your feelings of love for your personality, you can enlist the aid of friends and loved ones, particularly in the beginning stages of your work when you may be tempted to dismiss the work as being unimportant. Go forth to them and tell them that for a certain period of time you will be working diligently to love yourself more. Ask them to help you by noticing when you are speaking about yourself in a way that is unloving, and to gently stop you and remind you that you are not loving yourself. When the friend does stop you, then you may wish to speak about why you were expressing negativity about your personality. You may wish, if they desire to do it with you, to examine your feelings and thoughts about yourself in that moment, and communicate them out loud, in order to begin to identify some of the persistent negative criticisms and judgments that you make against yourself. After you have talked about such patterns, then ask your friend or loved one to remind you that you are a magnificent human being, and that you are worthy of love.

As you set about to accomplish your desires for healthful living by blending your inner work of loving yourself with your actions in the outer world, then, again, as with the other areas of your inner work, the next important issue is *persistence*. Are you willing to constantly do the inner loving of yourself in each day? Are you willing to persistently try to accomplish the outer actions that are necessary to demonstrate that love to yourself, including the actions of lovingly feeding, exercising, and resting your body? If you are, then you can combine the inner process of *loving yourself* with the *recognizing and healing of your fears*. Then, you can combine those two areas with *loving others* and *loving life*. Then, if you build all of this work upon a willingness to attune to the magnificence of your eternal being, and of God, you will be drawing the very energies of the universe together with a self-created wholeness within your human personality. The result will be the steady, day by day release of extraordinary, health-giving energies into your thoughts, your emotions, and your physical body.

Chapter 16

Conclusion

*—When you joyfully **choose** to align with the eternal energies of life, and you **choose** to make them the center of your human existence on earth, then you bring a magnificence and perfection into your human experience that is a true expression of the energies of God that have created you, and that sustain you.*

To conclude our teachings for this time, we would say that, as you have looked with us at the areas of your human feelings, thoughts, and physical body, as well as the many complexities involved in the interaction between your human personality, your body, your eternal soul, and the energies of God, we have painted a picture for you that you can hold before yourself to stimulate and motivate yourself toward greater health in this lifetime. We have shown you an *ideal* of goodness and love that you can hold in your mind and in your heart. This is an ideal that represents the *true perfection* that exists within all of

398 HEALING THE HEART, HEALING THE BODY

life, in all realms of being. It is an ideal that, when
fully acted upon, can bring about satisfying and fulfilling *ways of living* that will be more healthful for
you in your present human life.

This ideal of *goodness* and *love* that we have
pointed you toward is what your own soul is constantly trying to influence you to see, and to desire to
embrace. The energies of God itself also fill you with
impulses that are intended to inspire you to *choose*
to move toward this magnificent ideal, through your
own free will. Those eternal energies constantly urge
you to choose to weave love, wisdom, and truth into
your personal fulfillment of your desires for all
things, including health.

However, what you must understand, as we have
constantly emphasized throughout these teachings,
is that *you are free to do exactly as you please in your
present human life*. You are even free to ignore the
impulses of your soul and of God that prompt you
toward the magnificent ideal that we have described.
That will not make you a bad person. It will simply
make it more difficult for you to manifest the depth
of fulfillment that you desire in this lifetime.

If you do not feel the freedom that you have to
choose what you focus upon in this lifetime, then
even a commitment to higher ideals, and to the eternal energies available to you in your human personality, will tend to be confused. If you do not feel
that you are *freely choosing* a higher ideal in life because you genuinely desire it, then you will tend to
feel that the higher ideal is *imposed* upon you by life.
In other words, you might feel, "I *must* follow this

higher ideal in order to be a good person. There is no other way to manifest goodness. All other paths in life are inferior."

The truth of your life is this: Even if you pay no attention at all to higher ideals and eternal energies, and even if you live what seems to you to be a meaningless, superficial human life, *you* are not diminished or damaged. You are an eternal soul, and you continue to exist within a magnificence and perfection that is not diminished by your human choices. However, your *human* experience might be more painful and less fulfilling if you ignore the higher ideals and eternal energies. You will tend to feel incomplete and dissatisfied with life. Yet, *you* will not be diminished or damaged in your true being.

It is wise to try to follow higher ideals, and to attune to eternal energies, because you believe that making a commitment to such areas is the most satisfying and fulfilling thing to do in your human existence. The greatest health for you will come forward when you joyfully and creatively *choose* to discover the extraordinary eternal energies that feed you and guide you, because you believe that such a choice is exciting and fulfilling. When you joyfully *choose* to align with the eternal energies of life, and you *choose* to make them the center of your human existence on earth, then you bring a magnificence and perfection into your human experience that is a true expression of the energies of God that have created you, and that sustain you.

When you *choose* to express the beauty of God in

your life by focusing upon the ideal that we have tried to show you, then, not only will you create a joyful, magnificent, healthy human life, but you will also fulfill the larger purpose for which you were sent forth into human form. That purpose is: *To create on the physical earth, a perfect reflection of what you are as an eternal soul beyond earth.*

To bring forth the fullest truth here, we must say to you that you have come into earth to help create health, love, joy, and magnificence, not only for yourself, but also for all other human beings. You have come to make a healthfulness of the physical bodily forms, of the emotional expressions, of the mental lives of all ones. *You have come to help create ways in which the magnificence and perfection of God itself can be showered upon all beings on the physical earth.*

By joyfully and lovingly, and *through your own free will*, following the ideal that we have described in these teachings—which is essentially a willingness to believe that the magnificence of God lives within all of life—you can become an instrument in the unfoldment of the perfection of life on earth. You can accomplish this by showering that perfection into the physical world as your *thoughts*, your *feelings*, and your *actions*. Those thoughts, feelings, and actions, permeated with this idealism, become your gift to human life.

When all of you on earth are able to consistently hold this ideal and make it your personal *intention* in your day to day life—as many of you are now beginning to do—then you will all come together in your personal relationships, in communities, in nations, and in your worldwide trends of thought, feeling, and belief, and you will learn to *agree* upon the important purposes of human life on earth. By such agreement, you will begin to actually *accomplish* those purposes, thereby accomplishing the intentions of the eternal souls who did set human life into motion.

Day by day, as you work with yourself to create health in your life, remind yourself of this greater potential that you hold within you. Encourage yourself toward the *choices* that seem to you to be the most effective for releasing that potential into physical reality. Then, have the courage to commit yourself to those choices, and to live them as fully as possible each day of your life. By so doing, you will rejoice and fulfill yourself throughout this lifetime.

Appendix

Appendix

Further Study

With The Guides

For more than a decade, Ron Scolastico has brought the wisdom of the Guides to individuals and groups throughout the world. This work has helped thousands of people to understand their human life as a magnificent expression of their eternal soul, and the forces of God.

Dr. Scolastico's work with the Guides has created a vast body of spiritual and psychological knowledge that provides brilliant insights into many areas of life. You can request a general listing of available books and audio tapes of the work of the Guides by writing or telephoning:

Transpersonal Consultation Group
P.O. Box 6556
Woodland Hills, California, 91365
818-999-1557

There are many ways that you can work with the teachings of the Guides. You can request information on any of the following opportunities by contacting the Transpersonal Consultation Group.

THE EARTH ADVENTURE

If you wish to study the Guides' comprehensive teachings on the nature of physical and spiritual reality, you can read *The Earth Adventure: Your Soul's Journey Through Physical Reality*, by Ron Scolastico, Ph.D. In *The Earth Adventure*, the Guides take you on a journey with your soul through the underlying reality of the universe, from its creation, to the present, and into the future. This inspired book of wisdom from the Guides offers you an expansive new understanding of your life, from birth, through death, and beyond.

In *The Earth Adventure*, the Guides speak about the following areas, and much more:

—How and why the earth and the physical universe were created.

—How your soul has projected your present human personality into earth as a part of a vast adventure through physical reality.

—The purpose of your life on earth, and ways to fulfill that purpose.

—How you, as a soul, chose your human parents, created your physical body, and presided over your human birth.

—The process of human death, and what you will experience after your death.

—Your ability to gain conscious awareness of spiritual realities, and how to use that ability to enhance your present human life on earth.

—The impact of your past lifetimes on earth, and how you will choose your future lifetimes.

The Earth Adventure is available in paperback (published by Hay House) at your local bookstore, or it may be ordered in hardback from Transpersonal Consultation Group.

INNER ACTION TAPES

A unique opportunity is offered by the *Inner Action Tapes*. These tapes have been carefully created to lead you toward expanded consciousness through inner "programming." On each tape, the Guides speak directly to deeper parts of your mind to help you spark your growth in different areas of life.

Each Inner Action Tape begins with a gentle introduction by Susan Scolastico, and a musical accompaniment that sets the mood of relaxation and openness. Then, the Guides present a concentrated and focused stream of speaking that interacts with your mental and emotional patterns to inspire you to manifest your full abilities.

Each tape has a morning and evening side, with an average length of 15 minutes per side. By consistently using these tapes, morning and evening over a period of time, you can learn to activate your unlimited inner abilities to fulfill your desires in life.

There is an Inner Action Tape available on: (1) *Healing Fear and Negativity*; (2) *The Perfect Love Relationship*; (3) *Healing the Physical Body*; (4) *Loving Yourself*; (5) *Prosperity and Wealth*; and (6) *Experiencing God*.

SUBJECT AREA READINGS

There are many readings by the Guides, available on audio tape, that address a wide variety of subject areas, from personal growth and human development, to profound teachings about the vastness of spiritual realities. Each tape contains more than an hour of wisdom and teaching from the Guides. You can contact the Transpersonal Consultation Group for a complete listing of subject area readings.

The most recent additions to the library of subject area readings are: (1) *GODS AND SYMBOLS: Perceiving Spiritual Realities*; (2) *THE HUMAN MIND: Exploring the Mystery of Consciousness*; (3) *HEALING ADDICTIONS: A Spiritual and Psychological Approach*; and (4) *EDUCATION IN THE 90'S: Teaching Our Children, Teaching Ourselves*.

These four readings are also available in printed booklet form. The booklets have been edited by Dr. Scolastico for clarity and ease of reading. They can be ordered from Transpersonal Consultation Group.

PERSONAL LIFE READINGS

Since 1978, Dr. Scolastico has given *Personal Life Readings* for individuals throughout the world.

These life readings are conducted in person, or on the telephone.

In a personal life reading, Dr. Scolastico will attune to the Guides, and to your own soul forces. The Guides will begin the reading by giving you inspiring knowledge about yourself and your life that will provide deep insights into your personality and your soul patterns. You will receive sound and loving spiritual and psychological guidance that will help you understand the complexities of your life in a profound way.

After the opening statement by the Guides, you will begin to ask personal questions about yourself and your life. Through this question and answer process, you become an active participant in the reading, directing it where you wish it to go. The Guides' thorough and wise answers to your questions will help illuminate your life situations in such a way that you can gain a new understanding of yourself, and the knowledge will help you open new avenues of growth in your life.

The Guides will close your reading by lovingly guiding you through a deep attunement that will help you feel the beauty of your eternal nature.

Thousands of people have found their personal readings with the Guides to be a valuable, inspiring, and growthful influence in their lives.

RETREAT AND WORKSHOPS

In early November of each year, Ron and Susan Scolastico conduct a five-day spiritual retreat with the Guides in California. This is an inspiring experience in which 20 participants work directly with the Guides in a most beautiful setting.

The *Annual Spiritual Retreat With The Guides* presents an opportunity for you to take five days away from the bustle of your daily life to experience your spiritual nature, and to deeply feel yourself as an eternal soul.

During this very special and nurturing week, you will be actively involved with Dr. Scolastico and Susan Scolastico, and the other retreat participants, in many group readings with the Guides. During these readings the Guides will help you understand the deeper truths of life by weaving a complete tapestry of knowledge that is specifically tailored to the needs of the retreat participants.

You will also have opportunities to ask the Guides about your own personal life issues. You will be greatly inspired by what you learn for your answers, as well as by the answers to the questions of others.

There will by joyful, meaningful interactions and group activities with the retreat participants. There will also be time for private meditation and contemplation, and an opportunity to enjoy the beauty of nature.

In addition to the annual spiritual retreat, there are one-day workshops with the Guides held periodically in the Los Angeles area, and in various locations throughout the country. Information on these workshops, and on the yearly retreat, can be obtained from the Transpersonal Consultation Group.

THE STUDY GROUP

For ongoing inspiration and personal growth, you can join *The Study Group*. The Study Group is a subscription, audio tape series of special readings by the Guides, done on a monthly basis. These monthly readings provide stimulating and timely wisdom from the Guides on a wide range of important subject areas.

As a member of the Study Group, once a month you will receive a tape of new teachings given by the Guides, specifically for the Study Group members. These teachings will give you ways to enhance various areas of your personal life, and they will help you attune more deeply to your eternal nature. Each reading also includes fascinating and informative answers given by the Guides to particular subject area questions submitted by the Study Group members.

When you become a member of the Study Group, you can ask the Guides to explore the questions about life that are most important to you. And, as you listen to the Guides answering the fascinating questions asked by other Study Group members, you will gain valuable knowledge in areas that you may not have previously considered.

The Study Group is one of Dr. Scolastico's favorite projects with the Guides. He has said, *"In the Study Group, you have a chance to hear the Guides speak on many varied subjects over a long period of time. As a result, I believe that you will find yourself viewing your life differently. Your fears will lessen, your feelings of love will increase, and your ability to find purpose, meaning, and fulfillment in your life will grow.*"

If you would like to personally experience a Study Group reading by the Guides, as a special offer to readers of this book, you can receive an audio tape of the most recent Study Group reading by sending $3.00, to cover shipping and handling, to:

Universal Guidance Press
P.O. Box 6556
Woodland Hills, CA 91365

If you would like to receive a catalog of Hay House products, or information about future workshops, lectures, and events sponsored by the Louise L. Hay Educational Institute, please detach and mail this questionnaire.

We hope you receive value from *Healing The Heart, Healing The Body*. Please help us evaluate our distribution program by filling out this brief questionnaire. Upon receipt of this postcard, your catalog will be sent promptly.

NAME _____

ADDRESS _____

_____

I purchased this book from:

☐ Store _____

   City _____

☐ Other (Catalog, Lecture, Workshop)

   Specify _____

Occupation _____ Age _____

We hope you receive value from *Healing The Heart, Healing The Body*. Please help us evaluate our distribution program by filling out this brief questionnaire. Upon receipt of this postcard, your catalog will be sent promptly.

NAME _____

ADDRESS _____

_____

I purchased this book from:

☐ Store _____

   City _____

☐ Other (Catalog, Lecture, Workshop)

   Specify _____

Occupation _____ Age _____

```
------------------------------------------------------------------------
```

To: HAY HOUSE, INC.
P.O. Box 6204
Carson, CA 90749-6204

```
------------------------------------------------------------------------
```

To: HAY HOUSE, INC.
P.O. Box 6204
Carson, CA 90749-6204